D0801330

PRAISE FOR *COLD-BLOODED KINDNESS*

"A wonderful, intelligent, and engaging study that illuminates the disturbing relationship between some of those who appeal to our better instincts, as victims, and those on whom they prey, including ourselves—it will grip the general reader and should be compulsory reading for anyone working in the 'caring' professions. For many, the world will never look the same after reading this book."

—Psychiatrist Iain McGilchrist,
author of *The Master and His Emissary*

"Barbara Oakley has written the most ambitious kind of true crime book, one that goes beyond a story well told and takes the lid off the simmering conditions and psychopathology that cook up into a tragic killing. There are haunting warnings for all of us in *Cold-Blooded Kindness*, as well as a fundamental truth: Homicide is self-will run riot—even if it wears a smiley face."

—Lowell Cauffiel,
New York Times bestselling author of *House of Secrets*

"*Cold-Blooded Kindness* is a masterful fusion of analytic depth and powerful narrative. A singularly incisive exposé of the fallacy of simplistic moral dichotomies we routinely deploy to judge (and misjudge) the intricacies of human nature. And a gripping read to boot."

—Elkhonon Goldberg,
clinical professor of neurology, NYU School of Medicine, and
author of *The New Executive Brain* and *The Wisdom Paradox*

"Barbara Oakley sets her sights on a seemingly mundane act of domestic violence to reveal the many hidden layers beneath. To make sense of those layers, Oakley uniquely dissects the dynamic psychological, social, and cultural forces that led an artistically gifted and seemingly kind and caring woman to kill her husband. Was she an abused victim or a conniving victimizer? Read *Cold-Blooded Kindness* and find out."

—Mark Blumberg,
F. Wendell Miller Professor of Psychology, University of Iowa,
and author of *Freaks of Nature: What Anomalies
Tell Us about Development and Evolution*

"Finally someone has exposed the ugly, vicious underbelly of 'kindness.' Dr. Oakley reminds us that the expenditure of energy or emotion is not in itself naughty or nice, it's a question of how they are channeled or directed. So-called good and evil can look an awful lot alike—the devil is indeed in the details. *Cold-Blooded Kindness* is an excellent piece of investigative journalism and a riveting read all rolled into one. Dr. Oakley does Truman Capote proud, you won't want to put it down!"

—Dr. Margaret Cochran,
author of *What Are You Afraid Of?*
and host of "Wisdom, Love and Magic!"

"This brave and important book reminds us that even our best intentioned assumptions become prejudices if they go too long unexamined. Truth and justice deserve our rigorously honest attention and we must trust that they will protect us better, in the long run, than convenient lies. The book is also an excellent read—lively, suspenseful, strange, and as insightful as it is disturbing. You should read it."

—Jennifer Michael Hecht,
author of *The Happiness Myth* and *Doubt: A History*

COLD-BLOODED
KINDNESS

Barbara Oakley

COLD-BLOODED KINDNESS

Neuroquirks of a Codependent Killer,
or Just Give Me a Shot at Loving You, Dear,
and Other Reflections on Helping That Hurts

Foreword by
DAVID SLOAN WILSON

POQUOSON PUBLIC LIBRARY
CITY HALL AVE.
POQUOSON, VA 23662

 Prometheus Books
59 John Glenn Drive
Amherst, New York 14228–2119

Published 2011 by Prometheus Books

Cold-Blooded Kindness: Neuroquirks of a Codependent Killer, or Just Give Me a Shot at Loving You, Dear, and Other Reflections on Helping That Hurts. Copyright © 2011 by Barbara Oakley. All rights reserved. No part of this publication may be reproduced, stored in a retrieval system, or transmitted in any form or by any means, digital, electronic, mechanical, photocopying, recording, or otherwise, or conveyed via the Internet or a Web site without prior written permission of the publisher, except in the case of brief quotations embodied in critical articles and reviews.

Cover illustration © Media Bakery, 2011.

Inquiries should be addressed to
Prometheus Books
59 John Glenn Drive
Amherst, New York 14228–2119
VOICE: 716–691–0133, ext. 210
FAX: 716–691–0137
WWW.PROMETHEUSBOOKS.COM

15 14 13 12 11   5 4 3 2 1

Library of Congress Cataloging-in-Publication Data

Oakley, Barbara A., 1955–
Cold-blooded kindness : neuroquirks of a codependent killer, or just give me a shot at loving you, dear, and other reflections on helping that hurts / by Barbara Oakley.
    p. cm.
Includes bibliographical references and index.
ISBN 978–1–61614–419–7 (alk. paper)
ISBN 978–1–61614–420–3 (e-book)
    1. Alden, Carole, 1960– 2. Murder—Utah—Case studies. 3. Abused women—Utah—Case studies. 4. Battered woman syndrome—Utah—Case studies. I. Title.
HV6533.U8025 2011
364.152'3092—dc22

2010049898

Printed in the United States of America on acid-free paper

To My Beloved Philip

And whatever harm the evil may do, the harm done by the good is the most harmful harm.

—NIETZSCHE

CONTENTS

NOTES ON METHODS

*C*old-Blooded Kindness* is based on police records, trial testi-mony, and interviews. Dialogue is reconstructed from the best memory of those involved, or the best available sources, and rechecked wherever possible against testimony, documents, and other reliable sources. Statements presented as facts are taken from sources deemed reliable and have been checked wherever possible against other reliable sources. Every effort has been taken to eliminate error—as such, how-ever, human error may still occur due to the fallibility of human memory or my own misunderstanding. I would like to emphasize in this regard that any errors of fact or interpretation remain my own.

Carole Alden's own thoughts regarding the events recounted here are taken from nearly one hundred pages of letters she wrote to me over a several-month period, from November 2008 to May 2009. Carole's words have been paraphrased per copyright laws, but great care has been taken to retain the original meaning and context.

For convenience, I have referred to Carole Alden by her maiden name, although she has gone by other names.

I am not a healthcare professional—any observations made can in no way be taken as a clinical diagnosis.

The first use of a name that is a pseudonym is always in italics.

DRAMATIS PERSONAE

Note: pseudonyms are in **_bold italics_**.

Carole Alden: A Utah artist whose fanciful works and cloth sculptures have been featured in galleries and at the Utah Arts Festival. The mother of two boys and three girls by her first two husbands. When she was forty-six, on the morning of July 29, 2006, she called police to report that she had shot and killed her third husband, Marty Sessions.

Melloney Bozeman: Carole Alden's first daughter, from her first husband, Richard Senft. Age twenty-three at the time of the homicide.

Andy Bristow: Carole Alden's drug-addicted boyfriend between her second and third husbands. Died due to "combined drug intoxication" under mysterious circumstances.

Morris Burton: A sergeant in the Millard County Sheriff's Office—one of the first to arrive, along with Deputy Tony Pedersen, at the scene of the killing.

Patrick Finlinson: Deputy County Attorney in Millard County, Utah.

As a new arrival on the job, he assisted Michael Wims and Pat Nolan in the prosecution of Carole Alden.

Richard Jacobson: A star detective in the Millard County Sheriff's Office—key investigator in the homicide of Marty Sessions.

Allen Lake: A friend of Carole Alden's. Upon discovering Carole had killed Marty Sessions, Lake also called police the morning of July 29.

Michael McGrath: A forensic psychiatrist from Rochester, New York, who has researched battered woman syndrome.

Patrick Nolan: Assistant Attorney General for the State of Utah—a key player on the prosecutorial team in the State's case against Carole Alden.

Penny Packer: Carole's junior high school art teacher and a longtime friend and confidante.

Tony Pedersen: A deputy sheriff in Millard County, Utah—one of the first to arrive at the scene of the killing.

Brian Poulson: Carole Alden's second husband.

Emily Poulson: Carole Alden's third daughter, ten years old at the time her stepfather, Marty, was killed.

Jason Poulson: Carole Alden's second son, fourteen at the time of the killing.

Conner Rusek: Carole Alden's first son, from her first husband, Richard Swift; age twenty-five at the time of the homicide.

Krystal Rusek: Carole Alden's second daughter, from her first husband, Richard Senft; age twenty at the time of the homicide.

Anna Sessions: Marty Sessions's older daughter, age twenty-nine at her father's death.

Dennis "Denny" Sessions: Marty Sessions's brother—two years younger than Marty.

Edee Sessions: Marty Sessions's younger daughter, age twenty-seven at her father's death.

Marty Sessions: Carole Alden's third husband, whom she killed sometime between late evening July 28 and early morning July 29, 2006. Age forty-nine at the time of his death.

Richard Senft: Carole Alden's first husband.

James K. Slavens: Carole Alden's defense attorney—in a confusing turn of events, he had also previously served as Marty Sessions's defense attorney.

Lenore Walker: An academic who devised the term "battered woman syndrome" in the late 1970s to describe why women who are physically abused often remain with their abusers.

Michael Wims: Chief of the Special Prosecutions Section of the Criminal Division of the Utah Attorney General's Office. Chief prosecutor in the Carole Alden case. Wims also played a role in prosecuting extremist murderer Ron Lafferty, as described by Jon Krakauer in his book *Under the Banner of Heaven.*

Carolyn Zahn-Waxler: A distinguished researcher at the National Institutes of Mental Health whose career has centered around the origins and development of empathy and caring behaviors.

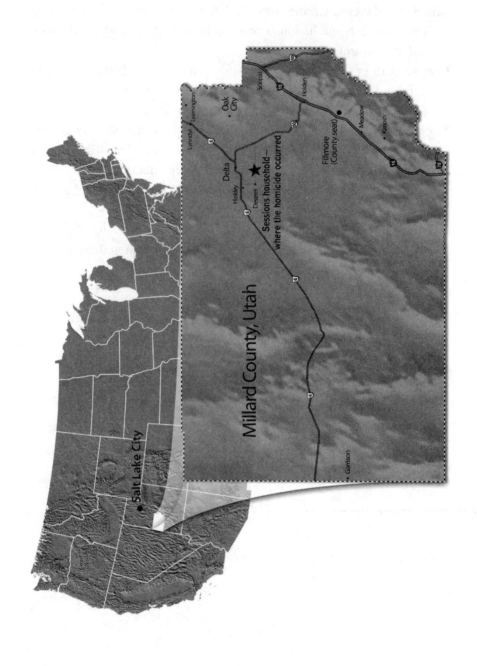

Salt Lake City

Millard County, Utah

Lynndyl
Leamington
Oak City
Scipio
Holden
Delta
Hinckley
Deseret
Sessions household—
where the homicide occurred
Fillmore
(County seat)
Meadow
Kanosh
Garrison

FOREWORD
by David Sloan Wilson

From William Shakespeare's *Macbeth* to Truman Capote's *In Cold Blood*, taking the life of another has been used as a lens for reflecting upon the human condition in general terms. *Cold-Blooded Kindness* continues the tradition with a twist: Barbara Oakley draws upon the best that science has to offer in addition to her extraordinary storytelling skills and grasp of human nature that all gifted authors bring to their subjects without the formal tools of science.

The case involves an artist, animal lover, and mother of five named Carole Alden who phoned the police to say she had killed her husband in self-defense. It seemed like a classic case of spousal abuse—Oakley was drawn to report on it as an example of how kindness can have a dark side. That's where I come in. I'm an evolutionary scientist who studies kindness as a strategy that can succeed or fail, depending upon the circumstances. When kind people lavish their kindness upon each other, life blooms. But kind people are also vulnerable to exploitation by people who aren't so kind. Conversely, selfishness and exploitation in all their forms provide benefits for the individual, at least over the short term, no matter what the collateral damage to others and even everyone over the long term. From an evolutionary perspective, we should expect a diversity of social strategies to coexist on the strength of their respective costs and benefits, the human equivalent of a multispecies ecosystem. This is the lens that I use to reflect upon the human condition, and Oakley is one of my valued colleagues.

Was Carole Alden too kind for her own good, a woman whose need to help others was so strong that she became easy prey for a social predator? That was Oakley's initial presumption based on the press reports. But when she dug into the case she discovered something more complex, dark, and interesting. In many respects, Alden had turned victimhood into an art form. *She* was the predator, and the man she killed was not her only victim.

Oakley is the perfect person to tell this story and to make it a vehicle for the exploration of larger themes that concern each and every one of us. As she was writing *Cold-Blooded Kindness*, she was also organizing an edited volume for Oxford University Press titled *Pathological Altruism*, which involved working with virtually every expert with whom she might want to consult about the Carole Alden case. *Pathological Altruism* has been praised as one of the most important contributions to the scientific study of altruism in decades, which means that *Cold-Blooded Kindness* is backed by more scientific authority than any other book centered on the diagnosis of a single killing.

The kind of science that you will find in the pages of *Cold-Blooded Kindness*, intermixed with the drama of the Carole Alden case, goes beyond forensic science to include the science of why people develop the personalities and relationships that they do and why some relationships are mutually destructive, even ending in a death spiral. There is no clear victim or victimizer in a mutually destructive relationship because each person plays a role in its maintenance. It is not as simple as a predator grasping a prey that is struggling to get away.

Although *Cold-Blooded Kindness* is richly informed by science,

Oakley would be the last person to say that science has provided all the answers. In fact, a second killing lurks in the pages of this book— the murder of objective truth seeking by passionate advocacy. One might think that an issue as important as spousal abuse would receive the most careful attention that science has to offer, but the crusade to raise consciousness about the issue has led to a black-and-white view of victims and victimizers that does not admit shades of gray. Thus, the authentic scientific study of mutually destructive relationships is only beginning, and much remains to be learned. Oakley's spirit of objective scientific inquiry stands in refreshing contrast to well-meaning but misguided crusaders.

Finally, it might seem that an objective scientific diagnosis of a killing would lack compassion, but nothing could be further from the truth. All of the characters in *Cold-Blooded Kindness* are trying to survive as best they can, surrounded by kith and kin who love them no matter how badly they stumble. Moreover, some of those most closely associated with the case have thanked Oakley for helping them achieve a kind of closure that eluded them before.

Taking the life of another has often been used to reflect upon the human condition, but with *Cold-Blooded Kindness* the image has never been sharper.

David Sloan Wilson
SUNY Distinguished Professor
Departments of Biology and Anthropology
Binghamton University
Author of *Evolution for Everyone: How Darwin's Theory*
    Can Change the Way We Think about Our Lives and
    The Neighborhood Project: Using Evolution to Improve My City,
    One Block at a Time

CHAPTER 1

A KILLING IN
MILLARD COUNTY, UTAH

**I don't know why we're here, but I'm pretty sure
that it's not in order to enjoy ourselves.**[1]

—LUDWIG WITTGENSTEIN

(Wittgenstein also noted: "A good guide will take you
through the more important streets more often than he
takes you down side streets; a bad guide will do the
opposite. In philosophy I'm a rather bad guide.")[2]

Carole Elizabeth Alden stood scared in the shadows, a sweaty target in the cool Great Basin evening. She had spent the evening slipping from room to room, always one step ahead, trying to remain unseen.

The caged rats, dead several days now, were drying. But the lizards were alive—alert and nervous in their separate cages. The snakes waited motionless, their pit organs attuned to the heat of potential victims.[3]

21

But rats, lizards, and snakes were the least of Carole's worries. She was a tiny thing—a whisker short of five feet. Her husky husband stood a foot taller—if he wanted to, he could wrestle her to the ground in a second. If that happened, there was no telling how things would unfold.

In their cages, the lizards skittered again.

She could hear Marty coming down the narrow hallway of the double-wide trailer that was their home. At least, until their real home could get built. Marty, she knew, was strung out on his favorite trio—alcohol, marijuana, and methadone. That was always when things would be their worst. Carole tried hard to keep her children shielded from the worst, which is why she had sent the ones still living with her away for the weekend.

Carole's children meant everything to her.

She tensed in the shadows.

Carole was handy with a gun; she had used one before to kill coyotes. Even so, her hands leapt up with the kickback, as if someone else had taken control of them. The blast happened too quickly for her to process—all she could hear now was the ringing.

When she looked at Marty sprawled on the floor in front of her, she was scared.

Marty's body was flaccid, as if he'd just passed out in a drunken, drugged stupor. Again.

She watched. A minute passed. Or maybe it was hours.

His shirt fluttered. A breath? An errant breeze from the air conditioner?

Maybe he wasn't really dead.

She had to make sure. Didn't want to come close until she was sure.

She needed a pillow.

Moments later, one was in hand.

She squatted low in front of Marty and propped the pillow against the top of his head, which was lying right eye down, tilted toward his chest. Then, still squatting, she aimed the muzzle of the Smith & Wesson .38 at the pillow and pulled the trigger. The bullet drilled parallel to the floor through the pillow. It bored through the crown of Marty's skull and into the softness beneath. In less than a hundredth of

Marty Sessions's side table.

a second, Marty's ability to speak, if it had even remained, was wiped clean. Vanished, along with his sense of logic, numbers, and ultimately, self. Damage done, the bullet slid through the roof of Marty's mouth, blowing out under the left side of his chin.

The gunpowder smelled oddly like urine. But it was hard to tell— the house itself smelled like death.

Carole covered Marty with a blanket so she wouldn't have to look. She was tired now. Very tired.

She awakened with a start. Sliding from the couch, she realized she had to get Marty out of the house. Fast.

Carole was petite, but she was also strong. She was used to carting Marty around when he'd passed out. She'd done exactly that when she'd picked him up from the middle of the street earlier that evening— with a little help from bystanders—and stuffed him in her Jeep to haul home. But she'd never realized before that dragging a living body is different from toting a corpse in rigor mortis. Marty's two hundred– plus pounds had become pure stiff dead weight. No matter how she tugged, pulled, or wrestled, she couldn't seem to move him.

Wait. Think.

Think.

Rope. That was it.

The new lariat was stiff—perfect for her purposes. She lifted the blanket and slipped the loop around his feet. Alternately pulling and pushing, she was able to inch the lasso farther and farther up his body. It rested finally just beneath his armpits.

Then she went outside to clamber into the Jeep—a gift from her sister and brother-in-law to lift her from her hardscrabble life. Counter-cranking the steering wheel, she backed toward the house, twisting to look through the dusty rear window.

With the Jeep now as close as she could get it to the back door, she jumped out to hook the rope she had snaked out the door onto a tow strap, then around the trailer hitch. She was back in the Jeep within minutes.

Bald tires whined against the gravel, spinning uselessly against the weight of the body.

Marty wasn't moving.

Damn.

Now what?

Try again.

No go. *Damn!*

Gun it!

The tires skidded and spun in the gravel, their last bit of tread finally gaining traction, thrusting the Jeep forward.

Inside the house, the rope sawed taut with a hissing *zzzzz* against the doorframe. Marty's body sprang into motion, careening in a momentary resurrection against the row of cages stacked against the dining room wall. The snakes recoiled, hissing. Marty's body bounced back toward the foyer, leaving a trail of blood and taking out a bookcase as it careened its way toward the back door.

At the threshold, the body stopped momentarily—jackknifed against the bulging aluminum frame of the doublewide. Then, with a *thwap*, Marty's torso gave just enough, his body sailing out into the yard, taking out a back porch support post on the way.

There. Marty was out.

She jumped out of the Jeep and went around to stare at the body.

The next part wouldn't be easy.

CHAPTER 2

MIKE McGRATH'S
DISTURBING REVELATION

**Codependent behaviors or habits are self-
destructive. We frequently react to people who are
destroying themselves; we react by learning to
destroy ourselves.**

—MELODY BEATTIE, *Codependent No More:
How to Stop Controlling Others and
Start Caring for Yourself* [1]

Psychiatrist Mike McGrath had a philosophy that went like this: No matter how bad your day goes, if you get home and your wife, kids, and pets are all okay, the day was not so bad.[2]

But one day, McGrath heard about the guy who went hiking and literally got stuck between a rock and a hard place, then eventually had to cut off his arm to save himself. Since then, McGrath's philosophy has changed. It is now: No matter how bad your day goes, if you get home and don't have to remove a body part, it wasn't that bad a day.

Nevertheless, Mike McGrath was having a bad day.

McGrath is a forensic psychiatrist, a clinical associate professor of psychiatry, and medical director and chair of a behavioral health department in western New York State. He also serves as medical director to a chemical dependency program and was supervising physician for a sex offender program. For the past twenty years, he has consulted to the Monroe County Socio-Legal Center, providing psychiatric care to inmates and providing forensic evaluations to the Monroe County courts on mental health issues, including competency to stand trial.

McGrath has a deep, personal, lifelong interest in and expertise on codependents.

CODEPENDENCY

A *codependent* is a shorthand term for *a person who enables someone else's highly dysfunctional behavior*. We've all known or heard of people like this—the hardworking secretary who supports a drug-addicted, abusive husband; the caring pastor who knows his wife stashes her vodka in the garage; the woman who works two jobs to afford cartfuls of food for her morbidly obese son. An old joke regarding Alanons (relatives and friends of alcoholics who are also affected by the addictive behavior) goes: *What happens when an Alanon dies? Somebody else's life flashes before their eyes.*

Codependency is intriguing because it is where compassion is between a rock and a hard place—at that counterintuitive point where pleasing other people makes matters worse. It's a kind of emotional obesity, where well-meaning observers say: *Just stop helping them, problem solved!*—while for the codependent, it's not that simple. A woman married to a drug-abusing batterer, for example, may literally find herself with a knife at her throat if she contemplates leaving. And if she has children, there is a whole new layer of complexity, particularly if the batterer is also the family's only breadwinner. Temperament adds its own twist to the puzzle. Perhaps some people are truly more sensitive to others' pain, so "no" is more difficult for them to say.

Currently, the concept of codependency is amorphous—it's a complex hodgepodge in which no one and everyone is guilty. Studying the phenomenon, McGrath has written: "In the codependent relationship, not all actors are equal. One who helps maintain the dysfunctional behavior of another is often referred to as an *enabler*. This term is relative, as it is possible for both players to enable each other in differing ways."[3] In codependent relationships, innocence is the first casualty.

Clinicians—psychology's frontline workers—were the first to frame their observations about codependent behavior. One of the earliest works on the subject was the 1989 book *Facing Codependence: What It Is, Where It Comes from, How It Sabotages Our Lives.*[4] Based on Pia Mellody's previous experiences in healing her own and others' symptoms, in this book the authors offered up five core symptoms of codependence. These involved difficulties in:

- experiencing appropriate levels of self-esteem
- setting functional boundaries
- owning one's own reality
- acknowledging and meeting one's own needs and wants
- experiencing and expressing reality in a moderate fashion—that is, avoiding extremes

Facing Codependence was the first self-help book of its kind—to this day many people still find it helpful. As one Amazon.com reviewer wrote: "[I]t seems to describe me to a T in some ways that I never thought anyone else would understand. All my life I have found most of my self-satisfaction only after ensuring that I am pleasing others."[5]

But *Facing Codependence* was just a start. Another writer, Melody Beattie, built on personal experiences that included abandonment, kidnapping, sexual abuse, and drug and alcohol abuse to write the multimillion bestseller *Codependent No More*. In Beattie's view, codependent behavior consists of extreme versions of perfectly normal behaviors. Therefore, it *is* possible to make changes in our personalities, to normalize them, and Beattie offers her life story as proof.

But as interest in codependency has grown, so has the tendency to make extravagant claims for it. Descriptions that were fuzzy to start with can be interpreted so broadly that almost anyone could be—and has been—described as a codependent.[6] Robert Subby's *Lost in the Shuffle*, for example, explains how showing *no* signs of codependency can be taken as proof that you are codependent.[7]

> ### Melody Beattie's description of codependency characteristics:
>
> - caretaking
> - low self-worth
> - repression of feelings
> - obsessing over things
> - attempting to control
> - denial
> - dependency
> - poor communication
> - weak personal boundaries
> - lack of trust of self and others
> - anger
> - sexual problems

BLINDED ME WITHOUT SCIENCE

The real problem is that we are in the midst of a neuroscientific revolution that is putting psychology and psychiatry on new, firmer foundations, but researchers and clinicians haven't begun applying those tools to help ordinary people make sense of things like codependent behavior. After all—while anecdotal stories can give a powerful start, findings from scientific research can add far more. Who can doubt, for example, the great strides made in understanding autism once it was rescued from the limits of psychoanalysts, with their pat explanatory story of cold parenting, and instead subjected to solid, scientific scrutiny?

But so far, codependency has proven too intractable—or perhaps simply too "female-oriented"—for scientists to have an interest in pursuing it. Authoritative descriptions in the usual handbooks are sparse: for example, in *Kaplan & Sadock's Comprehensive Textbook of Psychiatry* (which takes care to point out that use of the words *enabling* and *denial* in relation to codependence is not an endorsement of an actual syndrome), there are only four paragraphs on codependency.[8] *The American Psychiatric Publishing Textbook of Psychiatry*, *The American Psychiatric Publishing Textbook of Substance Abuse Treatment*, and the *DSM-IV-TR* have no mention of codependency in their indexes. *Principles of Addiction Medicine* and the *Clinical Textbook of Addictive Disorders* briefly mention the term, with no definition.[9] Academic books, in other words, leave readers to deal with this issue on their own.

Journal articles—usually at the forefront of scientific advances—are no better. As Mike McGrath has pointed out in his own research on codependency: "Most, although not all, peer-reviewed literature on codependency appears in relation to spouses and families of substance abusers. Articles tend to be either very critical or naively accepting of the concept. A significant amount of what has been offered professionally borders on unsupported speculation."[10] A big part of the problem has been the many different definitions of codependency—none of which has any systematic research basis.[11]

Without the rigor of science, we are left to simply go with what feels right when we try to define and understand codependence. The real problem is that what feels as if it must be right sometimes isn't right at all. It felt right during the 1950s (and '60s and '70s) to think that autistic children must have suffered from parental abuse. After all, at the time, everybody knew that personality was shaped by environment alone. And for decades, it felt right to think that ulcers were caused just by mental stress instead of by bacteria. The history of psychiatry is full of disproven syndromes and discredited therapies that once "felt right" to clinicians: penis envy, Oedipus complex, recovered memory therapy, rebirthing therapy, release of bottled anger to reduce aggression—the list is long and still growing.

The never-ending train wreck of felt-right syndromes has made psychology suspicious of purported new personality disorders. This has quashed efforts to include codependency as a personality disorder in the *Diagnostic and Statistical Manual of Mental Disorders*—the American bible of psychiatry. But this has also left codependency in limbo, since inclusion in the manual is the key to having the disorder be taken seriously and having it receive research funding and attention. Thus codependency floats, being referred to as if it's real but not actually being studied—a sort of psychological blank check.

Related to codependency is *battered woman syndrome*, a syndrome meant to describe the behavioral patterns seen in women who choose to stay in physically abusive relationships; a syndrome that would seem to describe Carole Alden and her relationship with Marty Sessions to a T. This is a syndrome that does not appear as a diagnosis in the *Diagnostic and Statistical Manual of Mental Disorders*. Instead, the syndrome appears in statutes. It must, by law, be considered in many states—Utah is one—as an aspect of the defense in cases involving battering.[12]

As inexorably as a migraine, battered woman syndrome and its "now you see it, now you don't" qualities led, beginning from the 1990s, to new legislative vistas. And, with relentless finality, to Mike McGrath's disturbing revelation.

CHAPTER 3

MAYBERRY WITH AN EDGE

In March 1911, the Delta Land & Water Company was organized. They surveyed a great many acres of Carey Act land known as the North and South Tracts, lying respectively northwest and southeast of the town of Delta. . . . The vast new land and virgin soil of the desert covered with a growth of greasewood, shadscale, and a little rabbit brush, lay flat in a valley bordered by blue mountains, a part of Pahvant Valley, so named for an early Indian Chief. This treeless, sundrenched, windswept land was a strange new venture to many of these early settlers. The soil, mostly clay, some sandy, proved a challenge in many instances to those unfamiliar with its nature.

—Francis B. Harman, "History of South Tract,"
*Milestones of Millard: A Century of History
of Millard County, 1851–1951*[1]

Sheriff's deputies are often tasked with the mundane: pulling over a drunk, checking on an old widow who heard her windows rattle, chasing the kid who was rattling the widow's windows trying to break into her house to score jewelry for meth. These simple variations on the same basic theme can go on year after year—the type of day-to-day policing that helps keep American society from Tallahassee to Tacoma running smoothly.

Every once in a while, though, something unusual happens. This can demand ingenuity in the immense, solitary reaches of Millard County, Utah, where police backup can be as far as a hundred miles away. Perhaps an officer is faced with putting handcuffs on a suspect who has two prosthetic hooks instead of hands. *Solution—remove prosthetics.* Or he's called out to investigate a car parked out on a stretch of hardpan, where he finds a vacuum hose was rigged to direct the exhaust into the passenger compartment and the desert heat is melting the suicide victim into a puddle on the front seat. *Solution— call for newest rookie, help him slop the body into a body bag. Don't tell him about the wrecker en route. Instead, watch his face when you casually mention he's got to drive the car fifty miles back to the nearest station.*

The deputies of Millard County are nothing if not resourceful.

Deputy Sheriff Tony Pedersen is widely regarded as one of Millard County's most resourceful officers. A lucky thing, as it turns out, because Pedersen, along with the equally capable Sergeant Morris Burton, was the first to respond to the two virtually simultaneous mid-morning calls on July 29, 2006. There was a shooting out in the area known as South Tract—a flat, desolate stretch of greasewood and rabbit brush on the southern border of the little town of Delta, some 135 miles south of Salt Lake City. What Deputy Pedersen would find that morning would draw him into one of the most unusual cases of his career—and along with him his childhood friend Chief Deputy Attorney Patrick Finlinson and their colleague Detective Richard Jacobson.

Millard County is an area rich in history, and that history is woven into the heritage of all three men. No less a pivotal figure than Mormon leader Brigham Young himself had chosen the little town of Fillmore to be the capital of the Territory of Utah. Although Fillmore ultimately became a simple county seat, the cream of all the early converts to the Mormon Church were sent there—their progeny spread as well to neighboring towns.[2] Finlinson, a slim, focused man with a sharp intelligence, jokes that none of those early converts were Finlinsons. This made little difference in his having acquired the local excess brainpower via other routes. Finlinson is a Millard County man five generations back on every line, his family tree filled with well-known local names like Shields, Church, Gillespie, Anderson, and Lyman. (Indeed, early church leader Amasa Lyman was notorious for his eight wives and nearly forty children—Carolyn Ely Bartridge Lyman, his third wife, was Finlinson's great-grandmother.) During its formative years, Fillmore's population consisted largely of polygamous double first cousins. Pedersen and Jacobson, too, share in that colorful early heritage. Nevertheless, the wild early era is long past, leaving Fillmore as the most conservative of the Millard County towns, where those who have lived in the area for nearly fifty years are still referred to as "move-ins."

Immigrants from south of the US–Mexican border like working in the Fillmore area because, outsiders or no, they are treated well and respected for a kindred work ethic. Democratic sheriff Ed Phillips was elected for seven consecutive terms—a testament to both his decency and the fair-mindedness of the citizens in this staunchly Republican town. Store owners who have moved in from the outside testify to the warm treatment they've received and friends they have made, despite their differing religions and backgrounds. It almost seems there is something agreeable in the waters that flow into this part of the Great Basin from the nearby Wasatch Mountains. Even 150 years ago, peaceful Chief Kanosh of the local Paiute band set a positive tone as he and a series of local white leaders clunked heads of those foolish enough to upset the peace.

But there is a viper in this paradise. Millard County straddles a major drug corridor reaching from Mexico to Salt Lake City. Fueled by the corridor, rural Utah has been in the forefront of addiction to crystal meth. Perhaps surprisingly, conservatism of the form taken in a modern smaller town like Fillmore has its advantages. The church offers a built-in social support system and way of viewing the world that is particularly helpful for those trying to find their way out of addiction.

In any case, drugs keep Pedersen, Finlinson, and Jacobson busy on a daily basis. Both in their late thirties now, Pedersen and Finlinson share the easy rapport of the Oak City boys they once were together. After making good on the outside with their college educations and established careers, each was happy when the opportunity arose to return home. It's probably just as well, however, that the statute of limitations has expired on their childhood escapades. Jacobson, the oldest of the trio, came back home to Millard County step by logical step. That's not surprising, given his rational, scientific bent—though none who've known him since childhood could have predicted what he would become.

Deputy Pedersen is a forthright, sandy-haired, sunburned man with the muscular build and sense of imposing presence you'd want in a tough situation. Which is precisely why, on the sunny morning of July 29, 2006, Pedersen found himself turning his patrol car toward the sheriff's substation in the sleepy little town of Delta, Utah.

On that morning, the first of two nearly simultaneous calls to dispatch came in, this one from a call box at Delta's public safety building. A man by the name of Allen Lake—a well-known local character—called in, extremely agitated, to report a shooting.

Once notified by dispatch, Sergeant Morris Burton contacted Pedersen, and within minutes, both were at the glass-paneled, vaulted entrance of the public safety building. Burton immediately began questioning Lake, who said that a woman named Carole Sessions— the wife of Marty Sessions—had told him she'd shot and killed her husband. Lake himself had apparently told Carole she needed to call the police to report the killing, and that if she didn't do it, he would. As far as Burton could tell, Lake was cold sober but so distraught he could hardly organize his thoughts.

The Millard County Sheriff's Office knew who both Carole and Marty Sessions were. Six months before, the couple had been caught late one night driving down the road with bales of hay stuffed in the backseat and sticking out like a cowlick from the trunk of their old Cadillac. This was odd enough behavior, but, even more damning, a neighboring rancher had registered complaints about hay that had been disappearing from his fields over the previous weeks. (Hay stealing is taken so seriously in Millard County that when thefts become large-scale, radio transponders are planted, LoJack-style, so the hay can be tracked.) On questioning, Carole had explained she was compelled to steal the hay to help feed the many animals she cared for—and that it had been Marty's idea.

Police had also known the Sessions couple because Marty had pleaded guilty to domestic violence the year before. The plea had been held in abeyance for a year, then the charges had been dismissed. Following the dismissal, Carole had called, complaining that Marty had disconnected a wire to the Jeep's ignition so she couldn't leave. A month later, Carole called again, saying Marty had illegally taken her Jeep to threaten Allen Lake for having an affair with her. In fact, the very evening before Pedersen and Burton responded to the reports of the shooting, officers had been called about a man lying drunk in the middle of the road. That man had been Marty Sessions. By the time officers arrived, Carole had picked Marty up and taken him home.

Sweating in the hot desert sun, Allen Lake continued his disjointed attempts to relay what he knew of the killing. While Sergeant Burton was busy with Lake, Deputy Pedersen took a second call from dispatch. Apparently, another call had just come into the station. This one had been from Carole Sessions herself, or, as her driver's license would reveal her to be—Carole Elizabeth Alden.

CHAPTER 4

TOUGH LOVE

There are four kinds of homicide: felonious, excusable, justifiable, and praiseworthy.

—AMBROSE BIERCE, *The Devil's Dictionary*[1]

Within four minutes of leaving the public safety building in Delta, Deputy Pedersen and Sergeant Burton pulled up on rural 4500 South, just short of the long, dusty driveway that led back to Carole and Marty's double-wide trailer.

Burton placed a phone call to Carole, glancing toward the house as he spoke. "I understand," he said with studied understatement, "you had a problem there last night."[2]

"Yes," Carole answered.

The trailer was set just far enough back from the road that Burton couldn't quite see what they were going to find. "Where are you right now?"

"I'm on the front porch."

Carole and Marty's double-wide trailer, as seen from the main road.

"Where is your husband?"

"He's in the backyard."

"Where's the gun?"

"On the front porch here with me. It's unloaded. I've got one of the bullet casings here, too, but I dropped the other one in the living room when I was unloading the gun and couldn't find it." Carole's tone was cooperative and apologetic, as if she understood the uneasy spot she'd placed the officers in.

"We're going to come up and talk with you," said Burton. "So I'd like you to walk onto the driveway as we're approaching, with your hands away from your body."

Carole did just that as Deputy Pedersen took the lead up the driveway, pulling in beside her.

Within minutes, Carole had been cuffed—for her protection, Pedersen assured her, as well as their own. She wasn't under arrest, but while the officers were trying to understand what had happened, it was best to proceed cautiously. Burton read Carole her Miranda rights and placed her in the backseat of his truck. Pedersen leaned down to ask whether she was all right—did she need any medical attention?

"No, I'm okay," she assured him. "He didn't hurt me because he couldn't catch me."

After a few minutes of conversation, Sergeant Burton decided he would take Carole back to Delta, where she could be interviewed. Deputy Pedersen would stay to investigate the scene.

Pedersen would soon encounter a crime scene he could never forget.

With Carole sitting quietly in the back of the truck, it took less than five minutes for Burton to get back to the substation in Delta. Once there, he placed Carole in a holding cell, bagging her shoes and socks as possible evidence. Within a few minutes, he brought her back out for routine procedures. Carole was next introduced to Deputy Josie Greathouse, who was given the task of "dressing her out." Dressing out was a routine job for female prisoners—it meant helping Carole change from street to jail clothes, and looking her over for scars, bruises, marks, and the like. Greathouse was an old hand at this—she was a popular deputy, well-known for her dirt-bike daredeviltry, her outreach to the community's Latinos, and her compassion.

Right off, the deputy noticed an odd lump on one of Carole's wrists. Looking up at Carole's face, Greathouse asked what it was from.

Marty Sessions—her husband—had put her in handcuffs, Carole explained, and they had been too tight.

Greathouse noted the lump and then continued. Brushing back Carole's hair, she noticed a little red mark behind her ear, right at the hairline.

Carole didn't know what had caused it.

Looking further, Greathouse noticed a red mark on Carole's ear. She asked Carole about that mark too.

Marty, Carole said, would grab her by the ears and squeeze her face together while he put his own face up to hers to yell at her.

Carole pointed toward the middle of her forehead, indicating that the bump there was from Marty head-butting her. Greathouse looked carefully and saw nothing unusual. But when she felt Carole's forehead, she could feel a knot under the skin.

Carole slipped her pants off, and a badly mottled bruise was visible on the back of her leg. Marty, Carole explained, had hit her with a board four days before. As Carole removed her shirt, a diamond-shaped bruise showed on the inside of her arm—she didn't know where that had come from—maybe Marty. There was an old scar in the middle of her back, half an inch wide and an inch and a half long, as if something sharp had pierced her skin. Marty, Carole said, had thrown something at her.

Moving on, Greathouse observed Carole's breasts. Her nipples were pierced. Carole said that Marty had pierced them when she'd been tied up.

High up on the inside of one of her legs, perhaps an inch from her vagina, there was what looked like an old laceration. Marty had done that, Carole indicated.

Carole moved to point something else out to Greathouse.

There were four piercings, two on each side of the lips of her vagina.

Although he'd never done it, Carole said, Marty had intended to run metal through the holes. That way he could put her in a chastity belt that only he could unlock.

Clearly this woman had not come from a peaceful rural home. What seemed to have been happening at the Sessions house verged on horror.

CHAPTER 5

MIKE McGRATH'S DISTURBING REVELATION, CONTINUED

**Despite articles and books on proper interpreta-
tion of statistics, it is still common in expert
reports as well as the scientific and statistical literature to see basic misinterpretations and neglect
of background assumptions that underlie all statistical inferences.**[1]

—SANDER GREENLAND, professor of epidemiology,
UCLA School of Public Health,
and professor of statistics,
UCLA College of Letters and Science

Mike McGrath's disturbingly bad day started out normally.[2]
Not one for breakfast or lunch, he revved himself on
coffee as he drove to one of the many sites he supervises in Rochester,
New York—a collection of inpatient and outpatient mental health
clinics and chemical dependency programs. McGrath's job involves

dealing with quality of care, client risk management, recruitment and retention of staff—each of these tasks is far more demanding than the bland corporate phraseology would make it appear.

McGrath has been a practicing psychiatrist and forensic psychiatrist for over two decades. He is a general psychiatrist who treats anyone age eighteen or older. Over time, however, he's developed proficiency with chemical-dependent offenders and sex offenders, and he's acquired a subspecialty in forensic psychiatry—the application of clinical expertise to legal questions. This means that when prosecutors or defending attorneys are trying to determine whether someone is competent to stand trial, or scratching their heads trying to understand a defendant's state of mind at the time of a crime, McGrath is the kind of expert they turn to. As the years passed, McGrath has worked with and treated many victims of domestic violence; he has also forensically evaluated both abusers and their victims. When offered honoraria for occasional local presentations about psychiatric issues, he has always asked that the money be donated to a battered women's shelter.

McGrath seems like the prototypical WASP, but his graying ponytail whispers of nonconformity. He writes:

> During my surgical residency I ran into a twenty-six-year-old Haitian girl who was employed as a unit clerk at the hospital. She had come to the USA at age seven with her younger sister to reunite with her mother who had emigrated years earlier. She had an associate's degree in finance and was working at the hospital for a few months where her mother was a nurse, trying to figure out what road in life to take next. I felt an immediate attraction to her, but she was so pretty I assumed she had several boyfriends. Slowly we got to know each other and I learned she had a five-year-old son and had come back from California (where she had been married and living for a few years) to make a new start. She was living at her mother's home in Brooklyn. The attraction between us grew and before long we were saying wacky things like "I love you." Leslie and I got married in February 1986. I adopted her son a few years after we married and we have two daughters, one a first year law student and one

a college graduate with a degree in history, trying to figure out what she wants to do, which I understand. Our son is an industrial engineer and he and his wife had a daughter—our first granddaughter—who was born on President Obama's inauguration day.

Between his wife, son, and daughters, McGrath is keenly aware of minority and gender issues—when pressed, he notes: "Just because I'm a white male doesn't mean that is my sole perspective on things."

Perhaps because of the nature of his work, it's difficult to catch McGrath in a smile. Pictures reveal a man with no need to ingratiate himself to the camera. Indeed, when asked to describe himself as a forensic expert, McGrath writes, "I think the way I would describe myself is that I am an advocate for the truth and get very annoyed when I see others twisting it, regardless of the way it may play out."

It was evening, as McGrath remembers it, when suddenly the crux of what he was researching struck him as having deep-rooted problems. It didn't seem right. It wasn't *fair.*

WHAT'S FAIR?

Even animals have a sense of fairness. Adult wolves, lions, and bears "play fair" with their cubs—keeping their claws and teeth in check as their tiny adversaries spring in mock menace. Monkeys will happily munch lettuce but will put on a monkey-pout if offered lettuce while a compatriot gets a juicy grape. *It's not fair*, their accusing eyes seem to say as they refuse the second-class treat.[3]

Unsurprisingly, our feelings of fairness arise through a complex tug and pull of neural music—blindingly fast synaptic rhythms and patterns that badger and chivy our brains into feelings of compassion for others in comparison with ourselves. But the neural music isn't the same for everyone. There's the rub.

If you grow up in a happy suburban home with a PTA mom and a dad who coaches Little League, you may stare at a picture of a broken-nosed, bloody woman and recoil in disgust. *That's not fair*, you think as you learn she was hospitalized because of her husband's Saturday night drunken outburst.

But if you grow up watching your mother being beaten every day by your father, you may not have the same reaction at all. The guys you hang around with may have seen the same patterns play out in their own families. Maybe you also got a good whipping when you did something wrong (and sometimes, even when you didn't). You and your brothers and sisters had some all-out clout wars to determine who reigned. Growing up like this, you are more likely to think a man beating a woman is normal behavior. After all, in your world, a woman has her place—how else are you going to keep her in line? And doesn't beating her show the depth of your feelings?

It's even more complicated, though. In some families, it's the dad who's beaten or emotionally abused. A child grows up thinking it's normal and fair to despise a weakling dad who never hits back—a man who instead drinks or takes drugs to strip away the pain.

Even more confusing, some children who have never been exposed to domestic violence engage in it, while some children raised in households with significant domestic violence grow up to be exceptional parents.

In the end, fairness isn't a perfect Platonic structure—like a sphere or cube—that lies outside us in some quintessential form. Instead, our own ideas of what fairness looks like are imperfectly woven into the very fabric of our brains through our lives and cultures. (The brain's two hemispheres seem to feel these effects in different ways—it is the right dorsolateral prefrontal cortex in particular that appears to underwrite our sense of justice.)[4] Genes have a powerful effect, obviously, but those genes are physically influenced—turned on and off—by the environment. "Environment" also includes other people and how they treat us—in a word, culture.

Culture can change, of course. Just over a generation ago, as researcher Linda Mills points out in the book *Violent Partners*: "[D]omestic violence was considered a private matter. Some people felt that a man's home was his castle and that it was no one's business what went on there. Others assumed that the violence in most marriages was either provoked (and therefore deserved) or rare (and therefore something to be endured, like bad weather). Why intervene?"[5]

But by the early 1980s, American culture was shifting. Open minds heard the impassioned words of women who had long been disenfranchised. The women's movement was becoming a radical force to be reckoned with.

By and large, people care. We're fair. So long as it's not too big of an intellectual leap from the culture we've grown up with, we can be brought by both emotional and rational appeals to change our outlook if others suggest something is not fair.

But who decides what's fair?

BATTERED WOMAN SYNDROME

Shadows flickered that evening in Mike McGrath's study—pictures of his smiling daughters looked down from overloaded bookshelves. McGrath's study is a tribute to his professional and private interests: Honorary plaques share the walls with a musket and collection of ornamental swords so sweeping that a tangle of extras tussle for room in the corner. Usually, the study was simply a comfortably untidy hangout where McGrath could lose himself in his work. But tonight, as he was scrabbling through his research papers, he felt a creeping sense of unease.

McGrath was reading Lenore Walker's *The Battered Woman Syndrome*, a classic for those who seek to understand the motives of women who stay in violent, abusive relationships. As a forensic psychiatrist, McGrath was keenly aware of the difficulties in psychiatric diagnosis of trauma syndromes. Indeed, that's why he'd been asked to write about battered woman syndrome for a new book, *Forensic Victimology*. (Since criminals have a discipline called criminology, it makes sense that there is also a field for victims called victimology.)

Battered Woman Syndrome

In Lenore Walker's *The Battered Woman Syndrome* she describes the syndrome as follows:

"BWS [battered woman syndrome] as it was originally conceived, consisted of the pattern of the signs and symptoms that have been found to occur after a woman has been physically, sexually, and/or psychologically abused in an intimate relationship when the partner (usually, but not always a man) exerted power and control over the woman to coerce her into doing whatever he wanted without regard for her rights or feelings. . . . The research has now demonstrated that BWS has six groups of criteria that have been tested scientifically and can be said to identify the syndrome. The first three groups of symptoms are the same as for PTSD [post-traumatic stress disorder] while the additional three criteria groups are present in intimate partner victims (IPV). They are:

1. Intrusive recollections of the trauma event(s).
2. Hyperarousal and high levels of anxiety.
3. Avoidance behavior and emotional numbing usually expressed as depression, dissociation, minimization, repression and denial.
4. Disrupted interpersonal relationships from batterer's power and control measures.
5. Body image distortion and/or somatic or physical complaints
6. Sexual intimacy issues"[6]

Walker's basic thesis implied that battered women are essentially normal—or at least were normal before the battering occurred.[7] These unlucky women have simply fallen in with abusive men. McGrath had no initial beef with Walker's thesis, knowing from personal experience that not all women enter battering relationships due to psychopathology. What didn't sit well with McGrath, though, was the methodology and extent of her research. As far as he could see, there were no independent control groups in Walker's studies.[8] How do we know, he asked himself, whether Walker's study subjects were similar to or different from non-battered women?[9] Wouldn't Walker want to know that?

McGrath shifted in his chair, as much to realign his thinking as his posture, then skipped back on the page to reread Walker's explanation of her methods.

> In conducting this research design, certain decisions were made that were appropriately influenced by the feminist perspective. For example, given the finite resources available, it was decided to sacrifice the traditional empirical experimental model, with a control group, for the quasiexperimental model using survey-type data collection. It was seen as more important to compare battered women to themselves than to a nonbattered control group. Comparing battered and nonbattered women implies looking for some deficit in the battered group, which can be interpreted as a perpetuation of the victim-blaming model.[10]

McGrath leaned back in his chair, looked up at the ceiling, then looked down again, dumbfounded.

In arcane, teasingly academic fashion, Walker was saying something extraordinary: that her findings related to battered women had never been compared to those of non-battered women. And possibly more important, those passages telegraphed that she had no intention of *ever* doing a study employing a standard control group—exactly the kind of research needed to demonstrate the validity of her claims.

She just doesn't think the rules apply to her, he realized.

As he began to burrow deeper, he began to see more. Walker's work, as it turned out, had never been replicated.[11] And she claimed she couldn't compare her group with normal women, because in thirty years, she hadn't been able to find an equivalent group of some four hundred *un*-battered women.[12] A psychologist might think, *So what? If normal women were shown to be different from battered women, this still wouldn't get at the quality and accuracy of battered women's perceptions.*

But that wasn't the point, McGrath realized. If the battered women sometimes carried a difference in their own personalities, then therapeutic efforts focused only on abusers might not repair the problem. If it took two to tango, with victims playing their own role in the dance— well, Walker's studies wouldn't reveal that, because Walker appeared to have started from the unproven assumption that battered women were different only because of the battering—otherwise they were basically normal. Therefore, the victim side of the equation could never be approached from a preventive angle.

Of course, McGrath realized, by wanting to understand whether there is pathology present in the victims as well as the abusers, there was always the danger of overfocusing on the negative qualities of the victim, which could not only oversimplify the problem but also turn it into an exercise in blaming the victim. After all, no matter how it's sliced, abuse is a slaughterhouse of the psyche. A woman (or man) can end up walking on eggshells trying to please a partner who can never be pleased. Such a spouse can be a Janus-headed nightmare—a publicly benign significant other who turns the spigot of emotional or physical abuse on behind closed doors. Regardless of how tangled the mess of blame and responsibility becomes, at some point, someone recognizes that he or she needs to get out of the situation. But escape is not a matter of snapping one's fingers and moving out—especially when children are involved.

How can these potential problems be avoided? McGrath wondered. *How can the rigors of science help women understand what got them into a battering situation in the first place and how to avoid it in the future?* A balanced approach that looked fairly at *both* partners was what was needed in Walker's research. But a balanced approach was not what she was providing.

Walker's approach isn't necessarily going to help battered women, McGrath realized. It was perfectly possible that an abusive man, for example, might be helped through therapy, but that the battered woman, who had no therapeutic attention devoted to her, might then move on to re-create the battering in a new relationship. (The "problem" for women in some abusive relationships, in fact, might be some of their nicest qualities—agreeableness, a trusting nature, enjoyment in helping others, and a desire to always look on the bright side.)

Ultimately, Walker's faulty scientific approach not only didn't address the whole issue, it might be creating a whole new slew of problems, because legislation in a number of states was based on Walker's approach. This meant prosecutors and defense lawyers had to take her assumptions about battered women, in some sense, as facts. To do otherwise courted appellate reversal.

In McGrath's analytical way, he slowly began to realize something more: everything he thought he knew about battered woman syndrome —a key aspect of litigation in murder trials involving battered women —was now suspect.

CHAPTER 6

A COMPULSION TO CARE

**79 years have passed almost like a dream and I
wonder how many opportunities for doing good to
my associates have I neglected. In all the years I
have lived my desires have been to do all the good
I could and as little evil as possible.**
—Carolyn Ely Bartridge Lyman, 1827–1908.
Buried in Oak City, Utah.
Great-grandmother of attorney Pat Finlinson.[1]

"I'm just so worried—so afraid for her," says *Penny Packer*,[2] Carole's junior high school art teacher, who retains a frank, clear-eyed beauty even now in her retirement years. The fiercely intelligent, free-spirited Penny shares Carole's love of animals—two rescued donkeys graze alongside a skittish half-blind horse back in the pasture beside her gray modular home.

A longtime friend of both Carole and the Alden family, Penny has swooped into the living room of the Alden family home where the interview is taking place; Carole's mother is bustling in the kitchen. Penny sizes up the couch and chairs and then plops herself unexpectedly on the floor in front of the fireplace. Like many of Carole's friends and supporters, Penny is distraught about Carole's prospects. She is still trying to reconcile the brilliantly creative teenager she once taught with the adult Carole has become.

"I am an art teacher, but Carole is an *artist*," Penny pronounces, smiling. She is perhaps thinking of Carole's *Desert Cradle*—a cloth creation featuring an empty cradle enveloped by a cactus, a lizard, and an all-too-realistic rattlesnake. The work earned notoriety in 1993 when it was selected as representative of Utah women's art for an exhibit at the National Museum of Women in Washington, DC. Carole told *Salt Lake Tribune* reporter Cornelia deBruin that "her piece symbolizes the way many women's lives are full of pain, including divorce and abuse."[3] The flap over the artwork was, Carole said, "moronic"— she pointed out that as the (then) mother of four children, she should be the last person to be accused of anti-motherhood.

Why were lizards and rats Carole's favorite animals? "It shocked people," Penny answers, eyes twinkling. "Carole looked and lived for *shock* value. She loved to wake people up and take them out of their comfort zone.

"You can have painters, but that's not necessarily an artist. In an artist there is something inside that allows their mind to just go out to the ether, where everything exists, and they're able to just draw this energy in and make something tangible, and . . ." Penny shakes her head, laughing. "I don't know how they do it. These ideas, visions, thoughts just come, pour in, and they're able to download these things and put them into a concrete piece of art that the rest of us poor souls can only look at and try to understand."

If anyone outside her family knows Carole, it's Penny Packer. Her mentoring friendship began in Carole's junior high years. Carole and a coterie of kindred students flocked to Packer's out-of-the-way Quonset hut art room during lunch period to eat M&Ms, listen to Neil Diamond, and discuss the meaning of life in Packer's nonjudgmental presence. Carole was the student ringleader—whatever her thoughts, the others would gather round to listen.

Between existential discussions, Carole railed in typical teenage fashion about her dad's restrictions and laughingly described the naughty things she did to get his goat. Carole's junior high school years in the 1970s coincided with the end of the hippie era, and she absorbed its ethos and hippie jargon, adopting personal freedom as her credo. She disliked organized activities unless she could take that activity's core idea and infuse it with what Penny called her "Caroleness."

"If you look at an artist's mental health," Penny muses, "it's always been different—to be an artist you see things differently because you're wired differently. Carole is ruled by emotions—overwhelmed by them. They bombard her in such massive quantities to tempt and taunt her. If she can just stop that onslaught of emotion and keep focus on a little tunnel of rationality . . ." Penny's voice trails off as she considers. "They

Carole submitted this "soft art" dragon as her self-portrait for the show "Constructing Self: Thirty Self-Portraits," at the Gallery at Library Square in May and June 2006, presented by the Salt Lake City Public Library and the Utah Arts Festival. She told others at the time that this dragon may define her.

should just keep her somewhere, where life can't get to her so she can just commune with the universe and create to her heart's delight. The everyday things that life has to do trip her up so."

Penny leans forward, nonplussed: "Carole is a fixer. She fixes sick animals. She fixes sick people. I'm worried for her because I don't know what kind of therapy it would take for her to not get back into this pattern of falling in with lost souls. A lot of the good that's come her way she's not allowed in. She's gone for the damaged goods. The ones that can be rescued by her. Remade by her."

EMPATHY

A compulsion to "fix" other people appears to be a part of that amorphous concept of codependency. In fact, one way to think of the syndrome is to remember that, just as abusers may have quirks in how their brains function, so, too, may victims. This recognition could be enormously helpful to treating both abuser and victim. Understanding the mental quirks that underlie codependent behavior is the first step toward changing them. As many therapists intuitively realize, the brain is greatly plastic, capable of enormous change.

Neuroscientists may not be studying codependency directly, but they *are* studying the fundamentally related behavior of empathy— that ability to peer inside another's brain and feel what someone else is feeling. It seems that codependent behavior may be related to excesses and glitches in our feelings of empathy.

But what is empathy? As it turns out, when we see, hear, or even simply know about another's situation, this can provide a trigger for our brain cells to weave their activity together in the particular pattern we experience as empathy. Variations in this pattern lie behind our unthinking impulse to comfort a crying baby, as well as more conscious decisions, such as deciding whether or not to help a friend move into a new apartment. Obviously, these empathic patterns are very useful in allowing the human species to survive.

Among the most interesting and as yet little understood components of empathy are special brain cells called mirror neurons. These spunky cells, like ventriloquists' dummies, spark in response to other people's actions. When a woman grabs for a handrail as she slips on a set of stairs, her neurons blast a signal to her hand that says *hold on!* Miraculously, as we watch the woman grapple for balance, the same neurons fire *hold on!* in our own brains. Likewise, when we see someone cry, tears well up in our own eyes because the mirror neurons in our brains are also signaling us to cry. In essence, we understand what another person is feeling, at least in part, because mirror neurons help us feel the same way.

But mirror neurons form only a part of the story. Jean Decety, a researcher at the University of Chicago, who could serve as James Bond actor Daniel Craig's husky, French-accented double, has looked carefully over the years at the constellation of neural patterns that underlie empathy. Like many other world-class scientists, Decety has a magical way of simplifying the impenetrable. He has found that empathy is best understood by breaking it down into four easy-to-understand components:

- The ability to share someone else's emotions.
- Awareness of yourself and of other people—and knowledge of where you "end" and others begin.
- The mental flexibility to set your own perspective aside and view things from another person's perspective.
- The ability to consciously control your own emotions.[4]

As Decety emphasizes, empathy is formed from a mixture of all four of these components. If any single component isn't quite right—because of a genetic predisposition, quirks in development, or even dysfunctional thought patterns that can arise from stress or simply hanging out with the wrong people—the resulting empathy begins to look different, even abnormal. Then that person's behavior can fray. He or she may have difficulties empathizing with others. Or people may feel too much empathy—unable to separate another's feelings and desires from their own.

LEARNING TO KEEP EMPATHY IN CHECK

But as Decety's work also shows, a person's brain is not fixed in stone when it comes to neural patterns related to empathy.[5] In a clever experiment, Decety's Taiwanese colleague, neuroscientist Yawei Cheng, showed that it is possible to turn on and off one's empathy for others by sheer conscious will. Cheng reasoned that it's simply not possible for surgeons, dentists, and nurses to go about their daily jobs if they feel the personal distress and anxiety that people ordinarily feel when watching someone in pain. These experts must develop some neural tricks to help desensitize themselves.

To study this, Cheng and her team used medical imaging to observe people's neural responses when they observed an acupuncture needle being inserted into another person's body. Normal people became uncomfortable watching the prick, and for good reason—their brains fired a pattern that echoed the uncomfortable sensation felt by the person being pricked.

But the brains of acupuncture experts reacted very differently. As soon as the prick occurred, it seems a part of the brain retrieved an *acupuncture* memory that in turn triggered the brain's command central to shut down the ability to empathize with another's pain. This command central did something else—it increased the signal to the part of the brain (the *temporoparietal* region) that makes us aware that someone else is different from us. Essentially, it was reminding the expert: *remember, that's somebody else, not you!*

Cheng's work shows that experts teach themselves how to disconnect emotionally from others when empathy becomes undesirable—and that they do this by tamping down their emotional reactions *as well as* by learning to amplify the *that's not you!* signal. Interestingly, it is the right hemisphere of the brain—specifically, the right frontoparietal network, that allows us to distinguish ourselves from others.[6] This is yet another example of the differing modes of operation of the brain's two hemispheres. Empathy itself, it seems, is rooted in the right side of the brain—lesions or low functionality on the right side of the brain has been associated with the lack of empathy seen in, for example, antisocial personality disorder.

No one teaches acupuncture experts how to make these changes in their brains. It's something they teach themselves naturally, just as babies teach themselves that moving their eyes can allow them to watch Mommy, and crying gets Mommy's attention.

But why would something like compassion arise in the first place? Evolutionists point to three possible advantages: that it would help vulnerable offspring, that it would be appealing in potential mates, and that compassionate people have more and stronger friends and alliances.[7] But this complex mixture of evolutionary forces would mean that a number of different genes could help support empathic behavior—meaning sometimes a person could inadvertently get an "overdose" of such genes. (Women in particular appear to be more empathic than men, not only because of the different ways their brains develop, but also because of the cultural reinforcements they receive for empathic behavior.)[8] Perhaps, then, codependents have varying mixtures of cultural, environmental, and genetic factors that have resulted in an overly strong tendency to empathize with others.

But the problem may be more fundamental, related to an inability to control emotions. Thus, learning how to tamp down their emotional reactions and amplify the *that's not you!* signal might be something codependents have trouble teaching themselves to do.

This, in fact, might lie behind codependency expert Melody Beattie's description of typical codependent behavior, where other people's moods control the codependent's emotions, and the codependent attempts to control her own emotions by controlling the other person's. "If my husband is happy," Beatty writes, describing a woman named Kristen, "and I feel responsible for that, then I'm happy. If he's upset, I feel responsible for that, too. I'm anxious, uncomfortable, and upset until he feels better. I try to *make* him feel better. I feel guilty if I can't. And he gets angry with me for trying.

"And it's not only with him that I behave codependently," she added. "It's with everyone: my parents, my children, guests in my home. Somehow, I just seem to lose myself in other people. I get enmeshed in them."

THE DARK SIDE

A door slams in the distance—Carole's mother is continuing her work in the background. After forty years, four children, and a fountain of grandchildren, she now lives alone in this, the family home. The idyllic garden she and her husband created on the once barren land reigns serenely around the house. But the Siberian pea pheasant cover planted long ago as part of a 4-H project is starting to become over-grown, and Carole's mother is in her mid-seventies. She recently took the plunge and bought a smaller patio home in town, near friends, and is now in the process of packing.

She peeks in the door to the living room to say hello, then politely heads off, back to sorting materials elsewhere in the house. She is tire-less—up at dawn and to bed near midnight. Even she is dismayed at the accumulation of family treasures she must sift through. But she's buoyed by constant phone calls—her three younger children keep tabs, and one friend or another seems to touch base every few hours. She also leads a popular aqua fitness class for those with arthritis and performs many volunteer activities in the community. "She volunteers because she just thinks it's the right thing to do," says her youngest son.

Penny, who paused with Carole's mother's greeting, resumes the conversation—her thoughts turning now to her friends, the Aldens: "Carole's parents were strict, but they gave their kids all sorts of growth opportunities. Whatever those kids wanted to do, those parents were right there for them—4-H, travel—you name it." Penny could have added sports, Brownies, Scouts, music, art, dog-obedience training, pheasant raising, and hiking. By all accounts—save those of Carole herself—the Aldens were as supportive a pair of parents as any child could wish for.

"Carole's first two husbands were pretty good. Smart—they were her equals. I think they just gave up on her after a while." Penny hesitates, then turns her thoughts to Andy, Carole's doomed, drug-addicted lover whom she was with during the years after she left her second husband, before she met Marty. "I don't know much about Andy. But he wasn't her equal intellectually.

"There is so much beauty in her—but there's that dark side that many artists have, that they have to deal with. Carole is a fixer," she repeats. "Fixes sick animals, sick people. She loves iguanas. But if one of them bit her, she'd strangle it." Penny looks up, startled, as if this was the first time she'd ever realized this. "She did something like that once before. She was pregnant; her goat tried to butt her. She killed it with a pitchfork right there."

Penny shakes her head, puzzled—clearly what she's just realized doesn't make sense to her. She changes the subject, summing things up. "I talk—she doesn't listen. A lot of people try to talk to her and give her little gentle nudges, and that's why she's in the mess she's in. She listens through her filter of reality.

"But anyway. Utah—no women's rights, a useless lawyer. Slam dunk, she was railroaded."

CHAPTER 7

EMPATHY'S ECHOES

When Lear cries, "Is there any cause in nature that makes these hard hearts?" we could reply, on one level, yes—a defect in the right prefrontal cortex.
—IAIN MCGILCHRIST, *The Master and His Emissary*[1]

Railroading of women is something preeminent empathy researcher Carolyn Zahn-Waxler knows all too well. As one of relatively few females to earn a doctorate in psychology in the 1960s, after receiving her degree from the University of Minnesota she headed to a postdoctoral position at the National Institute of Mental Health. Noticing her usefulness, her supervisors made the temporary position permanent. "There were few female scientists then," Carolyn noted, "and just two of them were in leadership positions, so I considered myself lucky."[2]

Science and rationality had served as her anchor during an emotionally turbulent childhood. Throughout Carolyn's early years, her depressed mother's self-focus had pulled Carolyn and her sister into her orbit, making it difficult for the sisters to pursue their own interests and dreams. When Carolyn was a sophomore in high school, her mother was hospitalized for depression; these hospitalizations were to occur several times a year and for many years to come. While the diagnosis of depression was clear, few if any effective treatments were available. Hostility and anger often accompany depression, and this played out in Carolyn's relationship with her mother when she returned home from the hospital. While Carolyn experienced the brunt of her mother's anger, Carolyn's younger sister frequently witnessed it as well, which added to the trauma for both youngsters.

Moving on her own from Wisconsin to Maryland, where the National Institute of Mental Health was located, was emotionally freeing for Carolyn, even as the freedom from family entanglements was replaced by intellectual demands. Her job was complex, and initially she was content to simply learn the ropes. This suited her bosses. Carolyn would eventually learn there was a gentleman's agreement in place that she wouldn't get resources to conduct her own independent research. A decade of serving in this role found Carolyn chafing at the constraints and limitations of her appointment. The rising tide of feminism hadn't yet reached the National Institute of Mental Health, which was still bound in a hierarchical and patriarchal research culture that looked askance at the idea of professional advancement for women. Carolyn found that a tightly woven institutional and cultural net of "sex discrimination, cultural constraints, child rearing, and early socialization" all combined to discourage her assertiveness, which meant her professional growth was unfolding in slow motion. Eventually, however, Carolyn began to publish influential first-authored articles in peer-reviewed journals. She gave talks, joined editorial boards, and served on committees. Gradually, her professional life expanded, and she overcame her own self-doubts: "Time and experience assured me that I was not an imposter," she wrote. "I stopped being so sensitive to others' judgments, quelled my 'internal critic,' and used self-criticism to effect changes in my life."

Carolyn Zahn-Waxler. Carolyn Zahn-Waxler's distinguished career at the National Institute of Mental Health has centered around the origins and development of empathy and caring behaviors. She is currently interested in translational questions, such as how scientific advances can inform the use of practices that encourage empathy, kindness, altruism, and positive emotions in children.

Carolyn Zahn-Waxler would eventually become head of the Section on Development and Psychopathology at the National Institute of Mental Health. She served as associate editor and, ultimately, editor of the prestigious journal *Developmental Psychology*. Carolyn's longitudinal studies—that is, multi-year studies that follow infants as they grow into adolescents—have allowed her to gain an extraordinary understanding of the development, and sometimes the overdevelopment, of altruism and compassion in children. Her research involving the children of depressed parents revealed that some of these children tried to take care of their distressed parents, a process known as role-reversal, or "parentification," of the child. She was struck by the extent to which her own personal experiences and those of her sister in trying to take care of the emotional needs of their parents paralleled patterns revealed in her research.

EMPATHIZERS VERSUS SYSTEMIZERS

In virtually every society, women, much more than men, are the ones who care for others.[3] Women drift far more naturally into the helping professions—they are also principally involved in the education of children. These roles, write Carolyn Zahn-Waxler and her colleague Carole Van Hulle, "require a deeply engrained sense of personal responsibility for resolving problems and distresses of others."[4] Women, it seems, may be predisposed on an evolutionary basis to be more empathic than men—although, of course, plenty of men are still highly empathetic.[5]

One researcher, psychologist Simon Baron-Cohen (a mild-mannered cousin of in-your-face comedian Sacha Baron-Cohen), has proposed a personality theory that divides people into two types—empathizers and systemizers.[6] Systemizers are people who like to figure out the rules embedded in systems. (The systems can be as different as car engines, train timetables, dance routines, and stamp collections.) Empathizers, on the other hand, are more interested in other people—what those people feel, and why they think what they think.

Baron-Cohen has devised tests to measure people's systemizing and empathizing abilities. These tests seem to indicate that if you're a good systemizer, you're usually not a very good empathizer, and vice versa. Translated into real-life terms, that might explain why a mechanical engineer could be clueless about his wife's pointed expressions of neglect when he forgets her birthday, while this same wife, a nurse-practitioner who worked nights to help put her husband through college, may have no interest in learning about the intricacies of her husband's work in designing engines.

In Baron-Cohen's perspective, these differing styles for interacting with the world have to do with which parts of the brain are shifted into overdrive while the baby is still in the womb. A few extra drops of testosterone at just the right time as a fetus is developing, he believes, can result in more systemizing and less empathizing ability by slowing the development of some areas of the brain.[7] This controversial testosterone-connected theory of brain development is called the Geschwind-Galaburda theory. It's thought by some that this theory knits together many seemingly unrelated findings, such as that boys

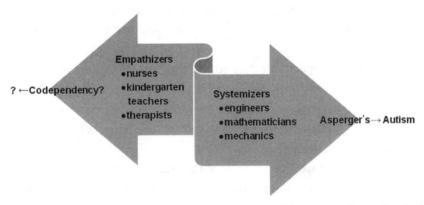

Empathizers-systemizers. Just as we can divide people up by their tendencies toward extroversion or introversion, we can also divide people up by their tendencies to *empathize* or to *systemize*. Empathizers are more interested in people—what they feel and why they think what they think. Systemizers are people who like to figure out the rules embedded in systems such as car engines, train timetables, dance routines, or stamp collections.

have more problems with stuttering, dyslexia, hyperactivity, and Tourette syndrome.[8] Although not often discussed, this theory may also support the incontrovertible evidence that girls suffer more commonly from syndromes related to relationships with others: depression, anxiety, and anorexia.[9]

According to Baron-Cohen, boys, with their homegrown sources of testosterone, are prone to becoming systemizers. But the amounts of testosterone involved are still tiny and can come from many sources—even from the mother herself. So some females can also receive dollops of testosterone at just the right time to help them develop better systemizing skills—and, of course, other factors play a role. Thus, Baron-Cohen posits that men tend to have stronger systemizing abilities, while women tend toward having more empathizing abilities.[10] Baron-Cohen believes that those with autism are über-systemizers. He hypothesizes that a child with autism can stare at a wiggling string for hours because of the pleasure he receives in understanding the dynamics of the string's motion. This might explain why traits of autism and its milder cousin Asperger's disorder are more frequently found in mathematicians and those working with other highly theoretical systems.[11] Roughly ten times as many men as women have autism.

These ideas appear to relate to the differing functions of the two hemispheres of the brain. As Iain McGilchrist notes in his seminal overview of hemispheric function, *The Master and His Emissary*, the left side of the brain serves as the seat of systemizing, while the right supports empathizing.[12]

Researchers have delved deeply into the extreme end of systemizing—that is, those with autism and Asperger's disorder. The conundrum of autism is clearly an important area of research—after all, a lack of ability to empathize with others can leave one in a difficult social pickle, even if this same lack of ability sometimes confers gifts like mathematical intuition. But those on the *other* side of the spectrum; that is, people who have extraordinarily high empathizing abilities and little or no systemizing abilities, have received little research attention.[13] Some feel this is due to bias—after all, medical research has a history of avoiding female-oriented problems, and empathizers are primarily women. But "hyperempathy" may also be little studied because having high empathizing and low systemizing skills is less obviously problematic. A woman who is great at empathizing but lousy at systemizing may not be able to follow a road map or program her VCR, but she will have plenty of friends who can help her whenever her lack of systemizing skills bedevil hers. Plus, she gets lots of praise for being such a caring person. So where's the problem?

DISEASES OF CARING

It's surprising how many diseases and syndromes commonly seen in women seem to be related to women's generally stronger empathy for and focus on others. For example, Rachel Bachner-Melman and her colleagues have found that the stronger the symptoms of anorexia, the more concerned for others and selfless a person appears to be—it's even possible to predict whether children will develop anorexia based on their selflessness.[14] (In a mark of the importance of setting personal boundaries and limits, it seems becoming more selfish helps protect against eating disorders.)[15]

"All of my life I lived for other people," writes one who had suffered from anorexia, "not out of choice, but because I didn't know any other way. It wasn't until years later that I found out that I didn't actually have a self. I became what other people liked, thought, said and did: without respect for myself, going day by day trying to please other people so that I could be good enough."[16] Interestingly, in an obverse of autism, nine in every ten sufferers of anorexia are female.[17]

Similar to anorexia in its predisposition for striking women is depression—a disease that also often grows from relationship issues. As it happens, our empathic responses to others can often bring guilt— which, overall, can have a positive effect. "Our ability to respond to one another with empathy, to experience guilt when we believe we have harmed another," notes psychologist Lynn O'Connor, "allows us to overcome many common social conflicts that might, without empathy-based guilt, destroy our relationships and render us isolated."[18]

But O'Connor has found that empathy-based guilt can explode into depression because of our all-too-human tendency to blame ourselves. Zahn-Waxler agrees, noting it is "hardly coincidence that guilt plays a central role in some theories of depression."[19] Cognitive theories of depression define it in terms of the tendency to "attribute negative events to internal, stable, and global causes: 'It's my fault,' 'I'm responsible for the bad things that happen,' and 'It will always be that way.'" Zahn-Waxler's research led her to conclude that such negative narratives can "become part of the fabric of everyday life, even in childhood"—and, moreover, that these extreme feelings of responsibility can in fact be an early sign of depression. Zahn-Waxler also found that these patterns were more common in girls than in boys.

Guilt. Depression. Anorexia. Female-oriented emotions or syndromes all—the feminine inverse of male-oriented autism. Perhaps, just as extreme systemizers have a compulsion to focus on understanding a physical system (while they ignore extraneous issues such as how people feel), extreme empathizers may be locked into focusing on how others feel—oblivious to how their own empathic responses can create difficulties for the very people they are trying to help.

In fact, people at the far end of the empathizing spectrum might form a key constituency of codependency. Such individuals would feel a deep-seated need to help others but at the same time be unable to see how, though their "help" might feel right, they are not really helping at all. In other words, such hyperempathizers might be so caught up in the sensation of "Oh, my goodness, they're hurting!" that they would therefore find it difficult to understand other factors—like what they really need to do if they want to be of assistance. Such a situation would be similar to the person who holds her hands to her face and screams instead of reaching out to pull a child to safety. Or they may simply be so caught up with helping others out of immediate emotional difficulty that they don't see how their help may foster dependency in others—or feelings of burnout in themselves—causing more damage in the long run.

Although such people might lack clear boundaries between self and other, making emotional inhibition difficult, there is yet another possibility. There are surely also many women in abusive relationships who are consciously aware of the destructiveness of the relationship but who are unable to control the centripetal emotional forces that pull them into such relationships. This may be something similar to many other types of self-destructive behavior—addiction of various sorts, poor eating habits, and bad exercise habits. So also with various cognitive or affective disorders, people suffering from bipolar disorder, schizophrenia, or Tourette syndrome might be conscious that they are impaired but still powerless to alter the impairment.[20]

Are all of these various issues relevant to Carole Alden? Perhaps. Or perhaps they are relevant to those who have surrounded her—her friends, supporters, mother, siblings, and children.

EMPATHIC DISTRESS

Neuroscientist Tania Singer and her graduate student Olga Klimecki at the University of Zurich have posited that there are two ways empathic people can react when they see someone else in pain.[21] First, they can transform empathy into compassion—a feeling of empathic concern and warmth toward others. This is shown in the upper path of the figure below. But people can alternatively react by becoming caught up in "empathic distress," which is often accompanied by negative feelings that can potentially lead to burnout—the lower leg of the diagram.[22] Turning empathy into empathic distress can be a natural consequence of an untrained mind—we may even feel guilty if we try to avoid it, as if we are somehow abandoning the hurt person. (This is part of how guilt can lead to depression.) But in fact, by allowing ourselves to be overwhelmed by the pain of the other, we are only hurting ourselves without actually helping the other person.[23]

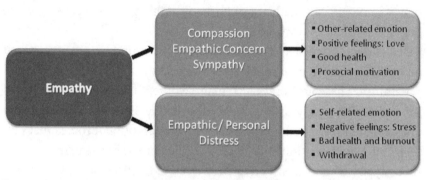

Two ways empathic people can react when they see someone else in pain. Buddhist monk Matthieu Ricard, who collaborates with neuroscientists Tania Singer and Olga Klimecki, says: "When we witness someone in pain, we suffer in resonance with his or her suffering. Neuroscience has proven that similar areas of the brain are activated both in the person who suffers and in the one who feels empathy. Thus empathic suffering is a true experience of suffering." This concept is illustrated in the lower leg of the figure. Ricard goes on to note that with the addition of "a powerful feeling of unconditional love and compassion, the negative, distressing aspects of empathy disappeared and were replaced by compassionate courage and a resolve to do whatever they could to soothe others' suffering." This is illustrated in the figure's upper leg.

Tania Singer and her colleagues plan to train caregivers, nurses, and doctors in secular forms of Buddhist loving-kindness techniques to allow them to help people in pain without suffering from empathic distress. Such techniques may also be useful for those grappling with issues of codependency.

"Burnout," in fact, is one of the most common and severe consequences of empathic distress in the healthcare professions.[24] It eventually leads to caregivers becoming more callous toward their patients, and to an increase in medical errors. It also leads to emotional exhaustion, depression, and general poor health.[25] More than any other factor, including how badly hurt someone may be or how much time is devoted to taking care of that person, "it is the *perceived* suffering of the patient that leads to depressive symptoms in the caregiver."[26]

This, as Singer notes, "suggests that compassion for a patient lies at the very root of compassion fatigue."

How could this be? After all, isn't the compassionate helping of others supposed to be healthy?

It all depends on which of the two empathic responses outlined by Singer that you might be feeling. Empathic concern for others without allowing yourself to become immersed in their pain can be a good thing for all concerned. But responding with empathic distress, particularly over long periods of time, can lead to trouble. As transpersonal psychologist Margaret Cochran says, empathic distress is "when somebody is down in a hole moaning, thrashing and flushing like a toilet and they call out to you to join them and you do. So now you're both down in the hole. Nobody wins."[27] Compassion, however, "is when someone is down in a hole moaning, thrashing and flushing like a toilet and they call out to you to join them and you say, 'No, I'll stay up here at the mouth of the hole. I've got some sandwiches and juice, come on up and we'll talk about it.' Everybody wins."[28]

BEING TRAINED TO BE TOO CARING— EMPATHIC OVERAROUSAL IN CHILDREN

Carolyn Zahn-Waxler went on to think deeply about the role of her family in forming her own personality and her parents' mutual role in inflicting suffering on one another. She eventually came to realize that it was not just her mother who was the problem in the family. Her seemingly rational, caring father, too, enmeshed her in his own difficulties, making her feel as though she was responsible for keeping him happy. "Because he seemed so victimized, anxious, and sad, I remained solicitous, but it also dragged me down," she wrote in her perceptive autobiographical essay "The Legacy of Loss: Depression as a Family Affair."[29] "The therapist thought that my father's more 'tender' emotions were sometimes manipulative. I began to see how he sometimes pushed my mother's buttons; problems in their relationship were not completely one-sided. Although he did not cause her depression, his pessimism, worries, and rigidity were likely to have interfered with her recovery."

Carolyn's education and employment made it possible to distance herself from the tempestuous family dynamics that had permeated her earlier life—this helped with her own personal growth. Gradually, as the years went by, her mother separated from her father—moving out on her own—and began to recover. When Carolyn became a mother herself, she worked to develop stronger ties with her own mother. Eventually, the two became close. Carolyn's new relationship with her mother was disturbing to her father, who had always perceived himself as Carolyn's favorite. Her father saw himself as a helper and refused help from others. Her mother felt guilty for leaving her increasingly isolated father. "They had been powerfully drawn to each other and maintained a mutual dependency throughout their lives that was unhealthy for both of them," Carolyn observed. "By now I had established more healthy boundaries that prevented their tragic relationship and needs from usurping my own."

Carolyn has learned a great deal about depression; in particular, that there are characteristics more common to girls than to boys that make them more vulnerable to developing depression (and, one might argue, to codependency): "a shy, anxious temperament; empathic overarousal and guilt proneness; a strong interpersonal orientation; submissiveness or lack of assertion; conformity to stereotypic feminine traits; ruminative coping styles (i.e., dwelling on problems); sensitivity to rejection; repression and internalization of anger; and poor self-image. Some children with a depressed parent take on the role of caregiver, girls especially, and this stance can increase their own depressive symptoms."

It may seem impossible to believe that children could be too caring about others. But Carolyn Zahn-Waxler's research has consistently shown this to be the case. Her colleague, Israeli researcher Ariel Knafo, has shown that some highly altruistic children take little pleasure in their own successes—perhaps showing early signs of behaviors associated with problems such as depression, anxiety, and codependency.[30] No one thinks of these caring kids as problems until it's too late. By then, the child's overly compassionate ways of dealing with others are deeply entrenched, and signs of possible self-destructive behavior patterns are already present.

One recent study has found that differences within a single gene may have a strong influence on our feelings of altruism—there may well be other genes with similar strong effects, and also a multitude of lesser genes that combine to also influence the degree to which we care for others.[31] And, of course, all this plays out with effects from the environment. A child with a compassionate and caring nature can be taken advantage of in situations of role reversal, when a "parent looks to a child to meet a parent's need for comfort, parenting, intimacy or play, and the child attempts to meet those needs."[32] In some sense, a child can be shaped by a parent into empathic overarousal, as the child tries to help and care for a parent, to become involved in "compulsive care giving," even as the child begins to suppress his or her own needs, and insecurities, under the guise of "grown up behavior."

One family friend describes how Carole Alden interacted with her own children: "She would talk to them as a peer, not as a mother, about her boyfriends. She would get them all upset—draw them into her drama."

She may have behaved, in some sense, as a codependent—and more certainly as a parent who was pulling her children into a web of codependency. But Carole herself had a very different upbringing.

CHAPTER 8

CARING STARTS EARLY

**A family story that threatens internal relation-
ships will be silenced by those wanting to maintain
fragile family bonds.**

—LINDA LAWRENCE HUNT, *Bold Spirit*[1]
(*Bold Spirit* is a favorite book of
Carole Alden's mother because of the
importance it places on passing along
a family's stories in full, rich measure,
even when the telling might be painful.)

Carole was born in 1960, at La Chapelle St. Mesmin, France,
some eighty miles south of Paris. Her father, then a lieutenant
in the Army Transportation Corps, had been responsible for trans-
porting materials to scattered posts around France. He served in the
reserves rather than the regular army and so didn't qualify for married
officer housing. But since he and his wife didn't want to be separated,

the pair scraped money together to live off-post. This meant that living conditions were rough—the two found themselves in an older home that had no hot water, no toilet, and no refrigerator. But the enterprising couple soon improved their surroundings enough to live comfortably.

Carole was their first child, and the pregnancy was a difficult one. Her mother nearly miscarried, and it is thought she was prescribed the artificial estrogen *diethylstilbestrol* (DES) to still the pangs. Several decades later, the drug would be associated with increased risk of developmental abnormalities.[2] Of even more interest, these "DES babies" have twice the long-term incidence of psychiatric disorders, even when those exposed had no idea they'd ever been in contact with the substance.[3]

Just as troubling, however, was the fact that Carole's mother came down with a severe case of chicken pox when she was eight months pregnant. Her fever went up to 104 degrees and remained high for several days. She had pox everywhere—her head, the palms of her hands, even the soles of her feet. A mother's exposure to chicken pox is always worrisome, not only because a pregnant woman is more severely affected by the virus (10 to 20 percent go on to develop varicella pneumonia, and 40 percent of those then die), but also because the virulence of the disease can cause neural damage in the unborn child.[4]

EPIGENETIC CHANGES

A baby's time while cocooned in the womb is extraordinarily delicate. One tiny cell becomes two, then four, then thousands, shape-shifting into a sort of lumpy pollywog. The cells in this neural-tube pollywog are particularly important because they each serve as an ancestor to millions of daughter, granddaughter, and multi-great-granddaughter cells. These offspring cells each methodically follow their genetically programmed instructions. Some nestle where they first appear, but many must work their way past other reproducing cells in an increasingly lengthy migration toward their final position within the newly forming baby.

Sometimes, like Hansel and Gretel, the migrating cells follow little chemical breadcrumbs left by other cells. But occasionally these breadcrumbs can be disturbed or the path can be somehow blocked—perhaps by a logjam of cells that were misdirected by missing breadcrumbs. This can happen if the mother is exposed to a heavy dose of ultrasound at just the wrong moment, which can cause tiny tears in the cellular fabric, or if she happened to ingest drugs such as diethylstilbestrol or suffered an infection such as toxoplasmosis from touching kitty litter, which inadvertently blocked or amplified chemical signals.[5] Or perhaps there was a sharp rise in body temperature that occurred at precisely the moment certain cells were dividing. Whatever the cause, certain genetic instructions can suddenly become impotent, like brakes that can do nothing to stop a truck that's gone off a cliff.

Sometimes the results of these epigenetic changes (that is, changes in genes' functions that occur without changing the gene's basic DNA

structure) are obvious—a cleft lip, for example, or left-handedness, or even, surprisingly, a gift for skills like music or math as the brain's neurons pour into and develop more strongly in some ordinarily second-fiddle neural area. Other times the change is much more subtle— perhaps the baby looks and acts normal at first, but as it reaches toddlerhood, it begins showing symptoms of autism or psychopathy. These changes can manifest at any age. As a teenager begins college, for

Carole in fall of 1960, at about six months old. She was a beautiful, happy baby.

example, he or she may fall victim to schizophrenia or bipolar disorder.

It is these epigenetic differences in how a baby develops that may help explain some unusual observations.

If one identical twin develops schizophrenia, for example, the other twin (who shares identical genes) has a 50 percent chance of also developing the disorder.[6] The fact that the twin of someone with schizophrenia is strongly susceptible to schizophrenia indicates an underlying genetic predisposition. But the fact that both twins don't always get the disorder may, at least partly, be due to those epigenetic factors that might have happened as far back as just after the big bang beginning of sperm meeting egg.[7] In fact, autism, psychopathy, and schizophrenia disorder all have something in common besides the fact that both genes and factors outside of genes seem to be able to kick them into gear. All three can entail quirkily missing or strangely expressed versions of empathy.[8]

*   *   *

Carole was of low birth weight—five pounds, six ounces, but she arrived pink and beautiful, and she soon began to thrive. At ten weeks old, the infant Carole came to America aboard the *Queen Mary*—a stylish entrance for a child who, even early on, enjoyed the spotlight.

Three siblings followed—a sister and two brothers. Her sister and the younger of her brothers were outgoing youngsters, never happy without a fleet of other children sailing nearby. Carole and the brother closest to her in age were socially more focused, having only one or two strong friendships at a time. All three of Carole's siblings, now in their thirties and forties with families of their own, are protective of their mother: an honest, thoughtful, and deeply compassionate woman.

Carole's father was of an old family: John Alden, her father's eleventh paternal great-grandfather, had come to the New World as a cooper on the *Mayflower*. ("The man responsible for bringing beer to the New World!" quip modern-day Alden descendants.) Although he had the difficult upbringing typical of those raised in the Great Depression, Carole's father was able to overcome this early disadvantage, going on to become a popular professor and well-known "force of nature" at a state university. Of the four Alden siblings, it was Carole who inherited her father's love of wildlife and animals of all sorts—although she was to take this love to extremes. As a youngster, she owned, at one time or another, virtually every animal a child might conceivably dream of, including dogs, cats, rats, lizards, gerbils, hamsters, mice, snakes, frogs, salamanders, and turtles—at one point she owned a total of sixty rabbits at the same time.

Carole's mother describes her as a delightful child; although even early on, Carole relished the unusual as a way to stand out and draw attention to herself. Whereas other girls simply played with dolls, for example, Carole developed an interest in taxidermy. Once she found a dead rooster alongside the school bus route. After persuading the bus driver to allow her to pick it up, she took it to school and performed taxidermy on it. But she forgot to process the comb, which rotted over school break, memorably fouling the school with its smell.

Carole stood out among the Alden children in another way. Although nearly everyone in the Alden family is artistic, Carole's artistry was of a different sort altogether. This was first discovered when two-year-old Carole was taken in for her annual checkup. Asked to draw something—which children that age generally accomplish by sketching out a few sticks and circles—Carole shocked the doctor by drawing a complete, extraordinarily detailed fire engine. In preschool and elementary school, Carole was a prodigy—her enormous artistic talent differentiating her from all the other children.

Carole differed in yet another way from other children. This difference earned her notoriety in the neighborhood.

The neighborhood where Carole and her family lived filtered out to hillsides where coyotes and hawks preyed on rabbits, mice, prairie dogs, and the occasional cat. Two doors down from the Alden household, a woman kept two freely roaming dogs. The dogs, as dogs are wont to do, set upon prairie dogs when they could find them.

The problem was that ten-year-old Carole adored animals in a fashion quite unlike any of the other Aldens except her father—indeed, unlike any of the other children in the neighborhood. Carole thrived on animals. She was lost in them. As her mother would say, while laughing at her own academic phrasing, "She had an early social consciousness about how both animals and people should be treated." Carole was horrified that the neighbor's dogs were killing prairie dogs in the course of their daily outings.

To stop the slaughter, Carole rounded up the neighborhood children, created signs, and set up a picket line in front of the neighbor's

Carole at dog obedience class at age twelve.
She was obsessed with animals.

house. Carole also offered a solution—the neighborhood's children would take turns each day walking the dogs on a leash.

But dogs will be dogs, and Carole found herself on the short end of a discussion with her parents about the impossibility of fixing all of the world's woes. Her parents' words fell on deaf ears. Dramatic efforts to fix—or appear as if she were fixing—others' woes would become a central issue in Carole's life.

CHAPTER 9

THE PRELIMINARY HEARING BEGINS

Murder is unique in that it abolishes the party it injures, so that society has to take the place of the victim and on his behalf demand atonement or grant forgiveness; it is the one crime in which society has a direct interest.

—W. H. AUDEN, "The Guilty Vicarage"[1]

The State of Utah, Plaintiff, v. Carole Alden, Defendant.
Preliminary Hearing.

Although no one knew it at the time, this crucial day of the preliminary hearing would be the first, last, and only day that Carole Alden would appear in court to determine whether she would ultimately be convicted of murder. It was this day, more than any other save that of the homicide itself, that would henceforth shape the direction of her life.

Trials are often thought of as the acme of courtroom drama. And of course, they can be. But while trials can be as intricate as a game of chess, they are, in some sense, set pieces. Preliminary hearings are very different—they arrive early in the adjudication process, at that Wild West stage when the rules of the game are being decided. In a case like that of Carole Alden's, the stakes of the preliminary hearing are high. Depending on how the hearing went, Alden would leave the courtroom either a free woman or facing the prospect of life imprisonment.

The objective of the preliminary hearing is not to establish whether or not the alleged culprit of the crime in question is actually guilty. The judge in a preliminary hearing has a task in some ways easier and in other ways more difficult than that of a jury. He or she has to carefully weigh the information about the case and decide whether there is enough evidence on each element of the defense that, if believed by the jury, would lead to a conviction.

In Carole Alden's case, things were a little trickier than usual. Marty Sessions was dead, no doubt about it. And Carole had killed him—she'd admitted as much. But underlying all this was the question of motive. Did Carole kill Marty to defend herself? If so, was there even enough reason to hold a trial? Or was there some other reason Carole killed Marty? Was she hallucinating, for example, perhaps as a result of possible abuse? Or were there darker motives?

Any reason for the killing provided by Carole's defense lawyer would be noted as an element of the defense—an element that would need to be proven or disproven. James Slavens, a Millard County defense attorney, had been appointed as Carole's public defender.

James Slavens's set of offices was situated in a run-down motel in Fillmore off Highway 15 Exit 163 (HBO, Rooms, Laundry, $29.95). Slavens himself is a ruddy, glassy-eyed man with a threadbare sense of fashion. But appearances notwithstanding, Slavens has a local reputation as a bully in the courtroom—his style is so aggressive that prosecutors go out of their way to avoid working with him. Yet he is known to be so effective that the very same lawyers who don't like working with him are quick to hire him when their sons are arrested for DUI.

Opposing Slavens was a prosecution team from the Utah Attorney General's Office in Salt Lake City. The prosecution would be led by Michael Wims, chief of the Special Prosecutions Section of the Criminal Division. Wims is a brilliant man—among his other coups, he had helped steer home the successful prosecution of Ron Lafferty, the polygamous wife-killer described in Jon Krakauer's *Under the Banner of Heaven*. Both Wims and his calm, astute colleague, Pat Nolan, an assistant Utah State attorney general, had been brought down to Millard County because Pat Finlinson had started his deputy county attorney job only a few days before the homicide and was too new and inexperienced. So it came down to Carole Alden, represented by Jim Slavens, versus the State, led by Mike Wims. These were the two adversarial groups who would be presenting before Judge Donald Eyre (pronounced "air") in the Fillmore County Court on the calm, clear, icy cold morning of January 8, 2007.[2]

As Wims, with his propensity for Latin, would say: "*Veni. Vidi. Veritas.*" "I came. I saw. The truth."

*   *   *

Judge Eyre cleared his throat, rapped his gavel, and pronounced: "We'll go on the record in the case of State of Utah versus Carole Elizabeth Alden. This is the time set for preliminary hearing in the matter. The Defendant is present with her attorney, James Slavens. The State is here represented by Mr. Wims and Mr. Nolan. Are we ready to proceed?"

> *Mr. Slavens:* "Yes, Your Honor. I would like Carole to be able to take notes and assist in this and so I'm asking for permission to have the chains on her wrists taken off so she can write."
> *Judge Eyre:* "Any security risk?"
> *Bailiff:* "No."
> *Judge Eyre:* "Okay. She may have that."

Mr. Slavens: "Thank you, Your Honor."

Judge Eyre: "Those individuals who have been subpoenaed to be witnesses here today, if you could all please stand and if you all will raise your right hand and take an oath?"

Clerk: "You do solemnly swear that the testimony you are about to give in the case now before the Court will be the truth, the whole truth, and nothing but the truth, so help you God?"

There was a solemn murmur of assent.

Judge Eyre: "You may be seated. Your first witness will be Sergeant Burton? Mr. Nolan, do you desire to make an opening statement prior to taking testimony?"

Mr. Nolan: "Yes. Good morning, Your Honor, Counsel. The Court will hear this morning from two witnesses in the State's case. Preliminary are Sergeant Morris Burton of the Millard County Sheriff's Office and what the Court will hear will be a discussion about events that took place at the end of July of last year, 2006."

Judge Eyre: "Thank you. Mr. Slavens, did you want to make an opening statement?"

Mr. Slavens: "I don't, Your Honor."

*   *   *

The prosecution was planning to put Burton on the stand as a sort of "master summarizer" instead of calling in all the police officers who'd been involved in the case. Normally, the prosecution likes to use only a few "star witnesses" to summarize their findings. This practice helps reduce the amount of time swearing in other people and establishing their bona fides. It also allows the prosecution to avoid laying all their cards on the table at the level of an early preliminary hearing.

Slavens's lack of opening statement was typical behavior for a defense attorney at a preliminary hearing. The standard for bindover—the judge's order that the defendant *will* stand trial on those charges—

was low. There simply needed to be *some* evidence presented at the preliminary hearing that *could* lead a jury to believe that a crime had been committed and that the defendant committed it. In this case, once both Sergeant Burton and Dr. Robert Deters, who had performed the autopsy, had completed their testimony, the standard would be achieved. The bindover would then occur, ipso facto, unless Slavens pulled some sort of extraordinary legal rabbit out of his hat.

Given the setup, then, this was not the time for Slavens to show his hand or to give hints about what strategies he might be employing at the later trial. Instead, this was when Slavens could listen to the prosecutor's theory, discover what the witnesses would say, and even use exploratory cross-examination. After all, no jury was present, so if he received an answer he didn't like, then he simply knew not to ask that question at the trial.

In some sense, the prelim was a freebie for the defense, giving Slavens a chance to observe the faces and demeanor of the government's witnesses prior to deciding whether to explore an agreed plea

Carole Alden in the courtroom with her attorney, James Slavens.

disposition or to go straight to a jury trial. This was all part of the usual legal kabuki process.

But meanwhile, Sergeant Burton gave testimony about the afternoon before the killing.

*   *   *

Mr. Nolan: "What happened after Carole Alden went over to get Mr. Sessions at Mr. Lake's house?"

Sergeant Burton: "She said she went outside—that when Mr. Sessions saw her there he was mad because he had seen her car at the house and was jealous. She said he went into an angry rage, walked out into the middle of the street, and fell down."

Q: "What did she do?"

A: "She drove her car around from behind Mr. Lake's house to the street next to Mr. Sessions with the help of others there. She loaded Mr. Sessions into the car and drove toward her house."

Q: "Did she get him home?"

A: "She did."

Q: "What happened when she got him back to their house?"

A: "She told me that she drove into the backyard, which was partially fenced, in order to keep him somewhat contained because she said when he was in that state he had been known to get mad and walk off—she didn't want him out in the street."

Q: "What did she say she did during that time?"

A: "During that time she placed a phone call to her daughter. She also obtained a blanket and pillow, put the pillow under his head and blanket to make him comfortable because he was laying on the ground there. She thought he would probably spend the night there."

Q: "Let's move forward to the actual shooting itself. Tell us Ms. Alden's explanation of how that happened."

A: "She said that after a series of events he was in the master bedroom of the house. He was throwing things around and throwing things at her, tearing things up. She left that room and stepped into the laundry room to hide from him. She said she obtained a gun she had hidden in the cabinet in the laundry room."

Q: "Let me stop you there. Did she say where she got the gun from?"

A: "Yes. She purchased the gun the day before at Beaver Sport and Pawn."

*   *   *

Nolan was making an important point. The town of Beaver was eighty-five miles south of Delta. Carole Alden had driven all that way to get the gun the day before the killing, when she could have purchased it in Millard County and avoided the expense and inconvenience of driving all the way to Beaver County.

*   *   *

Q: "And the gun was hidden where?"

A: "In the cabinet in the laundry room, above the washer and dryer."

Q: "What kind of gun is it?"

A: "Smith and Wesson .38 caliber revolver."

Q: "What happened next?"

A: "Before she went into the laundry room she said she had gone into the kitchen and turned out all the lights so he couldn't see her and then went back to the laundry room. As he came down the hall, as he passed the door to the laundry room, she thought he must have heard her or something and turned his head toward her. When he saw her, he raised his fist—he did not turn his body, and that's when she pulled the trigger and shot him for the first time."

Q: "Where did she shoot him?"

A: "She said she thought it was in the ribs, a little toward the back of the under left underarm."

Q: "Did she say how far away from the victim she was when she shot him?"

A: "She said about two feet."

Q: "What did she say that she did then?"

A: "She said that he stumbled back and she pushed the door of the laundry room closed."

Marty Sessions's grave was to have been under the koi
pond in the backyard of the Sessions home.

Q: "And then what happened?"

A: "She said she heard him say, 'I knew this is how I would go out.'
And she described him stumbling backwards and then falling
forward on his face."

Q: "What happened next?"

A: "She said that she waited for a period of time, she thought it
might have been five minutes. Then she opened the door and
found him lying face down in the hallway. She stepped out,
looked at him carefully; she was quite certain he wasn't
breathing, but she wasn't sure. She said the air-conditioning was
blowing right above him and blowing his jacket that he was
wearing. So she turned off the air conditioner, looked again and
was quite certain he was not breathing. She felt she needed to
make a phone call to her daughter."

Q: "So what did she do?"

A: "So that she could get past him to hang up the phone in the bedroom, get a dial tone, she said she placed a pillow over his head and then fired a shot into the back of his head to make sure that he was dead so he couldn't grab her and take the gun away from her."

Q: "After the Defendant shot the victim in the head, what did she do?"

A: "She placed a phone call to her daughter. I believe, the name is *Melloney*. And she said she did not tell her daughter that she had shot him. She simply said, 'It is over and I'm okay.' Her daughter asked if she needed to come over and get her. Her daughter lives here in Fillmore. Her daughter said, 'Do you need me to come get you?' Ms. Alden told her, 'No,' not to come over."

Q: "What happened next?"

A: "She said she went outside, that she had a fishpond in the back area where she had had some fish. She said she had intended to dig that deeper and use it for turtles. She had a lot of animals around the place and she wanted to get some turtles, wanted to dig that deeper so the turtles could hibernate. So she decided that would be a good place for a grave for Mr. Sessions."

Q: "Out in back of the house?"

A: "In back of the house. Then I asked her if the clothes she was wearing when I was talking with her were the clothes she had on when she shot him. She told me they were not—that after digging the grave she had undressed, hosed off in the yard and redressed in different clothes. She said that Mr. Sessions was too big for her to move by herself so she tied a rope around him and pulled him with the Jeep out to the fishpond."

The picture of the hallway where Marty Sessions died. An image was taken from a DVD recording of the crime scene made by Deputy Pedersen. The picture shows the hallway and the doorway to the laundry room (on the left). It also shows the bloody mark across the carpet where Marty's body was dragged.

Q: "And how successful was that?"

A: "She did pull him out of the house, and she had pulled over a large bookshelf and scattered boxes and items all over the living room area of the house, pulled him on out and his body was near the fishpond where she had dug his grave."

Mr. Nolan: "May I have a moment, Your Honor?"

Judge Eyre: "You may."

Mr. Nolan: "Sergeant Burton. Do you recognize this?"

A: "Yes, I do."

Q: "What does it show?"

A: "It shows the hallway and the doorway to the laundry room. It also shows a large pool of blood at the top of the picture and then a drag mark across the carpet and on down where the body was drug."

Q: "What did Deputy Greathouse relate to you, Sergeant Burton, about the Defendant's comments about the events of that night?"

A: "She said that Ms. Alden told her that Mr. Sessions had not hurt her, that he was too plowed to get her, that he kept falling on his face and that she always stayed at least 30 feet away from him."

Q: "Throughout that night?"

A: "Throughout the night."

Q: "At least until she shot him?"

A: "That's correct, yes."

Q: "Okay. Tell us about the next picture, what it shows."

A: "It is a close view looking right down into the grave."

Mr. Nolan: "We have no further questions on direct. Thank you, Sergeant Burton."

Mr. Slavens: "Might I *voir dire*[3] for just a couple of questions?"

Judge Eyre: "Go ahead."

Mr. Slavens: "Those pictures indicated that there was a pillow next to the body; is that correct?"

A: "That's correct."

Q: "And that pillow subsequently got destroyed, correct?"

A: "My understanding is the Medical Examiner's Office inadvertently destroyed it."

Mr. Slavens: "That's all I have. Thanks."

*   *   *

Slavens, in his wily way, had pointed out a flaw in the State's case. The pillow that Carole had placed against Marty's head had been destroyed after being photographed. This wasn't a major mistake, but still, it was a mistake—and Slavens had pounced on it.

Normally during the preliminary hearing stage, defense attorneys in Slavens's situation would play by the rules and simply accept the prosecution's presentation of what happened. But, as the prosecution team was finding, Slavens wasn't one to play by the rules. Instead, he was beating about the rhetorical bushes, trying to see what kind of testimony he could flush out. Slavens was apparently going to make them lay as many cards on the table as he could here at the early preliminary hearing level. For someone who came across as a country bumpkin, Slavens was holding his own against the powerful prosecutorial team.

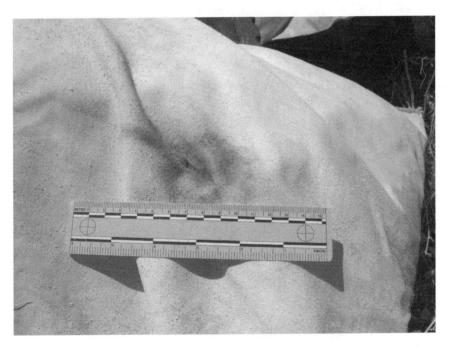

The pillow Carole placed against Marty's head
as she shot him a second time.

It might have been a recipe for exasperation for many prosecutors, but Mike Wims, mastermind of the State's case, observed without expression. Little fazed Wims, so it was easy for him to maintain a poker face in court. In fact, if Wims had been defending, he would have been doing some of the same "free" exploratory questioning that Slavens was now doing. Surprises can unfold.

Slavens continued his questioning—moving on to interrogate an unanticipated witness—patrol sergeant Rhett Kimball, who had been working the graveyard shift in Delta on the evening of Marty's death.

*   *   *

Mr. Slavens: "Could you describe for me what you were told about a disturbance on the night of the 28th and the 29th?"

A: "There was a subject in the street close to the intersection of 300 West 300 South in Delta."

Q: "When you got to that area, what did you find?"

A: "Nothing."

Q: "Nobody was there?"

A: "No, sir."

Q: "So is there any reason why you didn't go to the Sessions' home to see what was going on?"

A: "I think, as I recall, I had the dispatch attempt to make a telephone call to their residence while I was searching the Delta area."

Q: "You didn't put that in your report?"

A: "I didn't."

Q: "In fact, your last sentence in your report says, 'As there is not sufficient evidence to investigate a crime, this case will be placed into a closed status as unfounded'?"

A: "Yes."

*   *   *

In his own strategic way, Slavens had just brought out that the evening before Marty Sessions was killed, the police had apparently been called about Marty lying in the street. The implication, of course, was that if police had acted differently—if they had gone to Carole and Marty's home—the killing would not have occurred. Slavens was doing more— he was setting a strategy in place to show that virtually every time Carole had called the police, Rhett Kimball had been the one who answered. And, in good-old-boy fashion, Kimball had smoothed every- thing over. Maybe, Slavens seemed to be implying, the reason Carole had done what she did was because she knew she wouldn't get any help from the police if she did call.

As Slavens's sly attack also revealed, in some sense it was the mystery of Marty Sessions's true character that was, more than any- thing else, on trial.

CHAPTER 10

MARTY SESSIONS

People think it's all about misery and desperation and death and all that shite, which is not to be ignored, but what they forget is the pleasure of it. Otherwise we wouldn't do it. After all, we're not fucking stupid. At least, we're not that fucking stupid. Take the best orgasm you ever had, multiply it by a thousand and you're still nowhere near it. When you're on junk you have only one worry: scoring. When you're off it you are suddenly obliged to worry about all sorts of other shite. . . . You have to worry about bills, about food, about some football team that never fucking wins, about human relationships and all the things that really don't matter when you've got a sincere and truthful junk habit.

—RENTON, from the 1996 film *Trainspotting*[1]

I t was 1960, fall was weeping the last of its foliage, and Joan Sessions—the overwhelmed mother of four children under the age of six—had finally slid to the slippery end of her rope.[2]

Poplar Grove, the lower-middle-class neighborhood where the Sessions family lived, was one of the smallest and oldest neighborhoods on the west side of Salt Lake City—the family's bungalow had been built in 1894 by Marty's grandfather. As the sleepy decade of the 1950s folded to a close, and the sixties were in the naive calm before the Kennedy assassinations, life in Poplar Grove seemed to portend only a hardscrabble climb up to middle class proper.

But Joan Sessions's problem that fall day had nothing to do with Poplar Grove, a climb to middle class, the house, or even the kids (with whom she spoke Dutch, true to her heritage). Joan's problem had to do with stamps. The kind, in that pre-Internet era, that helped put the snail in mail.

Tom Sessions, Joan's husband and the father of her four children, was then a shop foreman at Gudgell Sheet Metal—he had an uncanny knack for the difficult art of heliarc welding. Of the Sessions children, Thomas Junior was five years old, Marty was four, Denny was two, and the baby, Janet, was only six months. The kids were a riotous handful— a handful that Tom expected Joan to keep under tight control.

Although Tom was then just an uneducated steel worker, he was also an intelligent man who was determined to—and did—use education to better himself. In determined fashion, he worked to put himself through college to become a teacher. Decades later, on Tom's passing, former student Bonnie Peters appeared to speak for many when she noted, "I attribute my ability to overcome the hard times I was born into by observing the example [Tom Sessions] set and how he went back to school to get his degree. His plain-spoken wisdom had a profound effect on people he came into contact with."[3] In his twenty-eight years as a teacher at Newman Elementary School, the senior Sessions touched the lives of thousands of children.

More to the point regarding Joan's problem, however, Tom Ses-

MARTY SESSIONS   **101**

sions was also a stamp collector—proud member 38 in the Utah Phi-
latelic Society. Tom's passion for stamps was so complete, so all-
consuming—so overwhelming—that eventually he would fill every
room and hallway of the old family home from floor to ceiling with
albums, boxes, and crates of stamps from every era and country, so
that simply passing from bedroom to kitchen became an exercise in
twisting, sidling, and sliding boxes around to clamber through
labyrinthine passageways. At Tom's death, his family would estimate
that the bungalow contained on the order of ten million stamps.

But in 1960, at what was soon to be the tail end of his marriage,
Tom's obsession was still nascent. All Joan knew was that Tom's
expectations of her—to keep the four kids quiet and out of his way as
he sat calmly piecing his way through his ever-increasing stamp
collection—were becoming more than she could handle.

On that fateful fall day, with studied firmness of purpose, Joan
Sessions took the vacuum cleaner out of the closet and screwed the
hose firmly on the wrong, "exhaust" end. Then, wheeling the vacuum,
she calmly walked out to where Tom sat in the middle of the living
room, surrounded by the thousands of loose leaflets of his collection.
Pointing the hose straight toward the stamps, she turned on the
vacuum. And laughed.

When Tom finally wrested the vacuum hose from her hands, Joan
grabbed the kids, her clothes, and her purse, then walked out the front
door, leaving Tom with a mess of stamps drifting like piles of leaves
across the hardwood floor.

She never returned.

*   *   *

Although Joan (pronounced in the Dutch fashion, with two syllables,
like "Jo-anne") tried to retain custody of the children, Tom hired a
lawyer and got them back within a month. Within six months, Tom Sessions had remarried. His new wife was far younger than he was, and he
later confided that he had remarried because he needed a babysitter.

Marty on his sixth birthday— a picture of boyish impishness.

Babysitter though she might have been, Tom's children thought she was also the equivalent of Cinderella's wicked stepmother. As far as the kids could determine, their stepmother outright hated them, taking every opportunity, even lying, if necessary, to get them into trouble. "She would lie even when telling the truth was easier," recalled Denny Sessions. Marty and Denny hung together—the youngsters were sometimes taken for twins, and even now, Denny's resemblance to his older brother is unnerving—especially for those who knew, and miss, Marty.

The three Sessions sons and their little sister were joined into a new, haphazard stepfamily with their stepmother's two young daughters. The boys soon found that they were expected to look after the three little girls. (A much younger stepbrother, Steve, eventually came into the picture—Steve would go on to care for his adopted father through Tom's final years.) In keeping with his role as a third-grade teacher, Tom was strict in his expectations—the boys were taught to never, *ever* dream of hitting one of their sisters—or any girl, for that matter. And if one of the girls ever did get hit, the boys were expected to hunt down the perpetrator and give him a lesson to remember. This idea of never hitting a woman, coupled with something of a "big brother" protectiveness that is the flip side of chauvinism, has remained with Tom Sessions's sons throughout their lives. It wasn't that they wouldn't argue with a woman—they would. It was just that they would no more dream of hitting a woman than, well, any well-brought-up American man.

This philosophy was part of what gave the Sessions family pause when Carole Alden began to make her claims of physical abuse against Marty after she'd killed him.

The three boys—Tom Junior, Marty, and Denny—often made mischief together. Denny was the principal troublemaker, but the three took turns accepting responsibility for the punishment that followed. In the sixties, paternal punishment often consisted of a thrashing, and Tom dished out no more and no less punishment to his sons than other fathers of the time. (Tom's own upbringing had been very strict—his mother in particular had been a no-nonsense disciplinarian.) Perhaps because Tom Junior and Denny were whip-smart like their father, their "whuppings" were generally lighter. Marty, who was less inclined toward scholarly pursuits and who muddled along with a C average in school, seemed to get picked on a bit more, his occasional trips to the woodshed a little more serious—although it was clear that Tom Senior loved all his children.

Even though Joan had left Tom, she had stayed in Salt Lake City. Denny, especially hated by his stepmother, migrated to his mother's house by age ten. Marty moved there a few years later, when he was sixteen—both boys found in their mother the understanding and compassion that their father rarely expressed. Away from their father, though, it was easier to ignore school. Soon, both Marty and Denny were dropouts, finding their way into the working world even as they also found women, partying, and, most important, drugs.

Marty started on opiate-based painkillers in the 1970s. He began with a prescription, and when the prescription ended, he turned to buying drugs on the street. By the early 1980s he made the switch to heroin—Mexican heroin. Of all types of heroin, "Mexican heroin is the worst. It looks like shit, and does your body like shit."[4] So says the dealer at the beginning of Steven Okazaki's powerful masterpiece *Black Tar Heroin*, a documentary that follows the disintegrating lives of five black tar ("Mexican heroin") addicts over three years in San Francisco, California.

Mexican heroin—that is, heroin turbocharged by selective acetylation—became Marty's and Denny's drug of choice. Whether called black tar heroin, black clown, *piedra*, or, as the Sessions boys knew it, *chiva*, it was all the same stuff. The peculiar processing methods resulted in a sticky black mass that looks like nothing so much as tarry baby poop. Hence another name—caca.

Marty began stealing to support his habit, which resulted in his first stint in prison. A chronic shoplifter, he would walk into Walmart or Kmart and tuck fifteen or so CDs around the waist of his windbreaker. Then he'd sell them at swap meets. When a particular method worked, Marty would do it again and again, which is why one of the stores finally got so fed up that they called the marshals on him, earning him another stretch in prison. And then another. And another. Sometimes Marty would paper out—meaning he'd finish all the requirements and not have any parole conditions. Other times he'd be out on parole and would miss a mandatory call-in or fail a drug test, and back to prison he'd go.

But although heroin would warp Marty's life, there was another side to the story.

*   *   *

"If I had the ability to look at everyone in the whole world to decide who my parents would be, I would still choose my father and mother,"[5] says Anna Ruttenbur, Marty Sessions's oldest daughter, age twenty-nine at the time of her father's death in 2006. Anna is a reserved woman who avoids the limelight—she has never before spoken publicly about her parents or her upbringing. Anna and her younger sister Edee spent a large part of their teenage years in foster homes as a consequence of their father's prison stints (their mother, a heroin addict like Marty, was given a compassionate release from prison to die of AIDS at home when Anna was fifteen and Edee was thirteen).[6]

"Anybody who knew my Dad liked him," says Anna, Marty Sessions's oldest daughter. "He was outgoing, soft-spoken, friendly, kind-hearted, very smart. . . . His biggest downfall was his addiction. *Everything* would have been different if it wasn't for that. He knew that, too. He was a genuinely good human being—his addiction didn't make him into a bad person."

If anyone should want to point a finger at Martin Sessions, it would be his daughters, whose difficult upbringing was markedly different from that of Carole Alden's comparatively privileged youth. But both women, whose high cheekbones and good looks mark them instantly as Sessions's offspring, retain an overwhelming love for their dad, even as they also retain a sense of his deep-rooted faults—or rather the single, overwhelming fault they saw in their father's life: heroin.

"My dad talked a lot to Edee and I about choices," Anna continues. "He was really hard on himself because of his addiction. He felt that he had missed a lot of us growing up because of that—it was one of his biggest regrets." Edee adds, "I wouldn't change how my parents were—I would want them, faults and all, because all of it helped me. Some of the biggest mistakes my parents made, I learned from, because my parents helped me learn."[7] One of Marty's most profound choices was that of allowing himself to fall deeply in love with the sparkling Susie Bunnell, who bore a striking similarity to actress Sally Field. It wasn't just Marty—*everyone* loved the vivacious, outgoing

Susie, including Anna and Edee, who found with Susie a relationship not exactly like that with their keenly missed mother, but akin to it. Marty found within Susie his soul mate. She understood Marty in a way no one else did; her own friendliness, good humor, and joie de vivre echoing with that buried within Marty himself to give renewed meaning to his life. Decades later, when asked about the relationship between the couple, the voices of other family members soften as they spontaneously volunteer the same heartfelt phrase: Marty and Susie fit together like hand and glove.

Not that the hand was necessarily always good for the glove. Susie, too, felt the siren call of heroin, although she managed to stay away from it for longer stretches than Marty. The two had actually married in prison, Marty's home away from home. "I don't think they would have healed one another," says Denny, "But they were soul mates. Both did drugs—they did their thing and were happy."

Marty's daughters recall him as a good father, at least when he was home from prison. He never laid a hand on them, although he had no qualms about getting up close with an accusatory finger or sending them to their rooms. Marty was strict, almost military, in his paternal role. If it was time for the kids to do the chores, it was time for chores—no waffling. But when it came to Marty's grandchildren, all disciplinary bets were off. His grandchildren adored him, and he loved getting down on the floor and rolling around with them, playing horsey and making funny sounds—Donald Duck was a particular favorite. He dubbed Ashley, his adorable little granddaughter, "Whooshy." The pair were ecstatic as he swung her through the air.

Although Marty had dropped out of high school, he made a point of getting his GED in prison, and he repeatedly emphasized the value of education to his daughters. He himself tended toward more visual- and systems-oriented interests: he was a talented artist and loved to create homemade cards to send with his correspondence. Wood-working was something he greatly enjoyed; he also reveled in learning about and working with computers. Marty's little-known side talent was a knack for making delicious homemade spaghetti sauce.

As Anna and Edee matured, they saw firsthand how their father interacted with Susie. The drugs made it an imperfect relationship, of course. But even so, the couple made a point of taking any arguments they had out of sight and earshot of the girls. More importantly, there was never, *ever* a hint of violence in the couple's relationship. *Could Marty get violent?* Absolutely. He wouldn't start a fight, but he would gladly wade in swinging—that is, if other men were involved. But in general, Marty wasn't a fisticuffs sort of guy, and, true to his upbringing, Marty never hit a woman—at least, not that the girls or anyone in the Sessions family ever saw.[8] In fact, one of the biggest issues Anna ever had with her father in the last two years of his life was when Marty heard rumors that Anna's then boyfriend had hit her. Both Denny and Marty set off at once to have a face-to-face talk with the miscreant. Marty's anger at the idea of a man hitting a woman— *ever*, for any reason—was an ingrained feature of his personality.

∗   ∗   ∗

On the evening of November 2, 1991, while Marty was watching television in prison, his world suddenly flipped topsy-turvy.

With Marty back behind bars, Susie and her son Scott—Marty's stepson—had been in the process of moving. An old family friend, Edgar Tiedemann, suggested that Susie and Scott stay at his trailer to save on motel costs. It seemed like a reasonable idea to Susie, especially since her sister Debra Pryor and her sister's boyfriend, Chuck Timberman, had already been living with Tiedemann for several months.[9] The evening was uneventful—the group made dinner and watched television until about midnight. Tiedemann had always seemed harmless, if slightly eccentric. But it was later learned that he had suffered a series of head injuries, had survived a left cerebral stroke, and had long sniffed glue and paint thinner.[10] He was, in other words, a ticking time bomb.

Debra Pryor recalled waking up that night to the sound of a loud pop in the living room. Chuck, lying beside her, got up to see what was going on. Tiedemann appeared in the hallway and shot him twice. Chuck collapsed, but, still alive at that point, he told Debra to lie still and play dead. Tiedemann meanwhile went back into the living room, fired more shots, returned, shot Chuck again, then went back yet again to the living room and resumed firing. In the other room, Debra could hear her fourteen-year-old nephew Scott begging Tiedemann not to shoot him again.[11] Shaking in terror, she listened over the next few hours as Chuck's labored breathing slowed to a stop.

Tiedemann then reentered Debra's bedroom and told her he knew she wasn't dead. He ordered her at gunpoint into the living room, where she found her nephew covered with blood and paralyzed from the chest down. Susie was lying still on the couch, covered with a blanket. Tiedemann pulled off the blanket and said, "Ain't she pretty now?"[12]

He had shot Susie point-blank in the eye.

Tiedemann then told Debra he was going to rape her.[13] Seven months pregnant, she begged him not to do it in front of her nephew, so he took her to the hallway, where he raped her as she looked at her dead boyfriend.[14] Eleven hours into the ordeal, Debra finally managed to escape. Police moved in to find Marty's stepson lying conscious, with a severed spinal cord, next to his dead mother. (Nine agonizing years later, Scotty's malnourished body would be found in a pile of his own excrement—the medical examiner would controversially rule his death a homicide from Tiedemann's paralyzing shot.)[15] Judge Judith Atherton would ultimately say, "I have seen many, many cases. I do not remember a case that is more brutal than this."[16] Tiedemann, as became apparent, killed Susie because he loved her but she didn't love him.[17] Of course she didn't love him—she was in love with her husband, Marty Sessions.

Marty was numb with grief and remorse for being in prison at a time when he felt he should have been with Susie, protecting her. As if matters couldn't get worse, the case dragged on and on. During Tiedemann's interrogation immediately after the murders, he told investigators that he thought he was Adolf Hitler and that he frequently spoke with the devil. As a consequence, Tiedemann was declared incompetent to stand trial and was instead committed to the Utah State Hospital. But over a decade later, in conjunction with budget cuts, the still clearly deranged Tiedemann was released. This forced the State to try the case—and to put Debra Pryor, by now the sole survivor, through hell all over again, as the unhinged Tiedemann blamed the killings on her. (The jury found the claim ludicrous.)[18]

Anna remembers: "My Dad just gave up after Susie died. He was sad for so long." Later, Marty would speak to his daughters about the killing and his feelings of anguish and guilt. God meant for him to forgive Tiedemann for what he'd done, Marty told Anna, but this forgiveness was something he struggled with. Ultimately, with much pain, Marty was able to find a way within himself to forgive Tiedemann—finding surprising solace when he did so.

Marty remarried several years after Susie's death. But that third marriage foundered on his drug use. Anna and Edee were happy when Marty married Carole. Whatever made him happy, they felt, made them happy.

CHAPTER 11

A DETECTIVE AT WORK

Murder is different because murder—unlike any other crime—permanently deprives the victim of everything. The victim of theft or arson might be able to regain or rebuild lost property. Even the victim of an aggravated assault or rape can sometimes and somewhat recover from the injury. But the murder victim is gone. Then there are the surviving family members and relatives of the victims. Because they have lost the victim forever, they know that murder is not the same as theft or robbery or any other crime. The defendant facing a murder trial knows this too, if for no other reason than the penalties for murder are more severe than for most other crimes. The police, the news media, the jury and the public all know that murder is different. So the trial of a murder case is different because the crime has raised the

111

stakes—for the victim, the victim's survivors, and for the defendant.

—CHARLES AMBROSE AND MICHAEL WIMS,
*How to Prepare and Try a Murder Case:
Prosecution and Defense Perspectives*[1]

Two days after Marty Sessions's death, Detective Richard Jacobson was planted in the middle of Marty's and Carole Alden's living room, staring at a trunk.[2] The arched top was covered with wooden planks. Metal eyelets dimpled the flat blue sides—a crude loop of rope handle emerged like an afterthought from the edge of the lid.

Jacobson—the quiet mastermind who would piece together the story of Marty Sessions's death—couldn't imagine having such a box anywhere in a house. Certainly not in a living room. Definitely not in a house with young children.

Carole Alden's children, Jacobson eventually discovered, were all too familiar with the box's contents.

Jacobson was a brown-haired man of medium build with the tanned and creased look of an outdoorsman. "I think he looks like Kevin Costner,"[3] says his wife, Relda, herself possessing the impish look of country singer Reba McEntire. And indeed, Jacobson shares Costner's earnest demeanor along with his good looks. Although Jacobson would be the last to admit it, he is widely acknowledged as the behind-the-scenes Sherlock Holmes of Millard County—an unlikely, soft-spoken genius at uncovering the truth behind the crimes he investigated. "It's not a detective's job to make truth out of non-truth," he would later tell a friend. "It's to follow the evidence." It was this ability to follow the evidence that made his talents so valuable.

Although born and raised in rural Millard County, Jacobson came by his sophisticated scientific approach naturally. His father, J. F. Jacobson, was a widely admired high school chemistry teacher—a salt-of-the-earth man who also won national and state awards for his teaching. Jacobson's brothers were also high achievers—one went on to receive a doctorate in genetics and move into the private sector, while another found his calling with the US Army as a lawyer in the Judge Advocate General Corps. Jacobson's sisters are well-educated nurses. A good detective has to have an analytic mind—to be able to break down the components, resynthesize them, and see through to the underlying pattern. Shaped in part by his father's scientific lens, Jacobson thrived on this rational approach.

Jacobson was a bright kid and an excellent student who had studied astrophysics in college—a result of his childhood spent as a "star-gazing machine" and avid reader of science fiction. But even though Jacobson's grades were good and the scientific underpinnings of the field fit him, astrophysics itself somehow didn't suit him. So he shifted to pre-veterinary studies—after all, he loved animals. Again, his grades were good and the science felt right—he also realized there

The trunk that sat in the living room of the Sessions family home. Police would later discover that Carole's children were all too familiar with the trunk's contents.

was something intriguing in the medical mysteries he would be solving. But ultimately, there was something still not right about veterinary medicine—an itch he couldn't scratch. Jacobson belonged in a scientifically oriented professional realm, he knew. His true calling, however, just wasn't among the professions he had *thought* he belonged in.

"Everything's about timing," says Jacobson. "Timing delivers itself to you. Most of the time, at least." Friends told him of a developing course—the first ever for level-2 certification to become a special function officer, which is a stepping-stone into police work. Jacobson took the course and became hooked on law enforcement.

His family was shocked at his choice, but in some sense, it was his family's devotion to both science and reason that had brought him finally to his life's career. Law enforcement, after all, is the ultimate blend of both science smarts and people smarts. Jacobson went on to pass the police academy through a year and a half of night courses—working during the daytime as a carpenter to help support both his family and his studies. He proceeded on up through the ranks in typical fashion- –doing a number of years on patrol and then serving as a SWAT team sniper and, eventually, instructor. He was fascinated by the scientific side of shooting—the importance of ballistic coefficients, air temperatures, and angle of trajectory.

But Jacobson hankered after more meaningful work—the satisfaction he received from taking a child predator out of society made other activities seem trivial by comparison. Jacobson was a family man with underlying values that centered on the old-fashioned virtues of industry and integrity. From Jacobson's perspective, he received two paychecks. One was from what his employer deposited in the bank each month, but the other was from the answer to two questions on his drive home each day. *Was my work today worthwhile? Was I pulling my weight?*

Because Jacobson had become a detective later than most—in his early thirties—his family had watched how the job had changed him. As his wife would later say, "Women who marry men who *are* cops

The back porch cum chicken coop of the Sessions house.
This photo was taken a few days after the homicide took
place, as were most of the photos in this section.

have it easier than women who marry men who *become* cops." Jacobson himself looks back on his early life as if it belonged to a different person. "It's difficult to see the absolute worst in humanity on a daily basis," Jacobson notes. "It will change you. You can only try to control how much."

Homicides usually take top priority in any detective's life. But Jacobson had been at a funeral on the far side of the state when Marty Sessions was killed. This wasn't just any funeral. "Buck," a retired Utah Highway Patrolman, had been very nearly a father figure for Jacobson since his own father had died many years before. If there was a single day in Jacobson's entire professional career that he wouldn't have missed for any reason whatsoever, this was the day.

Thus it wasn't until the day after the killing and initial interrogation that Jacobson ended up staring at the chest in the living room among the mountain of feces-stained clothing.

He doffed his hat and scratched his head, taking in the cages of dead rats and lizards—Marty's flying body had apparently sent them

A dilapidated Buick guards the garage
at the run-down Sessions household.

scattering. A family member would later estimate that over three hundred reptiles were living on the property at the time of Marty's death.

But beyond the live reptiles lurked rows of ceramic lizards and frogs filling nooks and ledges high and low. There were miniature versions of the welded lizard and dragon sculptures he'd seen in the yard. A large aquarium on the floor in the kitchen held a noxious brew of large, floating, very dead fish that added to the stink of chicken droppings wafting in from the sagging back porch. Cushionless couches and all, the latticed stoop apparently doubled as a chicken coop.

Outside, abandoned cars budded from the landscape. Bony llamas and a Shetland pony stared from beside a tilted barn with a caved-in roof; other animal pens contained unkempt alpacas and what looked to be emus. Roaming in the dust and weeds were chickens, dogs, cats, turkeys, ducks, and peacocks. A staked-out goat had apparently had quite a dustup earlier with some of the investigators.

The Sessions homestead was pure, unmitigated chaos. Jacobson's sense, intuited from the scene before him as well as from what he'd begun to learn from others, was that Carole Alden was a woman who exercised airtight control over whatever one thing was before her at that moment. But like a pilot disoriented in a storm, she'd lost all control over the big picture.

Jacobson backed away from the wooden box and moved to stand on one side of the massive bloodstain in the hallway just outside the laundry room. This was apparently where Marty Sessions had been shot. Given the spread and size of the bloodstain, it was hard to tell which way Marty must have fallen.

Looking past the bloodstains and bits of drying flesh, Jacobson could see into the laundry room where Alden had apparently been standing when she'd fired the first shot.

She *had* had a potential escape route—the laundry room had a side door. But it would have been impossible for her to get out that door—the room was stacked waist-high with fetid clothes.

But there were other doors in the house she could easily have escaped from.

The hallway where Marty Sessions was killed. The first door on the right is to the laundry room, where Carole hid the gun and herself. The carpet here has been pulled up for analysis by the crime lab.

How to truly understand who the victim was here?

Psychologist Dietrich Dörner's words resonated: "Those truly able to solve complex problems gather information before acting, think systematically, review their progress, and correct themselves often. Those who make the most errors tend to cling to preconceived theories, do not correct themselves, and blame others when things go wrong. The errors made in complex situations are a feature of poorly conceived reasoning and an overall human tendency for laziness."[4]

Dirty clothes were everywhere around the house, sometimes in mounds nearing eight feet high, often coated with urine and feces.

Thoughts intruded on Jacobson's observations. *How could anyone keep children in this kind of place?*

Picking his way down the cluttered hallway, Jacobson found himself in the dark master bedroom, backlit through a slit in the blankets that covered the windows. The bedroom door was hanging off its frame, a jagged hole punched through its middle. Closet doors lay over the bed—perhaps hurled there in a flash of anger. It would have taken a strong man to do this—Marty must have had an aggressive side, at least toward things, if not people.

Jacobson pushed past the closet doors to reach the far side of the room, where a half-empty bottle of Captain Morgan rum perched beside prescription bottles on a folding table cum nightstand. A nearby bureau indiscriminately housed dusty plastic bottles, Speed Stick deodorant, a canister of Icy Hot gel, empty cans of Shasta soda, dirty cups, and incense sticks. Oddly pristine among the rubble, lying over the edge of the bed, was a lovely crocheted afghan.

The clothes on the floor pointed toward more clothes hung in the closet—men's plaid shirts and pants on one side; flowing, seventies-style hippie skirts and blouses on the other. Pushing aside the skirts, Jacobson noticed several shelves of books. He moved closer to take in titles: *Screw the Roses, Send Me the Thorns: The Romance and Sexual Sorcery of Sadomasochism*, *Learning the Ropes: A Basic Guide to Safe and Fun S/M Lovemaking*, and *Bondage on a Budget*.

Ahh. A sadomasochist. So that explained the whips, chains, ropes,

One of the children's bedrooms. Note the tiny tick marks on the dresser drawers.

suspension harness, cuffs, and other gear in the living room chest. And that explained why Carole Alden showed signs of being abused.

Jacobson stood, pondering. Slowly, a new question arose. Why were the books on sadomasochism on *her* side of the closet?

He glanced around the room with fresh eyes. A glint of gold binding on the floor caught his attention—*A Treasury of Aesop's Fables*. The book was partly covered with a black silk band—a blindfold. Beside the blindfold lay a homemade whip made of wrapped leather and coat hanger wires with a smooth Plexiglas rod.

Jacobson rubbed his nose. The stench was appalling. Threading his way back up the hallway, he turned into a side bedroom—one of the children's rooms, from the looks of it.

This room, too, was in chaos—carpet barely visible beneath torn flaps of cardboard boxes, scraps of paper, plastic trays, and dirty clothes. A defunct oversized computer monitor sat forlornly on a desk, a disconnected keyboard on a chair cushion in front of it. Soda cans. A toy car. A horn.

Propped against the wall was a ragged bureau with a missing top drawer. Lower drawers lolled out to reveal their contents: dirty plates, bowls, cups, and glasses. Apparently the rules in the house were: no rules at all. Eat as you please, live as you please.

Next room—the daughter's, it seemed. Pages from a diary lay scattered on the desk, neatly printed in a child's block hand.

Dear Diary

I made a bracelet for the bus driver. She's nice. Marty says that I killed the sheep by starving it to death but I't been alive for at least four years! Maybe even more! I messed up my room really badly. I got everything.

A photograph beneath the writing showed a blonde, pigtailed girl—perhaps eight years old—with a rueful smile.

The ersatz wood veneer on the walls was covered with crossed-off tick marks, as if the days' slow passing was being marked in a prison cell. Writing showed up in fainter, lighter colors beside the hash marks:

Rock-a-bye baby,
In the treetop,
When the wind blows
The cradle will rock
When the bough breaks

The cradle will fall
Down will come baby
Cradle and all.

CHAPTER 12

CROSS-EXAMINATION BY MR. SLAVENS— WHY THE HOUSE WAS A WRECK

Terrorists are picadors and matadors. They prick the bull until it bleeds and is blinded by rage, then they snap the red cape of bloody terror in its face. The bull charges again and again until, exhausted, it can charge no more. Then the matador, though smaller and weaker, drives the sword into the soft spot between the shoulder blades of the bull. For the bull has failed to understand that the snapping cape was but a provocation to goad it into attacking and exhausting itself for the kill.

—PATRICK J. BUCHANAN,
Where the Right Went Wrong[1]

Jim Slavens, Carole Alden's public defender, is a man with a mission.[2] The mission was first revealed to him in elementary school, although he only rediscovered this on graduating from high school, when he and his fellow graduating seniors were handed envelopes from years before—envelopes that contained their own fifth-grade descriptions of their three dream careers.

One of the careers on Slavens's list was *singer*. "But if you heard me sing," says Slavens with a self-deprecating chuckle, "you'd know why this career was out of the question."

Actor was the second of Slavens's dream callings.

That profession, too, remained in abeyance—although one might think that any good trial lawyer treads one of life's most intriguing stages. But still, Slavens has retained his interest in the theater— several times a year, he and his wife travel to New York to enjoy Broadway and off-Broadway plays.

Thanks to Perry Mason, Slavens's third career choice was *lawyer*. That, of course, is what he is today. But it was neither an easy nor an obvious path to get there.

Slavens's heritage came, as Mormons like to say, through the

James K. Slavens, Carole's public defender. Slavens says, "Every person I defend has an aunt, or an uncle, parents, brothers, sisters, or children. . . . That's what I do in my practice. I take care of people who need defending. That's my job."

Hole-in-the-Rock. This meant that Slavens was descended from the original group of settlers sent by Brigham Young to southeast Utah, near the Four Corners area. The settlers included self-taught engineers who blasted holes in the rock and plowed through cliffs to carve a shortcut across the extraordinarily difficult terrain to Blanding, Utah. Among these hardy souls was Slavens's great-great-great-grandfather, the renowned Mormon bishop Jens Nielson. Nielson was an industrious, multitalented, blithely polygamous man who served as both spiritual and temporal adviser for his people, as well as American Indian translator for the neighboring peoples.

Jim Slavens, then, much like his courtroom opponents Pat Finlinson and "Jake" Jacobson, was a descendant of Mormon aristocracy —although his inherited community connections were to San Juan County, rather than to Millard. But an illustrious heritage still didn't make becoming a lawyer easy.

After receiving his bachelor's degree in English from Brigham Young University, Slavens first feinted toward a career as an English teacher on the Navajo reservation not far from Blanding; he taught there for several years. But law continued to beckon, slyly emerging from Slavens's subconscious often enough that his wife finally put her foot down—either get the degree or never mention it again.

Slavens went for the degree. He was accepted into a number of law schools but finally chose to attend the University of Idaho. It seemed a big step out into the world for a man who had never gone north of Utah's borders, but Slavens excelled—eventually becoming editor in chief of the *Idaho Law Review* and making the traveling Moot Court Team.

Indeed, Slavens had found his calling.

Slavens's first job, perhaps surprisingly, was as deputy attorney in Millard County—the position later held by his opponent, Pat Finlinson. Slavens worked there for a little over a year. But when the position of public defender opened up, there wasn't a doubt in his mind that he wanted it. He put in a bid, and next thing he knew, the position was his, with all its heartache, misery, and unacknowledged triumphs.

Being a public defender in a small town is no picnic. Slavens ruefully remembers a woman who stopped him at the post office to criticize him for defending a young man. "That guy's just plain no good," said the woman. "He needs to be going to prison—you should be helping him get there instead of standing in the way."

Slavens was shocked speechless—he still fumbles to describe his surprise even years after the incident. "It just wasn't very Christian of her, leastwise," he finally surmises. But two weeks after the first meeting, he happened to run into the same woman again. This time, however, the tables were turned—Slavens was representing the woman's niece. Now the woman had a new plea: "Please do what you can for my niece. She's a good young person. All she needs is a little help—a little guidance to get pointed into the right direction."

Slavens looked right at the woman and said: "Two weeks ago you were all over me about defending someone else—someone not related to you. But when it turned out to be your niece who needed defending, someone you know well, all of a sudden you find compassion. Let me tell you something. Every person I defend has an aunt, or an uncle, parents, brothers, sisters, or children. And they all care in just the same way you do about your niece. That's what I do in my practice. I take care of people who need defending. That's my job."

The woman, to her credit, got his point.

"If I paid attention to every person who criticized me for what I do, I'd never do anything," Slavens says. The battle-hardened defense attorney has a natural ability to look past legal issues, players, and defendants, to cleave to a higher calling: the Constitution. It is this magnificent document, Slavens feels, that holds the system together and makes the United States a truly great country. "Illegal immigrants do a lot of work in Millard County," he asserts. "And the Constitution protects those immigrants just the same way it does anyone else. That's part of what I'm proud of about our country. And that's part of my job. When it comes to writing my epitaph, that's what I want my gravestone to read. *He did his job.*"

His job was precisely what he was doing while cross-examining Sergeant Burton as the preliminary hearing continued.[3] This, in fact, was what the prosecution team was finding so annoying. It seemed as if Slavens was picking at everything. Things were beginning to get testy on the stand:

*   *   *

Slavens: "So Officer Pedersen was there at the crime scene, correct?"

Sergeant Burton: "That's correct."

Q: "So why are you assuming that he wasn't in charge of the crime scene?"

A: "I'm not assuming anything. It is you making the assumption. I told you, 'I don't know.'"

Q: "I'll tell you I don't know, that's why I'm asking the questions."

A: "Again, just to state what I've told you several times, I don't know what decisions were made as far as who was doing what there."

*   *   *

Slavens was attempting to show that there might have been disorganization in the police's approach to the case—disorganization that might have led to mistakes like the destruction of the pillow. Of course, the delay in Jacobson's taking over of the case was due to genuine human contingencies—it had taken the detective a day to travel across the state from the funeral and take over the Sessions homicide investigation. But it didn't hurt to pry. It was part of Slavens's job, after all, to look over the shoulders of the police and try to find flaws in whatever they'd done. Slavens had learned to ignore the dislike this automatically engendered.

He shifted tactics.

*   *   *

Slavens: "All right. Now, you indicated Carole told you that she and Marty had had domestic difficulties in the past; is that correct?"

A: "That's correct."

Q: "And she also indicated to you that Marty was out drinking with his friends the day before, the day of this event, correct?"

A: "Yes, that's correct."

Q: "Didn't she also tell you that she had some concerns about Mr. Sessions having contact with Allen Lake because of earlier threats?"

A: "Yes, she did."

Q: "And she went over to Allen Lake's house to find them?"

A: "Yes."

Q: "Let's talk about what she said happened in the street. She said that Mr. Sessions was wasted, correct? That he was stumbling, having a hard time standing?"

A: "That's correct."

Q: "That he was very angry at her?"

A: "That's correct, yes."

Q: "And that Mr. Sessions was laying in the road?"

A: "That's correct."

Q: "And they had some difficulty getting Mr. Sessions in the vehicle?"

A: "Yes."

Q: "Eventually he became less intoxicated than he was when he first came there, correct?"

A: "Yes. In fact, what she told me was initially he couldn't make ten steps without falling down. By the time of the incident when he was shot she thought he was making, maybe, twenty steps without falling on his face."

Q: "She also indicated that Mr. Sessions started throwing things, correct?"

A: "That's correct."

Q: "And tearing things apart?"

A: "Yes."

Q: "Punching walls?"

A: "Yes."

Q: "Making threats?"

A: "Yes."

Q: "Calling her names?"

A: "Yes."

The master bedroom a few days after Marty's death. The closet doors were apparently ripped off their hinges and thrown onto the bed.

Q: "Telling her he was going to get her?"

A: "Yes."

Q: "In fact, didn't she tell you that she was moving from room to room to keep separation between her and Mr. Sessions?"

A: "Yes, she did."

Q: "And at some point you asked her why she didn't leave, correct?"

A: "Yes. I asked her if she had access to the back door to get out and get away from him instead of going into the laundry room."

Q: "What was her response?"

A: "She said that she didn't dare leave him because in the past he has passed out and aspirated. She suggested that he had vomited and aspirated the vomit and it was necessary for her to resuscitate him because he was choking."

* * *

Prosecutors may have thought Carole was making up the self-serving "aspiration" business, but there was solid evidence to back up her claim. Although he didn't draw on his previous defense of Marty, Slavens had done his homework to defend Carole—he'd found an instance when Marty Sessions had aspirated in the Millard County Jail. It was a serious situation, for which medical treatment had been provided. Slavens's questioning was bringing this exculpatory evidence into view.

Q: "And she indicated to you that he was in the back bedroom and that for a moment of time there was no noise?"

A: "That's correct. Things got quiet, so she went back to check on him. She went in the bedroom, he yelled at her, threatened her, so she came out. She went into the kitchen, turned out the lights so she couldn't see him and then stepped into the laundry room and that's when she heard him coming down the hallway."

Q: "Okay. And he walked almost past her in the hallway, looked back, and made a threatening move toward her?"

A: "Yeah. Looked at her and raised his fist."

Q: "That's when she shot him?"

A: "That's correct."

Q: "And she told you her thoughts were: It was either him or her?"

A: "She said, 'I just felt like he was going to kill me.' She also told me she pushed the door closed after she shot him because if he got ahold of her . . . because, I can't remember the exact words."

Q: "History?"

A: "Yeah."

Q: "She would be history, right?"

A: "Yeah."

CHAPTER 13

FLASHBACK

... the fertile lands of the Pahvant Valley.
Thriving towns in this valley are Scipio, Holden,
Fillmore, Meadow, Flowell, and Kanosh. ...
Between these towns lie dry farms which yearly
produce bushels of grain.

The Sevier River enters Millard County near
the northeast corner and its waters are backed
into a large reservoir which furnishes water
during the summer months for thousands of acres
of irrigated crops such as alfalfa, lucerne seed,
corn, sugar beets, grain, and so forth. In the geo-
logic past the Sevier River was a much larger
stream which carried alluvial deposits from the
mountains and spread them over the desert,
finally emptying into Sevier Lake, which was part
of Lake Bonneville; thus this western part of the
county became known as delta country. ... The

towns are Delta, Hinckley, Oasis, Deseret, Abraham, Lynndyl, Oak City. . . . Average rainfall is ten and 7/10th inches in Millard County.
—STELLA DAY AND SEBRINA EKINS,
Milestones of Millard: A Century of History of Millard County, 1851–1951[1]

It was Thursday, July 27, 2006. The day before Marty's death.

Carole had a *lot* to do today. She stared at the monotonous road ahead of her, resisting the urge to floor the accelerator. The Pahvant Range was to her right, while cattle to her left grazed on Sevier River pastureland studded with sagebrush. She'd driven this road dozens of times before, but never with such an important task.

Delta, the sleepy little town four miles from her house, had all the usual amenities—groceries, sporting goods stores, banks. Carole needed money. She needed money *now*. But instead of stopping at the bank in Delta, her Jeep was heading up past Lynndyl and Leamington for Provo, a hundred miles up the highway toward Salt Lake City.

Bits and pieces of her past drifted with her, floating just behind consciousness. An e-mail from three years before, written to an old friend: *"I told my therapist today that if Marty didn't kill himself SOON, I was about ready to do it myself . . . have him taxerdimized to stand decoratively in the corner of the living room, with his head on one of those "bobble" things like the rear window dogs . . . so he could do nothing but 'yes dear' motions."*[2]

Another e-mail, sent the year before: *"By last night, I was ready to put him out of MY misery as well as his own. . . . I did my level best to suppress the urge to kill him while he pouted all day."*[3]

And yet another e-mail, about the same time, to another friend, *"I probably will get a gun someday . . . but I won't be using it on animals."*

She could feel the anger building. Marty Sessions. Her husband. She couldn't help but remember last year when he told her he'd purposefully overdosed on his medications. She'd gotten in her car and left, figuring that either he was bluffing and trying to see how upset she would get, or that if he did actually take all his pills, he could make himself throw up, call an ambulance, or lie down and die.

Either way, it was his decision, and she wasn't going to expend any more emotion over the whole thing. She was *done*.[4]

"And then he threatened me," she'd written a friend. *"Said if I did anything that caused him problems, he would go tell my ex a bunch of shit. And men wonder what drives women to kill them in their fucking sleep!*

"I believe I will go dig a great big hole in the back field, on the off chance that he does us all a favor and pitches over dead. Either way . . . eventually it will make a wonderful koi pond."[5]

Those were angry thoughts from over a year past. But the anger had been simmering.

Arriving in Provo, she turned off into the strip mall by Bulldog Boulevard, pushing through the double doors of the ungainly, two-story-high building that housed Check City. It took less than an hour to fill out the forms to obtain a cash loan for $450. The annual interest rate on the loan was a usurious 417 percent, but it didn't matter.

This money was important.

The house was quiet when she arrived home that evening. Marty himself had told friends he was planning to move in with a friend, Rick Searle, and he'd already taken some of his belongings over to Searle's place. Marty had left Carole a note: *"I'll be back to get more stuff."*[6]

But Carole had different plans. She told her older children not to expect Marty to be there after the weekend ended. She was taking him down to Arizona, she'd told them, back to the Indian reservation. Later, she would tell investigators she had planned to spend the weekend at home with Marty, patching things up.

But on that next day, Friday morning of July 28, she wasn't headed to Arizona with Marty or enjoying a quiet day with him at the house. She was in her Jeep, headed south with her son *Jason*.

As Carole drove, she passed Ashman's Pioneer Market in the distance, a well-known local gun store in Fillmore with a broad selection of shotguns, rifles, Colts, Smith & Wessons, Winchesters, and Glocks.

Heading farther south, she passed Meadow and Kanosh—quiet little towns where you could sleep on the main street and not get run over. The morning was a pleasant one, and the eighty-mile drive to Beaver went quickly. She walked briskly into the Beaver Sport and Pawn—an old-style two-story mercantile store with a large sign over the entranceway —"FLIES, LIVE BAIT," and a smaller wooden sign, "GIFTS."

She walked through the front door to find rack after rack of rifles and shotguns lining the exterior walls of the main entry room. Handguns were in the glass counter cases lining the perimeter of the room. She'd come to the right place.

"Can I help you?" asked the clerk politely.[7]

Carole glanced through the selection. "I need to do some shooting," she said.

"Anything in particular?"

"Coyotes," Carole answered. "They're bothering my animals." Jason was wandering silently among the racks of rifles.

"Well, you don't want a handgun, then. You need a rifle for coyotes, lady," answered the clerk, helpfully steering her toward the crowded racks.

"No," Carole said assertively, refusing to be drawn aside. "I want a handgun."

Her eyes traced the glass of the locked showcase, fingers close to the Smith & Wesson .38 lying below. "Like that one."

"But that's a handgun. It's no good for shooting coyotes. You want a *rifle*."

"No, I *don't*. He's a wily coyote. If he sees me with a rifle, he'll run. I want a handgun."

The clerk shook his head. This was gun country. People shot coyotes with rifles—not handguns. It was easier to make the kill at a distance. But it was her money.

Minutes later, .38 Special and box of rounds in hand, Carole exited the store and was on her way back toward Delta.

CHAPTER 14

THE SANCTITY
OF THE VICTIM

**We are all here on earth to help others;
what on earth the others are here for,
I don't know.**

—JOHN FOSTER HALL (1867–1945)[1]

W hat is a victim?

Forensic scientist Brent Turvey has pondered this question for years. Turvey is a broad-shouldered, dark-haired man with more than a passing resemblance to actor Robert Downey Jr. Indeed, like the superhero Downey portrayed, Turvey is something of a real-life forensic Iron Man who jaunts from his remote aerie in Sitka, Alaska, around the world to help solve some of the world's most difficult crimes. Turvey's website URL, http://www.corpus-delicti.com, sums up his criminological focus. *Corpus delicti* is Latin for "body of crime"; it refers to the principle that a crime must be proven to have occurred before a person can be convicted. Corpus delicti is one of the most important concepts in a murder investigation.

Turvey is the kind of quick-thinking, brash, in-your-face consultant who is a blessing if he is on your side and a hellion if he's on the other. But whatever work he does, and whichever side he works for, Turvey is an unabashed advocate of truth—regardless of how unpleasant, surprising, or dissonant that truth might be. In Malcolm Gladwell's brutal *New Yorker* essay on the chicanery behind FBI profiling techniques, Turvey pulled no punches as he vented, "The fact is that different offenders can exhibit the same behaviors for completely different reasons. You've got a rapist who attacks a woman in the park and pulls her shirt up over her face. Why? What does that mean? There are ten different things it could mean. It could mean he doesn't want to see her. It could mean he doesn't want her to see him. It could mean

In the small world of truth-seeking forensic practitioners, Brent Turvey (right) is friends with Mike McGrath (left)— the pair take a break from a series of lectures to detectives in Beijing as they stand on the Great Wall of China.

he wants to see her breasts, he wants to imagine someone else, he wants to incapacitate her arms—all of those are possibilities. You can't just look at one behavior in isolation."[2]

VICTIMOLOGY

Turvey's *Forensic Victimology: Examining Violent Crime Victims in Investigative and Legal Contexts*, written with Wayne Petherick, has already become a classic in the field.[3] The book complements Turvey's *Criminal Profiling: An Introduction to Behavioral Evidence Analysis* and a range of other books and articles.[4]

Turvey earned a master's degree in forensic science to go along with his double set of bachelor's degrees in psychology and history. He is an anomaly—he writes academic volumes, but he's not a typical academician. Rather than sit ensconced in an ivory tower, studying victims in an isolated academic petri dish, Turvey makes his living as a senior partner in Forensic Solutions, LLC, consulting as a forensic scientist in the investigative or trial phase for both law enforcement and attorney clients around the world. He focuses on the examination and interpretation of the crimes that make up people's worst nightmares—assault, rape, homicide, serial homicide, autoerotic death—and he is also an expert on fetish burglary and staged crime scenes. Turvey testifies in court about issues in all these areas and also about cases that involve criminal profiling, criminal investigation, crime reconstruction, and victimology.

Turvey and Petherick collaborated on *Forensic Victimology* because there was nothing like it available. The pair had found that, in an age where ideology has crept on little cat feet into many areas, professionals were being discouraged from approaching victims with the skepticism that good science requires. Victimization, Turvey notes, is not always simple.

An interesting example is that of twenty-six-year-old Tanja Morin of Lancaster, Ohio, who called 911 to report that her 2-year-old son, Tyler, was missing. She tearfully explained to the dispatcher: "The only way he could have went is through the back, and the only way you can get the fence open is if somebody kicked it from the outside. . . . Somebody had to come through the yard." The call was made at 10:51 a.m.

Tanja's husband, Michael, immediately came home from work to help in the search for Tyler. He found the couple's youngest child at 11:22 a.m., in a garbage dumpster less than a block away from their home. Had he been left in the dumpster much longer, the heat would have killed him; it was one of the hottest days of the year.

During the initial police investigation, the mother's kidnapping story succumbed to realistic victimology and fell apart. A nearby surveillance camera had captured the activity at and around the dumpster before, during, and after Tyler was reported missing. On the surveillance stills, Tanja can be seen walking hand-in-hand with her youngest son in the alley near the dumpster at 10:35 a.m. A minute later, she can be seen leaving towards her home alone.

Tanja confessed to detectives that she hadn't meant to hurt Tyler, only to create an emergency that would get her husband to come home from work. According to police, she told them, "He wanted to spend money today that we didn't have, and I was trying to think of a way he could come home so he didn't have to spend the money that he had."

Tanja was arrested that day, and charged with attempted murder, child endangerment, and kidnapping. At first, she pled not guilty. The judge subsequently ordered her to submit to a psychiatric evaluation. In November of 2007, she pled guilty to kidnapping, child endangering, and felonious assault charges.

In this case, the mother lived in a severely dysfunctional family where she was apparently convinced that the benefits of creating a false crisis outweighed the potential consequences to her or anyone else. Taken at her word, she was actually a victim of her husband's financial irresponsibility and was acting with good intentions. Certainly her actions were enough to warrant a psychiatric evaluation— something that would not necessarily occur to the court if a man were facing the same charges. In cases of domestic violence and even homicide, women are often treated by the justice system as victims in need of help, and men are viewed as aggressors deserving of punishment. Such distorted views, based on cultural archetypes, can result in diminished responsibility, or at least sympathy, for the mother.

The objective, scientific victimologist would [refrain] from taking this mother or any other alleged victim at [her] word, as this case and many others demonstrate that the institution of motherhood is not inviolate. Even a mother claiming to have the best intentions can put [her] child in a garbage dumpster and lie about it, if [she thinks] there is something to be gained.[5]

THE SANCTITY OF THE VICTIM

As Turvey cogently summarizes, *no* culture or institution is beyond doubt, examination critique, or redress in the study of victims and purported victims—not "the 'sacred bond' between a mother and her child; not the culture of law enforcement; and not the 'objective' forensic examiner. Within each there are those who are willing to distort or fabricate victimity because they perceive a cultural reward for doing so."[6]

The real problem, of course, is that some victims are truly victims in the classic sense of the word. Compassion for victims is there for a reason—there *are* often innocent victims. They have done absolutely nothing to contribute to the unfolding of a crime. Some cases are truly black-and-white. Who couldn't feel for a grandmother crying as she gazes toward the wreckage of her lifelong home left by a tornado? Or for the youngster who loses his beloved kid brother to cancer? Or the parents of a young woman abducted in broad daylight from a shopping mall, then raped and murdered?[7]

But sometimes the situation enters into various shades of gray. People can play different roles in their victimization—from something as simple as leaving a door unlocked to an act as darkly complex as a woman putting her own child in a Dumpster.

Every culture has different perspectives on crime and its victims. In modern Western culture, the dominant view at present is the "sanctity of victimhood." This "refers to the belief that victims are good, honest, and pure, making those who defend them both righteous and morally justified. Conversely, it suggests that those who doubt them are immoral and unjust in their tasks."[8] This sweeping cultural assumption is unwarranted and runs contrary to the scientific method. As Turvey notes: "Victimization is a method for absolving persons of responsibility. When trouble emerges, an 'innocent' party—the object of the injury or trouble—can be specified by assigning victim status to one or more persons, thus exempting them from blame."[9] In other words, "one is constantly reinforced with the notion that being a victim freezes the normal course of daily events and thereby shifts responsibility and accountability, if only temporarily."[10] At school or in the workplace, if people become ill, suffer a death in the family, or have a personal tragedy, they are treated with special indulgence.

The very fact that victims are perceived differently and given special dispensation means that there can be an incentive—whether conscious or subconscious—to be a victim. We cringe to even think victimhood claims could be false (what if we're wrong!), but false victims can be a real, and horrific, problem. The point is not to lay blame but to keep an open mind and to look at each situation anew. Sweeping, unchecked assumptions, in science, in the justice system, or in any realm, do a disservice to the truth we hold to be sacred and to the systems we rely on for their integrity, no matter how effectively they may advance some ideological agendas.

Systems can become bogged down responding to people crying "Wolf!" For example, as one *Eyewitness News* episode reported recently, Alfredo Garcia now makes a living as a serial plaintiff. He has filed more than five hundred lawsuits against small businesses who see him as a small-time thug and legal extortionist. Garcia, an illegal immigrant and convicted felon (for selling weapons and crack and for vehicular burglary), fell out of an avocado tree while drunk and has since been in a wheelchair. Garcia's "days are spent going from business to business looking for violations like a bathroom mirror or a paper-towel dispenser that's too high."[11] Garcia is not alone in his vocation—his lawyer has a roster of similar serial litigants scouring the region for businesses that can vest plaintiff's counsel with an entitlement to attorney's fees. Behavior like this could be useful in helping businesses see things from the point of view of people in wheelchairs, but violators of the Americans with Disabilities Act are not given notice or a chance to correct the problem—they are simply sued, often at taxpayers' expense. "Wouldn't conciliation and voluntary compliance be a more rational solution?" wrote Judge Pressnell in a Florida ruling related to this type of behavior. "Of course it would, but pre-suit settlements do not vest plaintiff's counsel with an entitlement to attorney's fees."[12] Elizabeth Milito, senior counsel for the National Federation of Independent Businesses, notes that the extreme expense of such litigation prompts many businesses to simply settle claims that are even without sound basis.[13]

Even some disabled-advocacy groups are beginning to speak out against such lawsuits. Andrew Imparato, president of the one-hundred-thousand-member-strong American Association of People with Disabilities, said: "There are these individuals and boutique firms that make a business out of filing 75 claims at a time. It leads to a strong backlash against the ADA, and it can do harm to the cause of increasing access for those with disabilities. The point of this law is not to shake-down businesses. The point is to improve accessibility."[14]

The unrelenting, one-dimensional focus on the sanctity of the victim, dismissing those who would take advantage as rare aberrations, has not only created problems for real victims—it has *created* new victims. The reporting of fake crimes, as Athens-Clarke, Georgia, police captain Clarence Holeman has noted, "is becoming an epidemic." Police departments are being forced to take a stance, since the increasing number of false claims of victimhood are drawing investigators away from legitimate crimes.[15]

In a more explicit example, Kristin Ruggiero recently bragged to her ex-husband, "I took all your money, I took your daughter, and now I'm going to take your career."[16] She then sent herself dozens of threatening messages on a phone she had purchased and registered in her ex-husband's name. It was only then that her criminal efforts to portray her husband as an incorrigible batterer were exposed. As columnist Carey Roberts goes on to note:

> This tale is not so much about a distraught woman sorely in need of psychological help. Rather, it's a story of a police department, a prosecutor, and a judge that allowed themselves to be duped by a conniving perjurer. And it's about a criminal justice system that has all but abandoned due process in a frenzied attempt to curb domestic violence.
>
> Like everything in the law, the problem begins with definitions. The Violence Against Women Act, passed during the first term of the Clinton administration, includes a definition of domestic violence that is so wide you could drive a Mack truck through it. States picked up on the loophole, and now most states include within their definitions of abuse, actions like making your partner "annoyed" or "distressed." The U.S. Centers for Disease Control and Prevention (CDC) likewise followed suit. The CDC's Uniform Definitions and Recommended Data Elements declares that partner violence includes "getting annoyed if the victim disagrees," "withholding information from the victim," and even "disregarding what the victim wants."
>
> Note the CDC's repeated use of the word "victim." In VAWA-speak, a victim does not need to be a prostrate body lying in a pool of blood. Rather, a mere accusation elevates you to the status of victim. No proof of violence is necessary.[17]

Again, some people really *are* victims. But we cannot operate a society and uphold its laws if we can't think critically. Unfortunately, critical thinking in this area is discouraged. If a person claims victimhood, to question that claim is regarded, in our culture, as unchivalrous. We are particularly programmed to view women as victims who need our sympathy, while men are aggressors who deserve to be punished. Such unexamined assumptions do a disservice to the truth inherent in each individual situation. Even in cases in which the assumption ultimately proves true, to have made the assumption, uncritically, is itself inherently unjust.

There are people, of course, who are comfortable questioning people who feel victimized. Skip Downing, a former English professor who also holds an advanced degree in counseling psychology, has developed a highly successful national program for teaching at-risk college students to change their behavior and excel. Downing's secret? He teaches students not to think like victims. You overslept the day of the test? *Why did you stay out late the night before? And why didn't you have two alarm clocks?* Couldn't get a ride to school? *Why didn't you have a backup plan?* Always had a problem with math? *Why aren't you going to the tutoring center?*

The slightest hint of victim-thinking—*I had to go babysit my sister's kids, so I couldn't come take the test*—earns a V symbol from Downing or those trained in Downing's "On Course" methods. In this case, the V doesn't stand for *victory*. It stands for *victim*—and it means "Stop it!"[18]

But Downing's down-to-earth approach to removing the unquestioned sanctity of victimhood, effective though it is, is an unusual phenomenon in a Western culture that prides itself on helping the less fortunate—a culture that is inclined to think that someone who claims or feels victimized is always innocent.

Real victims, whose hardships are beyond what many can fathom, deserve no less justice.

CHAPTER 15

HELL ON WHEELS

Success is how high you bounce when you hit bottom.

—GENERAL GEORGE PATTON

"If you don't stand for something, you fall for everything," says one Alden family member, still frustrated after all these years at the pain he feels Carole has inflicted on her parents and siblings. "Maybe that's true. Carole was held accountable until she had the kids. But once her kids were in the picture, Carole's parents couldn't turn her away."

Most people would call Carole's upbringing as she entered her teenage years idyllic. Carole's father brought his family along on two lengthy professorial stints to New Zealand. (Carole, by then married, missed the second trip.) According to outside observers—indeed, according to everyone in the family except Carole—both parents doted on all four of their children, trying to encourage and support

147

their passions and talents. Carole, the budding artist of the family, was allowed to take art classes—her interests also led her to piano, flute, and drum lessons. Carole's mother was largely a stay-at-home mom, while Carole's father, whose outgoing, gregarious nature made him a popular professor, encouraged the children in their love of nature, which they all adopted.

On a more fundamental level, the Alden family has an established outlook of helping others, particularly the less fortunate. All three of Carole's younger siblings have grown to become adults who are dedicated to helping the disadvantaged.

Carole did well until high school, when she stopped focusing on whatever didn't hold her interest. She became something of a loner, and because of her odd interests, she was noticed as being different, which appealed to her.

Carole appeared to have a particular problem with structure and order, despite, or perhaps because of, her parents' efforts to ensure she had reasonable organization in her life. Her room, for example, was often knee-deep in clothes and trash. Once a week or so, her parents would withhold privileges—Carole couldn't go anywhere until the room was clean, so she would polish the room to pristine beauty. But within a few days it would deteriorate, as if entropy worked double-time around her.

Carole's teenage years became hell for her parents. She began staying out late, lying about where she was and whom she was with. Both parents realized that teenagers will be teenagers, but there was something deeply antagonistic in Carole's attitude toward her parents, particularly toward her father. His attempts to instill accountability were seen as efforts to control her, to purposefully make her life unpleasant. Carole's conversations with friends involved her feelings of triumph as she fooled her father with yet another illicit escapade, making his life more difficult.

At the same time, Carole had some perfectly decent male friends. She made friends with genuinely nice young men in her early high school years in New Zealand. A memorable trio of friends she hung

Carole at age fourteen. There were happy times mixed in with what her parents hoped was simply a typically turbulent teenage phase.

out with in high school in Colorado were interested in music and art—one became a professor of philosophy at a midwestern college. Another became a successful maker of stringed instruments. The third had no chance to fulfill his early promise—he drowned in an accident in his twenties.

While still in high school, Carole easily won the annual Halloween costume contest every year. Carole's costumes were always spectacular—one year she dressed as an extraordinarily detailed dragon with a long tail. She stood out as having talents, which made her happy. Again, she wanted to be different—to be seen as someone extraordinary. In some sense Carole *was* a genius. Whereas most child prodigies display talents in art or math or dance (and indeed, Carole possessed unusual artistic talent), Carole was a genius with fabric.

It was as if she had been born with a sense for pattern that helped her cut and assemble cloth into whatever shape she wanted—no need for flimsy paper templates. Without instruction, she knew how to craft brilliant designs—elaborate wedding dresses would emerge like magic from her fingertips. Carole herself felt that her creations sometimes came to her in her dreams, which were almost like instructional videos. Even if the techniques and materials were completely new to her, she would wake up with the feeling she'd been doing it for years. She sometimes felt like a conduit—a sort of artistic "idiot savant."[1]

Carole won an art scholarship to a nearby university, but her uncanny ability with fabrics proved her scholarly undoing. Forced to take a clothing construction class, she found that part of the requirement for passing the class was to spend several hours a week hemming drapes for theatrical productions. For the independent-minded Carole—the Picasso of fabric creations—it was worse than drudgery. She adamantly insisted that she did not go to college to learn how to do something she had known how to do for years. This, of course, didn't endear her to the professor. But toward the end of the semester Carole stunned everyone during the student design "fashion show" by modeling a wedding dress she had made. "I had no idea she could create anything like that!" her professor exclaimed. Her professor also had no idea that Carole's lovely lace vests were on sale at one of the nicer dress shops in town; she was also sewing exquisite commissioned wedding dresses with Victorian flair, featuring muslin, lots of lace, and rows of fabric-covered buttons fastened by material-covered loops. To Carole, the designs created and modeled by others in the class seemed as unsophisticated as wrap-around skirts.

In any event, Carole's first attempt at the university didn't pan out, so her parents next supported her in a move to a school of arts. But this proved

Carole, age eighteen, models a dress of her own creation.

more commercial than Carole desired—she left that school, as well.

Carole was now eighteen and on the loose—she called the shots in her life, just as she had long wanted. And this is the juncture at which those free choices began to result in a life that has so mystified those who love her.

She struck up a friendship with a handsome twenty-two-year-old graduate student, Richard Senft, who was moonlighting at the local ice cream parlor to help pay his tuition. At that time, she took a job at a massage parlor with a shady reputation across the street from a popular strip joint. As Carole's old friend Penny Packer noted: "Was there stuff going on besides massage? Well, some of those clients wanted other things. Carole knew what she was doing—no normal massage person was going to make the kind of money Carole was making. But when I'd ask her directly about what was going on, she'd just lead me up to make my own decisions. She'd never use the word 'sex.' She did that a lot. She'd lead you right up to the verge such that that was the only conclusion you could come to—and then she'd leave you hanging."[2]

Richard Senft was good-looking in a square-jawed and muscular way. He was also bright, hardworking, responsible, and artistic—though he was too humble to boast of his talent. In high school,

Richard had been voted both Most Likely to Succeed and Class Brainiac. In other words, he was a catch. Carole was something of a catch herself—petite, adorable, impetuous, and possessed of an extraordinary artistic talent that, as much as her looks and sense of fun, caught Richard's attention. Richard recalls genuine love and real affection between him and Carole at that time. Two years after they first met, Carole and Richard Senft were married in 1980 in a home wedding.

After Richard received his doctorate in range science, the couple moved to Logan, Utah, where Richard worked as an assistant professor at Utah State for four years until his department was abruptly terminated due to budget cuts. Hardworking as ever, Richard next picked up a two-year hitch with the USDA Agricultural Research Service in Booneville, Arkansas. The couple moved to Ozark, about an hour's drive from where Richard worked. With the arrival of their third child, Richard began to grow exhausted from his triple duty—serving as the family breadwinner, cleaning up after Carole and the kids (a never-ending, thankless task), and babysitting.

Every other day or so, Carole would announce that she was off to the store for milk or eggs—then she'd disappear for three or four hours. This made it difficult to rely on her for critical childcare needs. Those three- to four-hour disappearances, as it turned out, allowed Carole to befriend an out-of-work neighbor. He began to come around during the day when Richard was at work. The furtive pair made plans to go to California together.

Meanwhile, Carole had also apparently been swapping sexual innuendos on the telephone while ordering lizards from a pet store owner in Cleveland. She suddenly found it necessary to fly to Cleveland to pick up some animals.

By this time, Richard was becoming overwhelmed with Carole's machinations and manipulations. The couple had spent many a sleepless night talking about their marriage, with Richard taking the tack that Carole must begin behaving like an adult. Finally, Richard offered her an ultimatum in the form of a choice—shape up or ship out. To

Richard's horror, she shipped out. Her new, reptile-loving beau drove to Arkansas to "rescue" her and the kids and move them up to Cleveland.

Richard discovered that the courts—generally sympathetic to women in any case—were putty in Carole's hands. Her accusations of abuse swayed the judge—Carole herself was utterly convincing as the perfect, doting mother. Despite Richard's best efforts, the children remained with Carole. Looking back now from the perspective of his twenty-years-and-counting track record of happiness in his second marriage, Richard notes, "Carole was never battered or abused by me"—a claim backed up by other adults in the Alden family. He continues: "As her modus operandi started to dawn on me, I would call her on her games and tell her that I wasn't interested in participating in those dramas. I asked, insisted, and finally begged her to be a grownup, to put her kids first, and to stop playing the victim game. If that's abuse, then I was an SOB.

"She learned with practice to thoroughly wrap herself in the cloak of the sanctity of the victim—and would go ballistic if someone pointed out that perhaps her problems were fabricated. No matter how reasonable a request I might have made, she had a talent for turning it around into a thinly veiled threat of ending the marriage."[3]

In any event, Carole's new beau was soon dubbed "Brutus from Cleveland" and later "a psychopath" by her family. Although mannerly, "Brutus" horrified Carole's parents with the values he displayed during one brief visit to Colorado. ("Just say the word," he mentioned in passing, "and I can have Carole's husband bumped off.") Carole eventually pulled the plug on this relationship by convincing a dealership to let her have a new truck—she escaped late one night, children and belongings in tow, and fled back to her parents' house. One family friend would wonder why, if Carole could run from one psychopathic relationship she'd entangled herself in, she didn't run from others she would later find herself in.

If life with Carole when she was a teenager had been difficult on her parents, life with Carole as an adult with children of her own was worse. After several months, a cute little house was found for Carole not far from her parents' house. Within weeks, the house began to lose its luster.

For years, much of Carole's income came from child support paid by Richard Senft, her first husband. Later, Carole's second husband, *Brian Poulson*, also added his contribution. One longtime family friend pointed to a recurring element in Carole's adult life—her avoidance of a steady job to support herself and her children. "Get a job—any job," her father told Carole when she complained of lack of money. To those close to her, it was a mystery as to why she would take on twenty rabbits to feed when her own children needed food.

Family friends noted that Carole was adept at using her children to gain sympathy. It's one thing for parents to set firm limits and refuse to enable errant offspring who have become mature. But when an errant offspring has children, it's much more difficult to say no. And after Carole had returned to Colorado, as before in Arkansas, her own needs began to come to the fore. She began disappearing in the evenings, leaving the two youngest children in the care of her oldest son, *Conner*, then eight years old. What little money there was for Carole and her children was apparently being used to support a burgeoning nightlife.

Those who loved Carole became increasingly concerned and sometimes risked speaking out to protect the children. But when Carole was told that having her kids sleep on the floor in a messy house and using an eight-year-old as a babysitter was *not* good parenting, she lit into her accuser, telling him to "get the fuck out" of her house.

Sadly, the children endured other hardships. One family member, for example, called Social Services upon finding three-year-old Jason sitting on the couch alone and hungry. The agency's response was that the situation would have to hit bottom before they could do anything. Another family member reported Carole's children to a school counselor, asking them to check to see whether the children were showing signs of neglect. But nothing came of the warning.

It seemed clear that Carole was struggling. And it was during this interlude in Colorado, living near her parents, at a time when her anger and frustration seemed overwhelming, that Carole began the first subtle insinuation to her family. Her problems, she hinted, weren't her fault. They arose from her father. From what he'd done to her when she was young.

But when pressed, she'd shy away, as if she didn't know what people could possibly be thinking.

CHAPTER 16

MIKE McGRATH
APPLIES CRITICAL THINKING

The history of our race, and each individual's experience, are sown thick with evidence that a truth is not hard to kill and that a lie told well is immortal.

—MARK TWAIN, "Advice to Youth"[1]

Forensic psychiatrist Mike McGrath's concern for battered women grew not only from his innate compassion and sense of fairness, but also from his critical thinking skills and ability to think independently. These talents had been honed through a series of frustrating experiences over the years.[2]

One of McGrath's watershed moments on critical thinking was related to the hot field of criminal profiling—a way of using clues from a crime scene to deduce the personality behind the crime. Understanding the personality, profilers supposed, would provide important clues to help catch the criminal.

McGrath devoured well-known profiling memoirs, reading books like *Mind Hunter: Inside the FBI's Elite Serial Crime Unit* by John Douglas and *Whoever Fights Monsters: My Twenty Years Tracking Serial Killers for the FBI* by Robert Ressler, as well as others by former FBI profilers. But something seemed amiss—McGrath couldn't help but note that the personality characteristics and other profiling offerings that were deduced to underlie very different crimes were suspiciously similar. Worse yet, the criminal profiles developed didn't seem to have anything to do with actually solving the crimes.

This was an area where McGrath's background in forensic psychiatry lent him a rich perspective far beyond that of most casual readers. Suspecting a problem, he analyzed the FBI study of serial killers on which their underlying theory rested—"organized" offenders (essentially, those who are more orderly in their life and crimes), versus "disorganized" offenders.[3] What he found astounded him. Results were based on the serial killers' own answers to a poorly designed questionnaire. *Anyone* should know that serial killers' own self-serving statements about *anything* should be the last thing taken on faith. To make matters worse, McGrath could see that the results of this "scientific" approach, and other similarly questionable conclusions, were being translated to advice for law enforcement on ongoing investigations. Yet anyone who disagreed with the developing FBI methodology was ignored if an outsider or considered a traitor if an insider. McGrath's hackles rose.

It was worse than he first imagined. McGrath could see other problems with state law officials using FBI-generated methods for investigating crime. A violent crime is usually only a federal offense when committed on federal property or when the crime is against certain people, such as federal agents or postal employees. The vast majority of rapes and murders and assaults are state—not federal—crimes. The FBI profilers, as it turned out, had little experience investigating violent crime before they started profiling. What the FBI profilers seemed to lack in experience, they appeared to make up for in hyperbole. For example, former FBI profiler Gregg McCrary claimed in sworn testimony to have drawn conclusions based on investigating hundreds of thousands of rapes. That would have meant that during his twenty-five years at the FBI he had an average (minimum) of twenty-two rape cases a day.[4] There's lying, notes McGrath dryly, then there's the FBI.[5]

McGrath was looking for the real science in areas that were critical to getting at the truth and protecting the public. And he wasn't finding it.[6] It was around this time that McGrath became familiar with Brent Turvey, the forensic scientist noted earlier who shared a disdain for criminal profiling.[7] They "clicked" as colleagues because of their ingrained skepticism, which they considered an essential ingredient for professionals truly interested in protecting the public.

Another critical-thinking moment occurred when McGrath began studying and then publishing the results of his research related to sexual assaults, in which he estimated that perhaps 25 percent, if not more, of all reported sexual assaults are simply not true.[8] However, as McGrath discovered, people's careers were being torpedoed when they made the mistake of trying to publish results that ran counter to such assumptions. Mike himself learned that if he brought up the rate of false reporting in sexual assaults, people wanted to know what he had against rape victims. As McGrath would later note: "I have nothing against rape victims. I just have this problem with scientific truth. It gets me every time."

As he looked further into the issue of sexual assault, he learned that, based on a 1988 study by Mary Koss, a psychology professor at Kent State University, it is widely claimed that one in four college women has been raped.[9] Again, McGrath applied common sense:

> If I sit in a college cafeteria, of every four female college students who pass by, one has been raped? I have daughters. How is it possible that they are at such risk? They have friends. Somebody must know the one out of four! Who has been keeping this horrible secret? My wife had completed graduate school within the last decade. Was she keeping this secret from me? Or were only undergraduate women being raped? How can this be true?
>
> Well, it ain't. The number comes from a questionnaire study, based on (purposely?) broadly worded and interpreted questions. It

seemed that feminist political agendas were getting some researchers a free pass.[10]

Such sentiments can understandably raise the hackles of any feminist.[11] But real feminism, of the kind McGrath knew and admired,
encompassed an honest ability to step back and look at how well-
meaning researchers with the best of intentions skew what are presented as facts.

Once established, assumptions die hard. An *ABC News* story from
September 2010 trumpeted, "A recent study from the Department of
Justice estimated that 25 percent of college women will be victims of
rape or attempted rape before they graduate within a four-year college
period."[12]

McGrath wasn't alone in questioning the data. Neil Gilbert, a professor of social welfare at the University of California, Berkeley, has
pointed out that the inflated numbers arise from a need for funding.
"These studies have been used to get funding for women's centers on
college campuses. I call it advocacy research, these people mean well
and have legitimate concerns. But at some point they exaggerate so
much that it is no longer a problem but the norm and with studies like
this they risk doing just that."[13]

As Gilbert insinuates, nobody is saying there isn't a problem, but
exaggerated estimates and a climate of well-intended but unquestioned
assumptions don't help the cause.

Not long after McGrath learned about the issues with research on
sexual assault, Brent Turvey asked whether McGrath would be willing
to write a chapter for a book that Turvey was editing on forensic victimology. In relation to his ensuing chapter, McGrath researched
trauma diagnoses and syndromes. He had heard of "rape trauma syndrome" and "battered woman syndrome" before, but he had little current firsthand knowledge, as psychiatrists didn't seem to refer to these
syndromes anymore. He'd certainly never learned anything about
them during his residency.

What McGrath learned, once again, astounded him. In her work,

Lenore Walker implied that battered women were simply normal people who happened to stumble into a relationship with an abusive partner. But there *had* to be shades of gray underneath Walker's insinuations. (Interestingly, Walker has long claimed legitimacy for battered woman syndrome by stating it has been officially listed as a subcategory of post-traumatic stress disorder in the American Psychiatric Association's *Diagnostic and Statistical Manual of Mental Disorders*. But the specific section she cites, as it turns out, is nonexistent.)[14] It would help if there were more substantive research in this area—research that went beyond the observations of counselors who generally study abused women only after those women have been abused. Walker certainly wasn't leading the charge for credible research here, though. Instead, she was insisting that scientific methods were not relevant.[15]

It could be that many young women made poor choices for mates and that problems developed over time as violence emerged. Some—or perhaps even many—battered women might not be totally "normal" (whatever "normal" actually means). It was just as likely, though, that they might not be disturbed enough to be clinically diagnosable as having a personality disorder. But nobody knew anything about all this—the lens of science had never been applied. Walker had started everyone off thinking that battered women were normal, then she'd battened down the hatches, attacking anyone who proposed a more nuanced, scientifically grounded view. McGrath observed:

> I think Lenore Walker and her original conceptions for battered woman syndrome came from a good place. Walker saw a situation she felt compelled to look into. Unfortunately neither she nor the good people thirty years ago who funded her at the National Institutes of Mental Health realized that without control groups the validity of her findings would be problematic. It's as if her pilot study became her study. Apparently only later when people started criticizing her did she realize the problem. But, rather than admitting the depth of the problem, it looks like she chose to frame it as "Oh, of course there were no real control groups. That's how I planned it and here's why. . . ."

Lenore Walker is a good example of perception as reality. No matter the criticism, people wanted to believe her work and, in fact, in some states *by statute* you must admit battered woman syndrome evidence at a trial if an assertion is made by the defense that a woman was battered. Walker has built her career around battered woman syndrome. She has become an icon. The victimhood she studies protects and enables her, deflecting criticism. It is very hard to get people to see past that.[16]

THE PARADOX OF FAMILY VIOLENCE

Feminists may bristle at the idea of feminist-based research being given a free pass. But researcher Murray Straus—himself a longtime feminist—has decades of personal experience with the phenomenon.[17]

The impish Straus, his research as influential as ever even now, into his mid-eighties, is no stranger to controversy. His extensive studies on the adverse effects of corporal punishment for children, detailed in his 1994 book *Beating the Devil Out of Them: Corporal Punishment in American Families and Its Effects on Children*, have brought Straus enmity from religious fundamentalists and organizations such as the Family Research Institute, which believes that preserving the "right to spank" is an important goal.[18] This same research has also, perhaps surprisingly, drawn fire from some on the left, who see Straus's findings related to corporal punishment as a distraction from wife beating, which they deemed the only "real" family violence.[19]

Through the years, Straus has been intently focused on what he has come to call "'the paradox of family violence'—the idea that the family is both the most loving and the most violent of all civilian institutions."[20] What causes violence within families? he wondered. Who commits it, and how? Are there ways it can be reduced—even eliminated?

Straus did not approach these questions lightly. He is an iconoclastic polymath whose life's work has involved the establishment of family violence as a field of scientific research. Straus has mentored some of the field's most prodigious scholars and served as the president of the Society for the Study of Social Problems as well as for the National Council on Family Relations. His widely cited research, supported by more than forty years of continuous grant funding from the National Institutes of Health and the National Science Foundation, has earned him many top national awards, including the Award for Distinguished Lifetime Contributions to Research on Aggression, from the International Society for Research on Aggression.

Straus's research helped provide solid evidence of the greater adverse effects that women experience in situations of partner violence. As Straus notes, "Attacks by men cause more injury (both physical and psychological), more deaths, and more fear. In addition, women are more often economically trapped in a violent relationship than men because women continue to earn less than men, and because when a marriage ends, women have custodial responsibility for children at least 80% of the time. The greater adverse effect on women is an extremely important difference, and it indicates the need to continue to provide more services for female victims of [partner violence] than for male victims."[21]

But Straus's evenhanded, dispassionate research revealed other, far more controversial findings. Although the public and research perception has long been that partner violence is inflicted almost exclusively by men, in reality, this is not at all true. In fact, men and women partners physically assault one another at virtually identical rates, as almost two hundred studies have confirmed over the past fifty years.[22] Women are hurt more often, because men are stronger, but even so, men are on the receiving end of a third of the injuries noted in partner violence—including deaths by homicide.[23] Rates of battering of women appear to have declined substantially in the past thirty years. But rates of problems for men—non-negligible to begin with—haven't changed at all.[24] It's as if, by focusing on men as the source of problems in partner violence, only half the issue has been addressed—like trying to help someone walk again by fixing only one of their two broken legs.

CHAPTER 17

A LOVE AFFAIR WITH ART, WOOING THE PRESS, AND A CONVENIENT DEATH

[Sarah] Bernhardt captured the world's imagination because she had a flair for self-promotion—Henry James called her "the muse of the newspaper"—but also because she was a genius . . . she didn't just out-Gaga Gaga, she out-Streeped Streep.

> —JEREMY McCARTER,
> "Drama Queen: Sarah Bernhardt Was
> Part Gaga, Part Streep," *Newsweek*[1]

Trapped in her once cute but increasingly neglected house in Colorado, Carole seemed at a loss. She'd left her first husband and fled her reptilian Cleveland beau, but now for those around her the question was becoming—*were efforts to help Carole really helping*? Or were those efforts instead simply enabling, at one level or another, the drama that increasingly swirled around her?

Carole scrambled—doing construction work, shoveling snow for people, and creating soft sculpture (fabric art) on commission. For some, Carole left the impression that with artistic talent of her caliber, menial labor was beneath her. But to others, she appeared to revel in the attention she brought to herself for doing what she considered "hard man's work." In any case, Carole was frustrated, venting in sound bites to her former husband back in Arkansas, using the moments before handing the phone to the children to insinuate that she and the kids were homeless.

More forthrightly, Carole claimed that during this time frame, she and the children were Dumpster-diving for food, an assertion she repeated in a sympathetic *Salt Lake City Tribune* article. This article turned Carole's trip from Arkansas to Colorado into an over-the-top six-month odyssey living in a shell built of scrap lumber on the back of a truck, with Carole and the children suffering eviction after eviction as she fled her "abusive" first husband, Richard Senft. *Krystal*, Carole's second daughter with Senft, comfortable in her role of backing up her mother's stories, chimed in to add: "It's been rough, bumpy, exuberant. . . . But there's always been constant love for all of us. She always made sure we had that."[2]

Others, however, remember Carole's journey from Arkansas to Colorado as being uneventful, save for the interlude with the quasi-psychopathic Cleveland pet store owner who apparently proved too dangerous for even Carole to handle. But the pet store owner was excised from the *Tribune* article. Carole was learning she could rewrite her life's story through credulous journalists.

Carole could often sound surprisingly cheerful when relating her travails to others. A family member once asked Carole how she could be so upbeat when everything in her life was in such a state of collapse. Her response was that she *had* to give the impression of being positive—that was how she coped with everything. But if Carole was cheerful, those she conversed with were often left in a state of depressed shock.

Carole rarely, if ever, directly asked for money. But in her conversations with others, it often seemed she was attempting to outdo the world in terms of how bad things were—glorying in the horrific miseries of her life. (And indeed, Carole's life was often objectively quite miserable.) Listeners sometimes couldn't help but feel Carole's unending laments were her way of indirectly asking for money, or simply one of her never-ending efforts to shock others.

In any event, Carole's return to Colorado to be near her parents was brief. Not long after her angry meltdown at being berated for her lax babysitting and nonexistent housekeeping skills, Carole came home one evening muttering of an even more traumatic experience: rape.[3] Carole didn't report the incident to authorities, but it was clear she once again felt victimized. One of Carole's jaded familiars notes that she must not have had much luck trolling for marks there—in any case, Colorado simply didn't seem to be working for her.

But something else *was* working: a growing long-distance relationship with Brian Poulson in Salt Lake City. Brian had known Carole since the time she'd lived in Utah while still married to Richard. When he discovered that Carole was no longer in a relationship, he came to Colorado to help her pack and to move her brood and her stuff to Utah. Carole's family was thrilled—Brian seemed a genuinely sincere, helpful, kind, and decent person. In fact, Brian would prove as much a catch as Carole's first husband. A stalwart six-footer with a nicely trimmed beard, blue eyes, and light brown hair, Brian was friendly and smiled easily. With his laid-back demeanor and deliberate speech, he never seemed hurried. Brian was a musician as well— he loved stringed instruments, especially the mandolin, and he enjoyed jam sessions with friends, along with bluegrass festivals. He also tinkered for fun with old VW's, had three sailboats, and was handy in his shop, where he made beautiful wooden kaleidoscopes.

Raised an observant Roman Catholic, Brian's second nature was trying to do the right thing. Not long after the move, the couple were married. A respectable time later came baby Jason, and four years after him came Carole's youngest, Emily. Interestingly, the fathers of Carole's children didn't seem to share the "loser" designation of her other swains—both Richard and Brian were each genuinely decent men. But these decent men didn't retain Carole's attention.

* * *

Carole's love of art is unquestionably at the core of her very being. Even those who have reason to despise her admit that she is consumed by a need to create artistically—they would find themselves contributing cash so that she could obtain the materials her creative processes demanded. Carole herself would say that her love for art was something she could no more turn off than stop her heart from beating. She felt her way of viewing the world was so radically different from the way others viewed it that she might as well have been an alien. It was as if her brain were a sort of "complex play dough fun factory . . . visuals in . . . interpretation out."[4] Entire projects, from start to finish, would unfold like videos in her dreams. This allowed her to work even with techniques and materials she'd never worked with before—a gift almost magical. Creation was, to Carole, a form of spiritual worship. She felt a responsibility to help others open their eyes to new ways of seeing and understanding. She especially enjoyed making people stop and smile with dazzled wonder.

Babies, with their "squeaky toy noises," were an indescribable pleasure. Her own babies, of course, were the most beautiful things she'd ever seen. Things iridescent appeared to hold a special fascination for her: the rainbow luster of embroidery thread, the evanescent sheen of motor oil on puddles, pheasant feathers, prism-type sun catchers with Tiffany-style peacock glass.

Carole's favorite painter was Frida Kahlo, who Carole felt was a brave soul for her exploration of both spirituality and personal anguish. Carole also loved what she felt was the "opulent natural sensuality" of Monet, Van Gogh, and the artists of the art nouveau period that peaked in popularity from 1890 to 1905. Inspiration was drawn, too, from Bernini's marble sculptures of the Greek goddesses, English book illustrator Arthur Rackham, the Wyeths, and fantasy artist Frank

Frazetta. Seeing feminist artist Judy Chicago's fiber art installations while still a student allowed Carole to realize her potential for making her needle art mean something. One of Carole's dreams was to someday meet Judy Chicago and participate in one of her projects.

One local artist and arts administrator, *Rebecca Smith*, who has known about Carole Alden for many years, is convinced that Carole is an artistic genius. Smith points out:

> I have seen plenty of artists in my day, and Carole Alden stands out from the field. I truly marvel at how her brain works. For example, I work with fabric myself, so I asked her one time about how she constructed her dragon. She told me that the design just unfolds in her head—then she whacks out the fabric to fit and sews it together. Well, I'm here to tell you, my brain could no more figure that out than fly. Now, an engineer's brain may work that way, so maybe she's "just" an artist with an engineer's brain, but she's leagues ahead of me when it comes to construction in her head.
>
> I think Carole is reasonably rare in the artistic field because she uses both sides of her brain to maximum capacity. A lot of artists couldn't find their way out of a paper bag, but they sure could make a masterpiece while they were in there. I think Carole would design the paper bag out of fabric, wrench it in a few directions, and then decide on her own terms when she was in the bag, and when she was out.
>
> What especially strikes me is how Carole will take anything at hand to create art because she is innately driven to do so. She creates snow sculptures, for example, because there's no other sculpting material to work with. Or, she just has really crappy acrylic yarn to make something out of, and yet she creates these huge pieces of fabric that are intricate and complicated and form a whole landscape. It might not even be that the end product art is genius, but her infinite capacity and drive to create something no one else has ever thought of is amazing.

It was in Utah with Brian that her art allowed Carole to begin cultivating what would become an ongoing relationship with the press. In fact, the eye-popping nature of Carole's creations made attracting the gaze of the media easy. In January 1993, the *Deseret News* printed a picture of Carole's family taking advantage of "plentiful snow and clear skies to create a 30-foot snow lizard."[5] In March, another journalist wrote about Carole Alden's one-woman show in the children's section of the Salt Lake City Public Library: "Chameleons, lizards, snakes and other reptiles scamper or slither across walls; a red-eyed tree frog clings to a window; and a turtle 'swims' over the librarian's desk. . . . She prefers to take artistic license when working with size, features, colors, etc. For example, the Tokay gecko generally measures 14 inches. [Alden's] is eight feet long."[6] Yet another article noted Carole as a "well-known fantasy artist" featuring fabric sculptures of "delightful dinosaurs and darling dragons."[7]

Carole Alden's ninety-foot-long metal-and-nylon-mesh "Library Square Sea Dragon" was ensconced on the Salt Lake City Main Library's reflecting pool during the thirtieth annual Utah Arts Festival. "I was going to have it done beforehand. But people really like watching you build it," Carole said to a newspaper reporter. "I haven't had any negative comments yet. I'll have to wait until my mother gets here."[8] Those who know her sweet-natured mother would be taken aback by Carole's gratuitous remark.

As Carole would learn, the media had unpredictable but often beneficent powers. In September 1991, she sent a letter to the *Deseret News* editorial page lamenting that someone had stolen her son's bicycle. "This particular bike," she noted, "had been a Christmas gift a year ago to my 10-year-old son from a church group who 'adopted' our family at a time when we were on the verge of being homeless, let alone worrying about gifts. This bike was his only possession."[9]

Checking back after several weeks, a reporter found Carole overwhelmed: "It's embarrassing to get this much attention over a bike."[10] Carole recalled she'd received at least eight calls a day for a solid week after the letter ran, with some people stopping by her house, pulling out their checkbooks, and donating money then and there. Others dropped bikes off anonymously. The title summed up the story's tone: "Replacement of Boy's Bike Proves Bad News Can Have a Happy Ending."

The reporter pointed out that Carole's son Conner was "'bowled over' by the public reaction to his plight. Conner was struck by the fact that his father—now divorced from [Carole Alden] and living in Pennsylvania—did not seem to care about the loss of his bike, and yet numerous strangers did care."[11] Carole, as it turned out, had never told Richard Senft—Conner's father—about the stolen bicycle.

In fact, Carole often applied to receive charity gifts such as the bicycle because, she claimed, she wasn't getting child support. She also apparently managed to convince welfare officials that she wasn't getting child support when in fact she was—she simply hadn't informed officials when she'd been evicted and forced to move, so the support checks stacked up in a neat, non-forwardable file. Through eviction after eviction the children were told they were forced to move because their fathers didn't love them and couldn't be bothered to pay to help support them.

Of course, nothing could be further from the truth. Both Brian and Richard loved their children very much and did everything they could to help support them—whatever the personal cost.

*   *   *

The bicycle proved but a dry run.

In 2002, Krystal Rusek, Carole's then fifteen-year-old daughter, found a lump on her breast. Later the lump was determined to be a bit of extraneous benign tissue, but Carole hit the media with a story they couldn't refuse. Her daughter, she announced, appeared to be dying of breast cancer, and one of her daughter's greatest wishes was for an emu chick.[12]

"Within a week, the lump doubled in size," Carole told Francisco Kjolseth, a reporter for the *Salt Lake Tribune*. "The prognosis didn't look good."[13] To *Deseret News* reporter Lynn Arave, Carole lamented that breast cancer ran in her family: "We always knew there would be a chance" that Krystal might get it, Carole noted, since two male relatives had contracted the disease.[14] (In actuality, the only member of Carole's family known to have had breast cancer was her paternal grandmother.)

Baby emus could be found by searching the Internet. As it turned out, a San Jose, California, breeder, Phil Lippe, had two chicks that were committed elsewhere, but after a few e-mails, Lippe not only pulled the emus from their previous commitment; he also insisted on giving the chicks to Krystal for free. With a few more phone calls, Carole had arranged the donation of a soft-sided sky kennel from PetSmart, while Delta waived all transportation fees. Altogether, the donations amounted to around $10,000.

Photographers and camera crews lined the wall at the Salt Lake City International Airport on New Year's Day as Krystal waited with her mother for a package—supposedly of artwork. Krystal was shocked when she found that the large package arriving from California was not for her mother but for her. She opened it, photographers snapping away, to find that it contained two emu chicks.

Hearing about the story later, however, the Alden family was even more surprised. They knew Krystal liked emus—but no more so than the many other animals she loved. Krystal herself disputes this characterization, saying she was a volunteer at Tracy Aviary at the time, where one of her tasks was caring for emus, and that she had told her mother that she wanted emus. It was Tracy Aviary, Krystal says, who wanted reporters to cover the story since the woman who delivered them to Krystal had been her supervisor there.[15]

The underlying issue, however, might revolve around whether Carole herself liked emus. As it turned out, she liked them very much indeed. In fact, it seems Carole had wanted to start breeding emus as a financial enterprise but had never had the financial wherewithal to get started. "That emu had nothing to do with her daughter—it had to do with Carole herself wanting an emu," says one of Carole's siblings.

In any event, the overwrought six-month odyssey, the bicycle, and the emus were but glimpses of still bigger media misadventures to come.

*   *   *

Carole was married to Brian just shy of eight years, during which time she added two more children to the three from her first marriage. Regardless of her love for her children, Carole's priorities did not put them at the top of the list. Conner's high school years often found him home caring for the younger children—a sad turn of events for this highly intelligent youngster, who now began to slip unsupervised toward a world of drugs and alcohol.

Inevitably, Carole's relationship with Brian began to sour.

Carole's modus operandi, according to many who knew her at various points in her life, was to search for a knight in shining armor to rescue her. Once the shining knight was hooked, however, she'd find ways to remain a victim, one who couldn't quite be saved. Disaster followed her every footstep in her self-created Jerry Springer world. As one person who felt blinded by her manipulations put it, "At some point, it became clear there were problems that were problems because she had created them. Everything happened around her. Every time we'd inch ahead, there would be a disaster. It took me a while to realize *she'd* made the disaster."

The shining knight would eventually begin to tire of the disasters and the victim-related antics and would react with frustration. The shining knight would suddenly flip to ugly ogre status, at which point Carole would begin the search for the next shining knight, slowly turning on the charm, grooming him.

Carole herself, on the other hand, felt that her problem lay, at least in part, in the fact that she went from "hi" to "soul mate" in a New York minute, skipping past the kind of casual pleasantries that allow people to get properly acquainted. She would latch onto each new soul mate's good traits, magnifying them even as she downplayed or ignored any bad qualities.

It was on the downhill side of her marriage with Brian that Carole fell in with a new group—Salt Lake City's sadomasochists. She apparently went to meetings three times a week—couples night, dominatrix night, and ladies night. Here at last, Carole found a compatible circle of friends with whom she could share her inner needs. Carole blossomed with the group, finding a sense of friendship and camaraderie that she had never experienced before and acquiring a special reputation as a dominatrix. Carole herself would say she found sadomasochism liberating—the sensory aspects allowing her to work through her own issues and providing her an "opportunity to conquer some of her fears and aversions" that came as a result of sexualization of pain by her father and her mother's taboo attitudes toward sex. Carole also wrote that she could control her feelings and dissociate during the pain.

Genital piercing has long been popular in the sadomasochism crowd—it is thought to both enhance sexual pleasure and express individuality. One article in the *British Journal of Urology* notes the irony of thousands of people identically practicing this type of piercing in order to express their individuality and adds "there appears to be no shortage of women who are willing to entrust their genitals to the hands of the piercer."[16]

One of the most popular types of piercings is known as the "chastity ring."[17] Perhaps surprisingly, genital piercings are no more painful than any other body piercing.[18] "Some women report feeling an endorphin 'rush' during the piercing. Piercers are not allowed to administer any anesthetics, so the essential concern is having a 'Master' piercer, one who has served a genital piercing apprenticeship, places piercings in anatomically correct ways, and performs swift and smooth procedures."[19] Carole had a particular fascination with genital and breast piercings, as indicated by the many drawings investigators found that predated the time she claimed Marty had forced piercings on her. One man who was intimate with Carole would tell an investigator that one of his early sexual experiences with her first involved a visit to the hardware store. As the investigator would eventually remark: "I didn't know there were so many uses for plastic, wood, and leather."

It was around this time that Carole began volunteering her services to assist with counseling prisoners and ex-convicts. It was in this way she met Andy Bristow. One jaded family friend would say Carole found prisons and halfway houses to be the ideal ponds to troll for erstwhile shining knights. As if to prove this point, Carole moved Andy into the house with her children and the distraught Brian. Another reliable source states that Carole moved Andy into the bedroom right next to the master bedroom where Brian and Carole had slept. This would have made it easy for Brian to overhear Carole and Andy when Carole moved into Andy's bedroom. But Carole, on the other hand, insists she was "diligently faithful" and "supportive to a fault" throughout her marriage to Brian, only becoming involved with Andy after she had separated.[20] Carole also felt that the more she tried to reach out to Brian, the further he withdrew, although others who observed the relationship point out that, rather than being retiring, Brian was far more confrontational about his disagreements with Carole than her first husband, Richard.

Andy, with his boyish face, appeared even younger than his age: nine years Carole's junior. He was a reserved man, not tall, but darkly handsome—to others, he appeared vulnerable and in need of help; in fact, he was a heroin user. Carole would later tell others that she felt Andy's "soul was pure"[21]—he was simply trapped in the shadow of heroin. If she could love him enough, she felt, the motivations he'd had for using drugs would lose their power. When Andy started his intervention—the first step on the road to recovery—Carole did whatever she could to help him, paying for his clinic visits, providing him with food, and giving him a place to stay so that he wouldn't have to worry about holding down a job or getting food as he faced the arduous task of going through withdrawal.[22] In spite of, but also perhaps because of, Carole's efforts—the type of unhelpful help so often seen in codependency—Andy continued using on the side. Needles began showing up in the laundry and around the house. Carole later wrote that she knew nothing of heroin addiction—she was looped into Andy's string of lies because she was clueless about drugs.

Andy's mother, LaRee, was a well-spoken woman who seemed overwhelmed with two incarcerated sons and an invalid husband in a wheelchair. LaRee was thankful for Carole's concern—she hoped Carole might truly be able to help her son. The two women developed a bond, sharing heartfelt conversations and providing each other with moral support. Carole would later write that she was far closer to LaRee than to her own mother or siblings. LaRee, it seems, was also able to provide some financial help.

Who is to know how conscious Carole's choices in love really were? In *Women Who Love Men Who Kill*, journalist Sheila Isenberg writes about the little-known and little-studied phenomenon of women who seek and fall in love with murderers. (Carole, it should be noted, fell in with hardcore drug addicts, not murderers.) Isenberg notes:

> Women in love with killers refuse to see faults in their men. And they bestow upon their inappropriate partners qualities that most objective observers can see are not real. These women do not allow themselves to admit their men have weaknesses. They deny the murders their lovers have committed. Their love is fed on illusion and fueled by fantasy so they naturally have false beliefs about the nature of the men they love.
>
> These women love a shadow lover of their own creation. It's as if each woman has taken a blank canvas and painted her ideal man, then fallen in love with him, making him come to life in the process.

He is an inkblot, a blank, a reflection of her inner needs; he, and the love she feels, are not real.[23]

Whatever Carole was doing, at least initially, in finding inappropriate lovers to place on a pedestal, it was a psychological tic that she shared with plenty of other women—none of whom, as Mike McGrath discovered, has been the focus of solid scientific research studies. Carole herself insists in her correspondence that it is simply against her personal belief system to walk away from others. The worse things become, the more she says that she feels duty-bound to show her unconditional love. She writes that she feels sooner or later the people she loved would come to understand her love was absolute—present no matter what flaws they had, and that the eureka moment of this understanding would be the catalyst that would allow them to change their lives. Her influence wasn't direct but rather through example—they would learn to emulate her behavior, and the relationship would blossom as a consequence.

Ironically, amid the same passages where Carole explains her unconditional love, she also explains that she left Brian for Andy because of Brian's constant complaints and her sense of lacking personal fulfillment with him.

In any event, Andy's continued heroin use once he was out of prison meant that he violated the conditions of his parole. Taking the two younger children, the pair struck out to Carole's parents in Colorado. Learning the real story behind the visit, Carole's parents insisted that the couple return to Utah. Andy was apprehended and put in jail, where Carole used her spare child support monies to make his life easier.

Journalist Sheila Isenberg continues:

It's surprising that a woman could relinquish her children because of her commitment to a man she has just met and begun to love. But the intensity of the obsessive love felt by women who love killers is incredible. These women have such strong psychological needs that when they think they've really fallen in love, they are willing to give up everything else in their lives for that love—including their children. Nothing can interfere with their love, nothing, not even children.[24]

But Carole did not abandon her children, although she often placed Andy's needs before theirs. And although she may have shared hybristophilic tendencies with those who lust after killers, Andy was by no means a murderer. Carole's old friend Penny Packer observes, "Andy did seem to be the most unintelligent and uneducated of all her men. Maybe he attracted her attention because he was a less strong person. He was the helpless one who couldn't respond back to her as an equal."[25]

Loving someone like Carole Alden who is free to make choices that affect others—particularly children—can be very confusing and frustrating. Family members recall that when Carole and Andy needed a U-Haul truck in order to move, Carole's parents put the charges for a two-day rental of the truck on their credit card. Several days after the truck was due, a U-Haul official reported that the truck had not been returned. Carole and Andy's address was given, and a U-Haul representative trekked over to discover the disemboweled truck sitting on the sidelines of the premises—its battery had been removed and placed in Carole and Andy's vehicle. If Carole's parents didn't agree to pay double the fee, the rental agency said Carole would have to go to jail. It was a taste of worse things yet to come, but Carole's parents, like thousands of other parents in similar situations, were trapped into enablement by love for their grandchildren.

Carole would ultimately say that she had been blind to Andy's extensive addiction as well as to his own free will—she hadn't anticipated his "side trips into depression, relapse, psychosis, [and] incarceration." She felt he had lied to her throughout their relationship, putting her in constant danger even as he manipulated and stole to meet his own needs. From her own perspective, she in turn had never held him accountable, instead always empathizing and reacting compassionately. Police records, however, tell a different story, showing the two becoming involved in frequent altercations.

And then, unexpectedly, death intervened.

The local police reported Andy's death in Spring 2001 as due to "combined drug intoxication." But strangely, the manner of death was reported as "unknown." In other words, the death couldn't be definitively determined to be an accident, a suicide, or a homicide—it was one of those head-scratchers where no one could quite figure out what had happened, so nothing could be ruled out. Interestingly, the officer who first arrived at the scene entered into the NationScan Criminal Index the term "NCI"—code for "suicide." Even Carole's daughter Krystal called it a suicide.[26] But the coroner didn't rule the death a suicide. Generally, what's not a suicide is deemed to be an accident—but the death was not ruled as accidental, either.

Carole sat beside the casket at Andy's viewing. She had made a tunic-style burial shirt and had designed deerhide moccasins, in which she placed prints of her feet. There was a band of her braided hair around his wrist. The day after the viewing, she gave a long, moving eulogy honoring Andy and his family. It was a very traditional, well-attended funeral. There were not many dry eyes.

Andy's mother belonged to the Church of Jesus Christ of Latter-Day Saints—a religion that discourages cremation. But Carole convinced Andy's parents that Andy had wanted to be cremated. Carole brought her daughter Krystal along so they both could witness the cremation.

Eight years after Andy's death, Carole would write that it took her all that time to be able to see Andy's behavior objectively. Occasionally, she is able to dredge up some anger, but then she can't help but forgive him, envisioning him the way she felt he truly could be. If Andy were to miraculously reappear before her, even knowing what she now knows, she is certain she would fall for him all over again—she simply doesn't "know how to not love somebody that much."[27] Perhaps, she muses, loving too much is a form of mental illness. Or perhaps she merely needs to find someone who loves as she does.

A curious detail is that Carole told others that she met Marty Sessions when he wrote a letter of condolence to her from prison about his friend Andy Bristow's death. But according to Rosemary Salyer, Marty's stepsister, Marty and Carole had begun corresponding before Andy Bristow died.[28]

Just as Carole's previous husband had been something of a third wheel, clinging to the relationship even when she moved Andy into their house to help "fix" him, this scenario may have found Andy repeating history, becoming the third wheel himself. Marty needed a place to stay, and his old friend Andy would have been in the way.

Later, Carole would herself allude to these allegations, angrily recalling a drug dealer she'd been jailed with who had told prosecutors that Carole had confessed to being involved in Andy Bristow's convenient, somewhat mysterious death.[29] (Indeed, the Millard County prosecutor's office would later discuss with the Tooele police the possibility of reexamining Andy Bristow's death—an investigation that would have been admittedly made more difficult by the cremation.) Carole's biggest concern in this regard was that Andy's mother would learn of it and think the worse of her. But Andy's mother, LaRee, who presided over the tragic deaths of all three of her children as well as her invalid husband, still thinks fondly of Carole. LaRee also recollects that her son Andy died of an accidental overdose of a medicine he had been prescribed.[30]

Marty's devoted daughters, Edee and Anna, both feel that Marty and Carole did not begin to correspond with each other until after Andy's death. But however the relationship began, when Marty was let out of prison, Carole moved him into her house.

CHAPTER 18

WHY SO DIFFERENT?

Above all, artists are men who want to become inhuman.

—GUILLAUME APOLLINAIRE, *The Cubist Painters*[1]

People from small towns can be the first in line to point a finger at someone who has done something wrong. But they are also the first to forgive—never denying an opportunity for redemption. After all, long after a crime has come and gone, everyone in the town still has to find a way to get along together.

Irene Scott, a deputy clerk for the Fillmore District Court, has known Carole for years; their daughters were friends. Irene sits quietly in the spacious courtroom as a late-afternoon retirement party swirls around her; she has watched the long, slow progress of the proceedings with an insider's perspective.

"Carole? She was a little different. Dressed a little different. They call her the Dragon Lady. She'd drive around with a big dragon on the

181

top of her car. She wasn't well accepted because she was different. She is brilliant—maybe that's part of what made her seem eccentric."[2]

Irene pauses, words emerging haltingly as she remembers. It's clear that Irene is a kind person who looks for the best in everyone.

"She loved animals—had odd ones—ostriches. Loved the outdoors. She was going to build a straw bale home." Irene looks bemused. Pensive.

"She's getting the help she needed. She went downhill once she got with Marty. The kids all recognized that she needed help. She needs to understand what she did and why.

"There were days it appeared she never combed her hair. She had long, flowing clothes. She was just in her own little world. But she didn't care what people thought, either.

"Her art is so detailed. Everything she did was *so* detailed. That was just her way."

*   *   *

Carole Alden was different.

She is different even from her brothers and sister—each of whom is a stable, respected member of the community.

How can that be? Nature? Nurture?

Neither?

SHARED GENES, DIFFERENT PERSONALITIES

Some of the world's most infamous killers have come from horrific upbringings. Charles Manson—mastermind of the infamous Tate-LaBianca killings in 1969—was once given to a waitress by his mother for a pitcher of beer. Ed Gein, the model for Norman Bates in *Psycho*, had an alcoholic father and a mother whose bizarre child-raising techniques and religious fanaticism should have had her frog-marched to an asylum. Russia's Andrei Chikatilo, who killed over fifty women and children in his efforts to achieve orgasm, grew up in the midst of World War II listening to his mother's stories about his older brother being kidnapped and cannibalized by the neighbors.

It's no wonder we think the family environment lies at the root of murder.

But if families create the child, why do the children in a family differ—often remarkably? Ed Gein's first kill, for example, was his own brother Henry, who, unlike Ed, had begun to question his mother's strange beliefs.[3]

The Unabomber, mathematics prodigy Theodore Kaczynski, was tipped off to authorities by his gentle and sincere younger brother David, who recognized Ted's style of writing and beliefs from the manifesto reprinted in prominent newspapers as part of the FBI's efforts to track down the killer. David ultimately donated his reward money to the families of those Ted had killed.

Both boys had received warm upbringings.[4]

John Hinckley, Ronald Reagan's would-be assassin, was a troubled young man from a picture-perfect family. Hinckley's parents wrote a moving account, *Breaking Points*, of their attempts to help their son—it would be difficult to find a more supportive couple.[5]

Even in the deeply abusive Gilmore family, one son, Gary, would grow up to be a spree killer executed by firing squad, while the other, Mikal, would become an award-winning writer for *Rolling Stone* and the *Los Angeles Times*.

A shared environment, whether harmful or beneficial, can produce very different outcomes. Of course, part of this is because an environment is never truly shared—children will be treated differently depending on their sex, their birth order, and their personality—whether winning or obstreperous. A big part of why children turn out differently, however, also relates to their genes. But if parents and siblings share genes, how could genes help influence them to sometimes act so very differently?

Perhaps the easiest way to think of it is to think of a quilt. The same blocks of quilt (that is, genes) can be sewn into patterns that look very different, simply depending on how they are laid out. Thus, daughter and son quilts can look quite different from those of the parents—and from that of each other. This, indeed, is why siblings can be so very different from one another, despite their similar upbringing. But even so, we can still see the resemblance between the family members—after all, the same colors and portions of the same patterns are used in making the different quilts. (Keep in mind that this is an analogy. Having a different quilt pattern—that is, a different arrangement of genes—only influences your tendency to behave in a certain way. It doesn't dictate your behavior.)

In fact, we can think of environment's effect on a personality as being analogous to its effect on a quilt. For example, just as bleach or grape juice can leave an accidental stain in a quilt's fabric, or a seam can rip wide, just so our genes can be stained and ripped by the vicissitudes of life.

Some of these effects are the result of our own choices. If we choose to learn to play the guitar, for example, our sensorimotor cortex changes along with our finger dexterity. If we choose to work out at a gym, certain genes will turn on and others off as our muscles strengthen. (The ability to artificially enhance those natural processes has spawned the industry of illicit doping.)[6]

Researchers are finding that as people grow older, the environmental effects on personality seem to fade—rather as if the quilt has been washed so many times that the stains fade and its true colors are all that remain. This means the original color and pattern—that is, the underlying genetics—are what gradually becomes most influential and visible in adult personalities. Perhaps surprisingly, this grownup peeling away of environmental effects to reveal the underlying influence of genetics is especially noticeable in people's altruistic tendencies.[7]

Some changes in our genes take place despite anything we might wish to happen. Even something as simple as your mother getting a fever from a bout of chicken pox can have subtle effects on genes during particularly sensitive times of fetal development. (That's why pregnant mothers are asked to avoid hot tubs). Drugs such as diethylstilbestrol, which Carole's mother took, can perform a tie-dye effect on the genetic quilt, leaving an indelible mark.

*   *   *

The courtroom retirement party is drawing to a close—there are only remnants of the oversize sheet cake left on the aluminum foil–covered tray. Irene says sadly, "It's just when she got with this guy—she just lost her will."[8] According to Carole, Irene, too, once made the mistake of letting a felon into her life.

Did you meet Marty?

"Yes. He was kind of creepy. I couldn't understand why she was with him. But her kids loved and accepted her just the way she was.

"You could be jealous of her," Irene continues, fingering her skirt in the cool environs of the courtroom. "Carole could live on nothing and survive. She doesn't need money to be happy."

Carole herself would later write that she wasn't concerned about material items such as cars or clothes. She was determined to be a full-time, stay-at-home mother, working her career around that central, motherly mission, which was what she felt she was best at. Entertainment in her household was not centered around electronics or toys—there were neither video games nor Barbie dolls. Instead, her children's play involved exploring the land and using creative skills. Her children, she noted, "might as well have been Amish."

Irene continues. "Carole wasn't a people person. Not sure she had friends. People thought she was odd, but if you sat back and watched, you'd think so, too."

Irene shakes her head and looks up: "I hope you can see her creations, just for the detail. For the perfection."

CHAPTER 19

CAROLE AT WORK

Richard Smith was among the first settlers coming here from Spanish Fork, Utah. He had the first threshing machine. He became ill and his sickness was something the doctors couldn't diagnose. Tests were made and medical men from Washington came to observe and study the case. Mr. Smith died before they found the cause and cure. It was the first case of tularemia, or Pahvant plague, an infection contracted from the bite of a deer fly which had fed on diseased jack rabbits.

—STELLA DAY AND SEBRINA EKINS,
*Milestones of Millard: A Century of History
of Millard County, 1851–1951*[1]

It was while working for the City of Delta in the year before Marty's death that the seams of Carole's tortured personality began to unravel publicly.

"Carole would show up here for work with her two kids in tow—it was weird. Like straight out of *The Addams Family*,"[2] says Randy Morris, a straight-talking park employee for the City of Delta. "The boy was quiet. The girl was a natural survivor. Quick with a comeback." A holy terror was more like it—park employees commented that nine-year-old *Emily* seemed to dart everywhere, always looking for someone to talk to. She'd plant herself in front of workers on the job and talk endlessly, driving them crazy. Thirteen-year-old Jason was more sedate.

"I have lots of good things to say about Marty Sessions, but *nothing* good to say about Carole Alden," Morris continues. "There are four kinds of people I don't like: liars, cheaters, thieves, and lazy people. Carole was all four. It's no wonder we didn't get along. When she did work, she worked one-handed. She'd pull a weed and then take it home to give her goats or emus or alpacas or something. We called her 'Lizard Lady.' Once I called her 'Dragon Lady,' because people called her that sometimes, too. But she corrected me. Lizard Lady is what she wanted to be called."

Morris's coworker, Scott Ross, adds, "She brought her kids, her dog, and a blanket to work here. She'd show up to work in the park in flip-flops and stretch pants—she spent more time chasing the kids and the dog than doing any real work."[3]

While Morris, with his calls-them-as-he-sees-them demeanor, could come off as something of a grump, Ross was more of an easygoing listener. Carole gravitated toward him, riding roughshod over facts with her tale of woe. She had had two husbands who died, she said. One had been a professor. But she'd managed to put herself through university working in a massage parlor.

Carole was unhappy with Marty and obviously angling to find a way out of the relationship. "She was just strange," Ross remembers.

"She told me she brought her kids with her because she couldn't leave 'em alone with Marty. That he was watching her. I'd see Marty come riding around the park with his bicycle. Every time I'd see him, he looked lit."

But the grumpy Randy Morris spent more time with Marty and came to like him. "I can't remember if it was Carole or him that told me he was a Vietnam vet. But he'd had some problems," Morris said. "Marty would come and wait for Carole sometimes. He was a nice, likeable guy."

Morris and Ross worked on the outdoor side of the parks department. Their colleague Leonard Hardy, on the other hand, worked at the shop as a mechanic. Hardy recalls, "Carole was different—when most people saw her coming, they'd split. But Scotty and I, well, we're just nice to people, even people maybe who are a little different. I dunno, but whatever the reason, Carole made a special point of trying to get to know me. She was very straightforward. *Very* straightforward."[4]

Hardy pauses as he remembers.

"Randy first brought her over to introduce her to us in the shop. I was standing there with my buddy. Randy went off, and my buddy and I were left talking to her, sort of 'get acquainted' talk, and she asks if we were married. We said yes. Then what she said shocked me. It was something along the lines of 'Well, my husband just doesn't put out like what my needs are. I need some young studs who would take me out for a ride.'

"I mean, we were just shocked. *Shocked.* We didn't know what to say—we just suddenly found we had other stuff to do."

Despite Carole's subsequent attempts to corral Hardy, he steered clear, helped by the fact that the shop was physically distant from where Carole was supposed to be working. But one day, Carole rushed into the shop in a state of emotional meltdown.

"I thought maybe a family member had died," Hardy said. "She was just losing it. Crying her heart out—she could barely walk. Come to find out her little dog—the one she'd bring to the park—had gotten hit by a car that morning. Somebody took it to the vet, but it was too bad hurt and the vet put it down. The body had already been hauled off to the flesh pit." Hardy was referring to the part of the dump where animal bodies were left. It was July, and the flesh pit was a charnel house of maggot-ridden, fly-infested, stinking decay.

"Well, she was bawling and crying and carrying on. She said the dog's soul couldn't cross over without a proper Indian burial. With sage and stuff to keep away the evil spirits. I told her, 'It's July! Have you ever *seen* a flesh pit? The dog's dead—just let it be.' But no, no, she said she was going to go out and get that body to bury it right.

"Well, I couldn't imagine her climbing down into the flesh pit to get that dog's body out. She just didn't know what was out there. And I didn't want to see her driving in her state. So I told her I'd go get it."

Hardy reflects, searching for words. "I just went for a short little ride with her. Fifteen minutes out to the dump. She's an artist—I know artists are eccentric. But she's *way* over the top eccentric. After my little ride with her I realized she wasn't just eccentric. She was psychotic, horribly depressed, and got more skeletons in her closet than anyone you've ever met."

Hardy pauses again, remembering.

So we get there and sure enough, it was just godawful out there. Horrible. I climbed down in and poked around until I found her little dog. It was already all bloated and shit was oozing out of it. So I stuffed it in a bag and climbed back out. Here I am, poking around this hellhole, and the whole time she's just sitting up on a hill, staring into space like she was in a trance. Weird. Just weird.

So we get back in the truck. And she starts talking to me. She's an artist. You can tell she's an artist because she can do things to your mind—paint pictures in it with words—pictures you don't want to see. She had two husbands, she said. Both of them committed suicide. She said she went into the other room and took a nap and she knew she shouldn't have. And when she came back he was dead. She described it to me, how she walked back into the room, and she just knew instantly that he was dead. It was so nice—serene and calm.

I was just weirded out. I mean, if my wife killed herself...

[Hardy pauses, the idea too horrible for this compassionate man to imagine.] I just—just don't know what I'd do. I'd be beside myself. I sure as hell wouldn't be standing there thinking how nice and calm it all was.

And then she started talking about when he was cremated. That she'd watched it—it was the most beautiful thing she'd ever seen in her entire life. Wonderful—all these beautiful colors! Beyond belief! It was his soul crossing over, she said. I couldn't believe it—I don't think you can even watch cremations.

She made it sound like everybody in her life had committed suicide. She had all this misery. A dark spirit. She's got issues I can't even comprehend. I've never been around a person that affected me like that. She has unbelievable powers to drag people down. I can't imagine living around her. I thought—it's no wonder these guys killed themselves!

It was basically the most horrible fifteen-minute ride of my life. It was the way she could explain things. I couldn't get away from her painting those pictures in my mind. I kept thinking I should just stop the truck and get out and walk just so I could get away from her. I finally started just mentally blocking what she was saying. It was more than I could take. I have never heard anyone more depressed in my entire life. Horrible.

"I'm normally a happy person," Hardy says. "I never get depressed. I've never had anything affect me quite like that. Unbelievable. I got back to the shop and couldn't work anymore that day. Took me two days to get my mind back to business. I only hope she is the only person like that on this earth.

"To tell you the truth, we all couldn't help but wonder what a nice guy like Marty was doing with a woman like Carole." Hardy sighs.

"She really is a good artist," he concludes. "I just thought she was eccentric. Whoa—not anymore. But could be I was just in the wrong place at the wrong time. Maybe it just had to do with the dog dying. Maybe it all bubbled to the surface then."

*   *   *

Indeed, Carole's relationship with animals somehow seems to lie at the very heart of her dysfunction. "Carole used animals to self-medicate whenever she was under stress," says one longtime family friend. "Sort of like comfort food. She was always drumming up stress states so she could play the victim. So she always needed more animals."

Just before leaving Colorado for his first professional job at Utah State University, Richard, Carole's first husband, came home to find that Carole had purchased a couple dozen recently hatched ducklings. "Buying animals just before an interstate move is perhaps not the best thing to do," Richard recalls. "I quickly cobbled together an enclosure that fit in the back of our Chevette and we drove out to Logan, Utah, with the ducklings."[5]

Much as others might stop by the convenience store to pick up a chocolate bar, Carole would stop by the pet store to pick up a crea-ture—a rat, a turtle, an exotic snake. Sometimes she'd bring home something far larger. Perceptively regretting his own long-ago role in abetting Carole's behavior, Richard recalls:

> After living in Utah for a few years we bought a house in a small town near Logan. The lot had 1/3 acre pasture in the back, which is pretty common in small Utah towns. A lot of families have a horse or maybe a calf in a back paddock. Not long after we moved in, I came home from work one evening to find that two horses and a bull calf were being unloaded from a stock trailer. No previous discussion. No plan to feed them. No fully fenced pasture. Melloney, age three, was leading the bull calf around by a leash while the calf made every attempt to not step on her. So I quickly built the fencing and bought enough hay to feed all three animals through the winter. (Can you say 'enabler'?) Guess who ended up taking care of these animals all winter?

More telling was a later episode that took place when the family lived in Arkansas. Carole placed an ad in the local *Thrifty Nickel* asking for turtles. Richard remembers:

Grungy-looking guys with missing teeth came out of the woodwork to deliver the animals for a buck or less. The prize catches were a few gigantic snapping turtles. Somehow Carole was able to obtain huge aquariums, which were placed on tables and stands. My fear was that one of our kids, who were very young at the time (6, 4 and 1), would push a chair over to an aquarium and try to play with a snapper. These turtles can stretch out their necks at lightning speed and have powerful jaws that can snap off an adult's finger, and probably a toddler's hand and forearm. I managed to get covers put on the aquariums, but there was really nothing in place to stop an unwatched kid from trying to play with the snappers.

Arguments with Carole about precisely this type of obvious danger, with Carole adamant about keeping the turtles and Richard livid about the dangers, ratcheted up the tension in the marriage. Carole seemed to have a way of targeting men for long-term relationships who genuinely had decent hearts—men who simply wanted to make her happy. Then, in essence, she'd "paint pictures in their mind" (as Hardy so neatly put it) and only later would they realize they'd been manipulated far beyond what they would ordinarily have agreed to.

Observers noted that Carole would sometimes seem to regress to a childlike or adolescent emotional state. It was at these times in particular that she would begin gathering animals, which sometimes seemed better cared for than her children. Carole once purchased a dozen hedgehogs in an ill-fated hedgehog-raising adventure. The older girls were moved out of their sunny bedroom to a closet—the hedgehogs got the girls' room.

Richard notes: "There was every kind of animal you could imagine while we were together (or so I thought). Afterwards, there were many more. My kids would mention some of them when we spoke on the phone. I couldn't help thinking that the child support money I was sending was going towards buying exotic reptiles instead of buying food, clothing and school supplies for the kids."

ANIMAL HOARDING

Wiry veterinarian Gary Patronek is perhaps the world's leading expert on animal hoarding. He and his colleague, social worker Jane Nathanson, have spent years trying to understand how and why some people have a compulsive need to obtain and control animals, even when it is clearly counter to the animals' best interests.

Such animal "rescuer-hoarders" usually have a normal relationship with animals during their childhoods. However, a pattern develops whereby animals begin to serve as an emotional crutch. Why?

One of our most basic human needs is to "attach"—that is, to become particularly affectionate with another caring human being. It seems our brains can develop properly only when in a relationship with another guiding brain. It's a little like learning how to play catch. A kid throws the ball toward his mommy, and his eye gives feedback about whether mommy caught the ball. Then mommy gets the ball and throws it back. At first, this process is made very easy—mommy stands close by and holds her hands out. Through practice, kids develop and refine the necessary hand-eye coordination. After a while, mommy doesn't need to stand so close. And still later, the kid may be on the run throwing the ball to a teammate also on the run in a complex dance that's a far cry from the initial clumsy throw. Underlying this whole process are the changes neurons are making as they shapeshift to help the kid become attuned to how his body interacts with the ball and with others.

Attachment processes mimic these activities in that we've got an attachment figure as soon as we're born who's willing to play catch with us. Usually, it's the mother, although any loving caregiver will do.[6] Our eyes and our sense of our body give us feedback about whether, in some sense, we've made a successful throw. We smile—and mommy smiles too. Mommy laughs, and so we laugh, and that makes mommy laugh more. If Mommy frowns and looks away, we don't feel so good.

Clinician-scientist Allan Schore has given theories of attachment a new neuroscientific foundation. In some sense, a child attaches to her mother (or any principal caregiver) through a complex reciprocal exchange of glances, bodily caresses, frowns, hugs, kisses, tears, and cuddles that awaken genes and cause neural structures to cascade into normal human development processes. What we call attachment is actually, in a very deep sense, the neurons being shaped and pruned by reciprocal interactions with another person into the pattern we associate with parental love.[7] An important part of this process is not only the encouragement we receive from being in sync with our caregiver, but also the shame we experience when we do something the caregiver doesn't approve of. This is all a part of the give-and-take that enables the first brain (the caregiver's) to teach the second (the child's), in some sense, how to be a brain. As Schore writes: "There is widespread agreement that the brain is a self-organizing system, but there is perhaps less of an appreciation of the fact that the self-organization of the developing brain occurs in the context of a relationship with another self, another brain."[8]

Social worker and counselor Jane Nathanson has found that many animal hoarders report either trauma in early childhood or poor bonding with their childhood primary caregivers. We don't know why this is so. But it is true that animals provide unconditional acceptance and love—a sort of training-wheels version of love for someone who can't grapple with the full repertoire of human attachment, which includes shame. More than that, an animal is something of a blank screen on which owners can project whatever they'd like. After all, pets aren't in a position to argue.[9] Finally, as Nathanson and her colleague, veterinary medicine specialist Gary Patronek, note: "Channeling their excessive caregiving tendencies and energies toward the rescue and shelter of animals, Rescuer-Hoarders are prone to experiencing a 'caregiver's high' as needy animals are in ever-abundant supply and the hoarder derives a sense of being a savior, contrary to the reality which their animals experience. . . . Rescuer-Hoarders essentially create an exclusive domain with animals within which they strive to fulfill their own needs to feel highly valued, loved, and secure."

It may be that animal hoarders frequently report poor connections with their early caregivers because their caregivers were truly unsupportive. (Although even in a highly chaotic and disturbed family it seems having a single good caregiver can be enough to help provide resiliency.)[10] Or it could be that animal hoarders had difficulty making any attachment to humans at all—the best they can do, given possibly funky neurological equipment, is to fulfill their attachment needs with a training-wheels, light version through bonding with animals.

Interestingly, Nathanson and Patronek note that:

> [h]oarders often report social histories characterized by dysfunctional human relationships from adolescence into adulthood. [A]nimal hoarders frequently note their attraction to girl/boyfriends, partners, and spouses whom they knew to be troubled or needy. They are unable to see the connection between their partners' apparent neediness and propensity to become highly dependent upon them and their own need to achieve relational security through their caregiving role. . . . It is typical to observe affective instability, intense and unstable interpersonal relationships, and even dissociative symptoms in hoarders. . . . Hoarders appear to become enmeshed in a pattern of excessive need to acquire, possess, and control. Perceived unconditional love from animals serves as a path, albeit a futile one, towards healing.
>
> Although Rescuer-Hoarders profess unselfish motives, they themselves derive the benefit from the human-animal relation. When asked 'why have you become mission-bound to rescue unwanted, homeless animals?' Rescuer-Hoarders consistently express their motivation is to love and care for helpless and deserving animals. While this well-intentioned motivation or concern for animals is understandable and may hold true at times or in specific cases, it is important to [note] the identification the hoarder is most likely making with helpless animals.[11]

Animal hoarders, it seems, often neglect themselves, live in squalor, and have untreated mental health problems.[12] At the same time, despite abject squalor surrounding them, with animal excrement covering floors and furniture, hoarders may insist that "it's just a little dirty" or feel that if they themselves aren't bothered, the animals are fine with it, too. Clinical psychologist Sue-Ellen Brown, who specializes in attachment issues with animals, observes, "Animals are unable to disagree with a human's interpretation of how they feel or what they want. People can believe animals feel and think exactly like them whether they actually do or not."[13] Nathanson and Patronek perceptively conclude:

> Rescuer-Hoarders' apparent obliviousness to their animals' deplorable conditions may be conveyed by way of defensiveness, minimizing, denial, or dissociation. This lack of empathy belies any altruistic behavior or motivations. By seeing their animals as extensions of themselves, hoarders fail to acknowledge or understand whether or how their animals might have needs that are distinct from their own. In other words, by failing to acknowledge and appropriately respond to the animals as 'others,' Rescuer-Hoarders become, essentially, self-serving. Therefore, it would be erroneous to conclude that the hoarder's state of self-neglect is self-sacrificing—that is, that they are unselfishly foregoing their own needs in order to provide for their animals—and their motivation and actions cannot be rightly viewed as demonstrating the altruistic criteria of an unselfish concern for others.

*   *   *

Randy Morris, Scott Ross, and Leonard Hardy all look back on their interactions with Carole Alden as among the strangest they've ever experienced. Perhaps the strangest thing, all three men agree, was that once Hardy brought the little dog's sad body back to the shop in Delta, Carole ignored it. It sat forgotten in its bag, gradually stinking up the shop. Carole casually came by again to pick it up several days later. No one knows what became of it.

Someone who has known Carole for decades writes, "Nothing about this incident surprises me. This is Carole in high gear, trolling for her next man, using the ploy of extreme emotional distress and bending people's minds while trying to draw them into her world."

But Carole was older now—not the dazzling young woman she once was. And her repertoire of stories was growing increasingly bizarre.

Scott Ross relates, "When Carole's defense lawyer, Slavens, came to me, I told him, 'Look, if you want me to testify for her, you're crazy, because I think she did it on purpose. It was way premeditated. She thought about it for a long time before she did it. She *told* me she'd like to kill him and bury him in the backyard.'"

When asked whether Carole might have been joking, Ross responded, "Well, we all say those kinds of things when we're kidding around. 'I'd like to kill that guy' and such. So that's how I took it. It didn't set in on me until after the killing, what she really meant. She knew what she was doing."

CHAPTER 20

ALLEN LAKE

I try to do the right thing at the right time. They may just be little things, but usually they make the difference between winning and losing.
—KAREEM ABDUL-JABBAR (considered one of the greatest basketball players of all time)[1]

F inding Allen Lake takes work.

First you check out the tan apartment building on the outskirts of Delta, knocking on doors answered by weary women who stare when you ask for Allen Lake.

So you walk randomly into stores and restaurants—Delta is a small town, after all—asking after Allen Lake. You come back, day after day, talking to people, getting little clues. *I saw him yesterday, down near Curley's. At the Loft. At the Chevron station. At J. J.'s.*[2]

Finally, you drift by Lake's apartment building again, trying to guess which one of the four clustered apartments in front of you might be Lake's, when a couple of teenagers pull up in a Chevy pickup.

The girl gets out first, slams the door. The boy follows—the slim frame of youth, baseball cap turned backward. They stand a bit away from you, focused on each other. "*Dad!*" says the girl.

The man turns questioningly to you, as much to get out of the argument as to find out who you are. You look closely. The boy is actually a man, maybe forty-five, good looks still apparent behind the pugilist's nose. His thatch of hair is bleached gold—even his pale blue eyes seem bleached.

"I'm looking for Allen Lake," you say.

Long pause. Finally, "You're looking at him."[3]

*   *   *

J. J.'s, as it turns out, is set well back from the road in a squat, neatly built 1940s-style box home with a large sign over the front porch: DELTA.

Inside, glass cases of antique teacups and 1950s toys line the walls. Faded Oriental carpets cover the hardwood floors. Pool players pause their game to stare silently at Lake. "It's okay," Lake reassures them.

Lake steps up onto a shag carpet stoop at the bar and pours himself a drink. For his visitor, he pulls out a gallon jug half full of rosé, blows the dust off the top, and pours a glass.

"I met Carole when we worked at the cheese plant," he says. "She was always bringing me sandwiches and the like. She was a hippie sort of flower child—like she was straight out of the seventies. Flowing dresses and such."

He pokes at the varnish on the wooden bar. "She was just a great human being, you know. Very good mother.

"She would do stuff for me all the time. I'd come home and she'd be cleaning my house. She painted my derby car. She was a good artist—real good.

"Got to be like she was stalking me," Lake continues. "She didn't want to go home. Once she gave me a pair of sex handcuffs. She used to say—God, I'd love to make love to you right here, right in the cheese vat."

Lake grimaces. "But she was a good mother—a real good mother. People used to call her the Lizard Lady. She had this thing about lizards, snakes, and such. Even the seat covers in her Jeep had lizards on them.

"She'd talk about Marty sometimes. How he beat her. She'd tell everybody, 'You want to see my bruise?'

"She'd have done anything for me. Kept making me things. A big quilt. Curtains. If I needed a hundred bucks, she'd lend me a hundred bucks. She was coming on to me. But I'd tell her, look, you're married now.

"I'll be honest with you, if Carole had been drop-dead gorgeous, it wouldn't have mattered a bit if she was married. But she was an awesome person. I didn't want to make her feel bad, you know? By telling her she wasn't my type.

"Marty was an okay guy. I never saw him hit her or anything like that."

When asked what happened the night of Marty's death, Lake pauses.

"After work, a few other guys and I got drunk out at the lake. Filthy drunk. We were having a *good* time. Got a little loud. A little rough. Marty ended up on the road in front of the house. Just lying there. Somebody called Carole. She came with her Jeep—picked him up and shoved him right in it, took him back home.

"I went to bed. She came back over for a while. Drank some orange juice, I guess. Then she left again. The next morning she came back. I was in the shower. Came out, had a towel on. She looked funny. Real funny. I said, 'You look bummed. Where's Marty?'

"Her eyes just looked empty. Black. Spooky. That's when I realized it. She'd killed Marty. She wanted to tell me. I was freaked out that she told me. I told her to call the police—and if she didn't, I would.

"You know the rest." Allen spreads his hands and gives a sad grin.

CHAPTER 21

I'M RIGHT AND
YOU'RE WRONG

**Every form of addiction is bad, no matter whether
the narcotic be alcohol or morphine or idealism.**

—CARL GUSTAV JUNG[1]

Wh150hat gives us that frisson of certitude, as in I'm *right*?
Neurologist Robert Burton has long wondered about precisely this
feeling, as described in his brilliant, elegantly readable *On Being Certain*.[2] A feeling of certainty, Burton muses, is important from an evolutionary perspective. How else can we quickly make a life-or-death
decision such as which tree is best to climb to escape a hungry lion?

There are, in fact, disorders of certainty. Obsessive-compulsive
disorder, for example, involves the inability to be certain. *Did I really
turn off the stove when I left?* Some people can take certitude to self-
righteous extremes, as with suicide bombers, those who kill doctors
who perform abortions, or ecoterrorists.

Burton saw that even good intentions can go terribly wrong when people dig their heels in because they believe they are right. One of Burton's most frustrating memories concerned Dr. "X"—a prominent oncologist who was well-known for his aggressive approach to treatment of even the most terminal patients. Dr. X asked Dr. Burton to do a spinal tap on an elderly man with advanced widespread cancer. "He's not as mentally clear as he was yesterday," said X. "Maybe he has an infection—meningitis, a brain abscess—something treatable."[3]

As Burton recalls:

I've known Dr. X. for years and have no doubt about his clinical skills and his utter dedication to his patients. Medicine is his life; he's available 24/7, and, when all fails, he even attends his patients' funerals. And yet I dread working with him. Driven by a personal unshakeable ethic of what a good doctor *must do* for his patients, he wears his mission on his rolled-up sleeves, his full-steam-ahead attitude challenging and often shaming those of us who favor palliative care over prolongation of a life at any cost. He has the intense, uncompromising look of someone with a calling.

Upon entering the room, spinal tap tray in hand, I am confronted by the patient's family. "Please, no more," they say in unison, backed up by the frail patient's silent nodding. "Could you talk with Dr. X, tell him that we're all in agreement."

I page Dr. X and explain the family's wishes. "No, I want the spinal tap done now," he says. "And don't try to tell me how to practice medicine. I know what's best for my patients."

"Please," the wife pleads, her hand gripping my arm. She'd overheard Dr. X on the phone. "I know that he cares, but it's not what we want." But moments later Dr. X rushes in with his characteristic air of urgency, and explains why the test is necessary. No one really believes him, not the patient, not the family, and certainly not the nurse who turns away to hide her look of "how could you?" And yet, the family accedes. Even the patient agrees to the test, resigning himself to more poking and prodding, pain and suffering, in order not to offend his doctor. I, too, give in.

The spinal tap is difficult and painful, and reveals nothing treatable. The patient has a post-spinal tap headache that lasts until he lapses into coma and dies three days later. Afterwards, in talking with Dr. X, it's clear that he's learned nothing from this experience. "It could have been something; you can't know if you don't look. End of discussion."[4]

But how and why do we feel that ineffable feeling we know as certainty? As it turns out, hidden from our active consciousness are underlying neural calculators—a "hidden layer"—that help us grapple with the reality that surrounds us. You might think of this hidden layer as a little like the chip that underlies a computer's computations. You may not know anything about the machine code and assembly language that underlies a computer figuring out the square root of 289. But you can apprehend the result—17.

As a consequence of the computations of your hidden layer, you can look at a face and instantly feel a sense of certainty about whether or not you've seen it before. Everyone's hidden layer is different, due to previous experiences, previous thoughts, genetics, and a multitude of other factors. As Burton points out, the hidden layer "is the anatomic crossroad where nature and nurture intersect and individual personalities emerge. It is why your red is not my red, your idea of beauty isn't mine, why eyewitnesses offer differing accounts of an accident or why we don't all put our money on the same roulette number."[5]

But notice that the feeling of certainty we get—the feeling of *I know that face!*—is *outside* our conscious control. Like it or not, certainty is a feeling—an emotion—*not* a rational conclusion. That feeling can lead you astray—as when you say hello to an old friend and find you've surprised a complete stranger. "*Without a doubt*," as Burton notes, "is nothing more than an involuntary sensation of a perfect match."[6]

As an illustration of how rational, "objective" knowledge and "felt" knowledge can collide, Burton points toward the Müller-Lyer optical illusion. On the one hand, we can see objectively that the two horizontal lines are the same length. But yet, other unconscious factors scream a different certainty based on other visual cues. Indeed—there are different and conflicting ways of knowing.

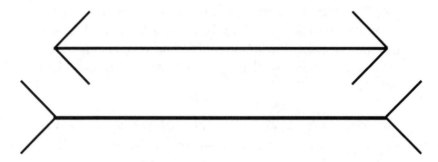

The Müller-Lyer optical illusion.

This feeling of certainty springs, it seems, from the pleasure-reward parts of the brain—the same areas that are triggered by drugs such as heroin and cocaine. Our feeling of certainty is a sort of circuit breaker that "stops infinite ruminations and calms our fears of missing an unknown superior alternative. Such a switch can't be a thought or we would be back at the same problem. The simplest solution [is] a sensation that feels like a thought but isn't subject to thought's perpetual self-questioning."[7]

But, as polymath science fiction writer David Brin observes, this feeling of certainty can feel so good that it can sometimes become an addiction. We can see this addiction firsthand in self-righteous people, who are keen to wallow in the wonderful feeling that they are *right* and their "opponents are deeply, despicably *wrong*. Or that [their] method of helping others is so purely motivated and correct that all criticism can be dismissed with a shrug, along with any contradicting evidence."[8] Good intentions don't somehow elevate us above this perceptual conundrum.

In fact, we often behave in an altruistic manner because we are certain that our actions are morally sound and will indeed help others. But no matter how we might think we have reasoned our way to a particular moral conviction, that conviction was arrived at subconsciously, through an *emotional* feeling.

This same set of conclusions applies to our feelings of certitude regarding our moral choices. "What feels like a conscious life-affirming moral choice—*my life will have meaning if I help others*—will be greatly influenced by the strength of an unconscious and involuntary mental sensation that tells me that this decision is 'correct.' It will be this same feeling that will tell you the 'rightness' of giving food to starving children in Somalia, doing every medical test imaginable on a clearly terminal patient, or bombing an Israeli school bus."[9]

CERTITUDE AND DOING GOOD

Elisabeth Kübler-Ross wrote the seminal book *On Death and Dying*, which describes her theories of how people psychologically adjust to death. Her work was enormously valuable in opening a dialogue with dying patients that showed that contemplating and talking about death could be beneficial for everyone involved. But Kübler-Ross's devotion to helping others came at enormous cost. She provided "extraordinary care to her patients, often personally paying for ambulances, against medical advice, to transport dying children home for Christmas."[10] After founding—and funding—a healing center for the dying, she "obsessively devoted her time to her patients, becoming consumed by her work and essentially living at the healing centre so as to be available to her patients at all times."[11] She claimed she saw the ghosts of her patients, and she became deeply involved with psychic channeler and self-ordained minister Jay Barham. "He has so much integrity," she said. "The truth does not need to be defended."[12]

Time magazine described the unfolding scandal as follows:

Barham conducts group sessions where, he says, spirit entities materialize by cloning themselves from cells of his body. The entities are unusually interested in sex, sometimes pairing off the living participants for fondling or mutual masturbation. In private sessions women are selected for sexual intercourse with an entity. Participants in the sessions, many well-educated, if gullible, middle-class professionals, have had occasional doubts about the entities. . . .

Four women in the group developed the same vaginal infection after visiting an entity on the same night. A few of the participants noticed that entities made the same mistakes in pronunciation (such as "excape" for escape) that Barham did. But most put aside their doubts. "I needed to believe," admitted one woman in the group. "It was a sense of being loved unconditionally."[13]

*   *   *

Kübler-Ross's faith in Barham is unshaken. A friend, Deanna Edwards, says she attended two darkroom sessions in hopes of changing the psychiatrist's mind about Barham. Edwards says she ripped masking tape from a light switch and flipped on the lights, revealing Jay Barham wearing only a turban. "I never heard such screaming," says Edwards, who hastens to explain that it was not the sight of Barham that caused the alarm; the other participants believed that light destroyed an entity. Edwards was sure the demonstration would convince Kübler-Ross that Barham was a fraud. No such luck. "This man has more gifts than you have ever seen," says Kübler-Ross. "He is probably the greatest healer that this country has." The current furor does not appear to disturb her. Says she: "Many attempts have been made to discredit us. To respond to them would be like casting pearls to swine."[14]

Kübler-Ross was as obsessed and certain about the importance of her work as she was about Barham's innocence. Kübler-Ross's husband finally became so disturbed that he gave her an ultimatum—she needed to choose either work or family. She "chose work, disappointing her husband and family and receiving a harsh judgement by the divorce court, which ruled against her in custody proceedings."[15]

*   *   *

It is within that *feeling of rightness* that the problem nestles. As Burton concludes:

The strength of a moral decision can be seen, at least in part, as the synergistic action of unconscious cognition, involuntary feelings reflecting the rightness of this decision, and a powerful sense of pleasure in knowing that this decision is correct. It isn't in our nature to willfully abandon feelings of rightness and sense of purpose, especially when you add in the moral dimension of such actions making you "a good person."

I cannot imagine a more powerful recipe for potential misguided "good behavior." The only defense is the understanding that we can't know with any objective or even reasonable certainty that what we consider an act of altruism is actually of overall benefit to others.

For me, acting altruistically is like prescribing a medication. Believing that you are helping isn't enough. You must know, to the best of your ability, the potential risks as well as benefits. And you must understand that the package insert as to the worth of the medication (your altruistic act) was written by your biased unconscious, not by a scientific committee who has examined all the evidence.

Back to Dr. X. Despite many attempts on the part of other medical staff, Dr. X continued to his dying day working non-stop to help his patients—whether or not they wanted his help. No contrary or tempering advice sunk in. At his memorial service, I sat through an outpouring of poignant testimonials to his dedication and devotion. No one spoke for those patients who suffered from his well-meaning excesses. Years later, I remember Dr. X mainly for what he taught me about uncritical acceptance of believing that you "are doing good."[16]

LEFT SIDE–RIGHT SIDE

Perhaps surprisingly, misplaced feelings of certitude fall right in line with research involving the differing roles of the brain's two hemispheres.

The two sides of your cerebrum are *different*. They are so different, in fact, that if the two were separated (as is occasionally done by slicing through the connecting tissue in epilepsy patients), they sometimes tussle over what they want. Roger Sperry, who won a Nobel

Prize for his pioneering research in neuropsychology, found one of his patients "struggling to pull his pants up with his right hand while at the same time yanking them down with his left. Another assaulted his wife with his left hand while defending her with his right."[17] Truly it is as if we each have two completely independent minds fighting to control our body—two "wills," as it were—although we always have only a single consciousness. (Interestingly, it is always the left hand that "misbehaves"—a telling reminder of the fact that the word *sinister* itself comes from the Latin word for *left*.)

What to make of all this? Wouldn't it be more logical, from an evolutionary perspective, for there to be a single, unified brain commanding our bodies?

As it turns out, right from the beginning of the animal kingdom, creatures have evolved to grapple with two simultaneous, highly demanding tasks. A bird, for example, must be able to simultaneously focus on the food in front of it, as well as warily scan to surroundings for danger. These different ways of seeing the world are tough to do at once—rather like patting your head and rubbing your tummy simultaneously. Specialized cerebral hemispheres seems to be the solution evolutionary processes have hit on, because it is widespread in vertebrates. And it must have developed very early on in evolutionary history, because animals from plovers to marmosets to humans specialize in the same way—left hemisphere for focused attention (pecking at food), right for breadth and flexibility of attention (keeping an eye out for hawks).[18]

As psychiatrist Ian McGilchrist notes in his masterpiece on the differing left and right hemispheres of the brain, *The Master and His Emissary*, this particular division of neural labor "has the related consequence that the right hemisphere sees things whole, and in their context, where the left hemisphere sees things abstracted from context, and broken into parts, from which it then reconstructs a 'whole'; something very different. And it also turns out that the capacities that help us, as humans, form bonds, with others—empathy, emotional understanding, and so on—which involve a quite different kind of attention paid to the world, are largely right-hemisphere functions."[19]

It's easy to discount brain-lateralization theories as so much pop psychology. But as McGilchrist's staggeringly erudite synthesis shows, there's real power in the theory. How we understand the world is a function of which hemisphere gains dominance—or whether the two reach an amicable balance. Or, in more unusual cases, whether one or the other hemisphere gains hyper-dominance.

Studies of split-brain patients, those who have suffered strokes, and those who have had one hemisphere or the other of their brain anesthetized all give us fascinating insight into the very different attributes of the two hemispheres. It seems that the right hemisphere is what gives us an understanding of what's going on out in the world (an expanded version of "watching out for hawks"). In a very real sense, then, the right hemisphere is in touch with reality. The information it collects is passed on to the left hemisphere. This second, "major" hemisphere (so called because it has the ace-in-the-hole powers of speech), is the one that specializes in focusing ("pecking at food"), dividing into categories, and viewing the world more abstractly. Patients with right-hemisphere strokes (which leave the left hemisphere intact) report a peculiar distancing from reality—their world seems flat, and the ability to empathize can disappear.[20]

Left to its own resources (that is, when disconnected for whatever reason from the right brain), the left brain is a blithely self-satisfied, upbeat Pollyanna that is perfectly willing to make up stories so as to maintain a sense of certitude. This explains the strange phenomenon whereby patients with right-hemisphere strokes that paralyze the left side of the body can refuse to believe there is anything wrong. Such patients will make up the most outlandish stories to explain why their left arm isn't moving. As McGilchrist observes, "Note that it is not just a blindness, a failure to see—it's a willful denial. Hoff and Pötzl describe a patient who demonstrates this beautifully: 'On examination, when she is shown her left hand in the right visual field, she looks away and says 'I don't see it.' She spontaneously hides her left hand under the bedclothes or puts it behind her back. She never looks to the left, even when called from that side.'"[21]

As famed neurologist Vilayanur Ramachandran notes, these stroke patients show "an unbridled willingness to accept absurd ideas."[22] McGilchrist goes on to point out that left-hemisphere dominance seems characterized by "[d]enial, a tendency to conformism, a willingness to disregard the evidence, a habit of ducking responsibility, [and] a blindness to mere experience in the face of the overwhelming evidence of a theory . . ."[23]

Experiments where one side of the brain was anesthetized result in interesting conclusions.[24] For example, if told

1. All trees sink in water;
2. Balsa is a tree.
3. Implied conclusion: Balsa wood sinks in water.

The subject with only an active right brain will point out that what he has been told seems to suggest that balsa wood sinks—but the reality is, it floats. The right brain, McGilchrist points out, appears to be the seat of our innate bullshit detector. But the patient with only an active left brain will insist that wood, most notably balsa wood, sinks—"that's what it says right here!"—real-world facts be damned.

Could deficits in the ability to dial down the influence of the left hemisphere account for some people's unwillingness to see facts that contravene their own perceptions? Could it also account for the almost outlandish stories some can believe—in the face of overwhelming evidence to the contrary—if it confirms their initial impressions?

CHAPTER 22

A VICTIM'S SUPPORTERS

In all matters of opinion, our adversaries are insane.

—Oscar Wilde[1]

On August 14, 2006, Carole Alden was formally charged with first-degree felony murder, second-degree felony obstruction of justice, and desecration of a body, a third-degree felony. But supporters rallied to her defense, filling the judge's mailbox with sympathetic letters, excerpts from which also made their way to the *Deseret Morning News*:

> *"This letter is in support of leniency for Carole Sessions,"* wrote the Rev. Stanley DeLong of the Delta Community Presbyterian Church. He performed the marriage of Alden to her husband, Martin Sessions.

> *"She is HONEST and TRUSTWORTHY!!! NOT A MURDER-ER!!!!!!!!!,"* wrote friend Angela Western. *"And may shame come*

upon those who have taken it upon themselves to deem themselves worthy of judging her in this manor (sic), they too shall pay the wages of sin in GODS eyes and what a heavy price they will pay!!!!"

"She has paid a heartbreaking price for her act of desperation brought on by chronic, intense stress and abuse," wrote friends Rebecca Heal, Kristen Merrill and Michelle Nunley, members of the performing group known as the Saliva Sisters.

"Carole still has a vibrant career awaiting her, a history of success, and the ability to make a positive contribution to society," wrote friend Joy Emory.[2]

"Friends hope that Alden's penitence is enough to persuade the judge to release her," the article concluded.[3]

*　　*　　*

Millard County Jail volunteer chaplain Sylvia Huntsman, who also served on the area's domestic violence commission, was quoted in the *Deseret Morning News* saying: "Marty, her husband, frequently threatened to kill Carole and her children, describing in graphic detail how he would do it."[4]

But behind the scenes, more nuance appears.

Sylvia Huntsman's knowledge of Marty and of the homicide, as she reveals in a telephone conversation, came from Carole herself. Huntsman had come to know Carole through weekly Sunday meetings at the Millard County Jail during the two-year period before Carole went on to the Utah State Prison in Draper.

"Carole is one of those people who will take in every stray dog," says Huntsman affectionately. "She liked men who had bigger problems than kindness could fix. Marty had a terrible violence. She had hidden a gun in her laundry room that the police had told her to get to shoot coyotes.

"When she shot him the first time, she shot him in the head,"

Huntsman says. "Carole believed he wasn't dead. That he was going to somehow get back up. So that's when she shot him again. That's why the second shot was in the back." (This contradicts the physical evidence—it would have been impossible for the tiny Carole to have fired directly down through the top of Marty's head unless he was already down. And Carole herself told police that the head shot was the second shot.)

"So she decided to give him a Native American burial in her backyard," Huntsman continues. "She just wasn't thinking. In her view, it was self-defense. Shooting him again and moving the body just wasn't logical. But she was traumatized—she wasn't thinking logically at the time.

"Carole's relationship with her kids is incredible. She has one older son she isn't close to. He's washed his hands of her. Her daughter Krystal is extensively educated, though—is graduating from college. And Carole is very close to her youngest—Emily. Her relationship with her kids is great and very honest. She hasn't put up a lot of excuses with them.

"What are her best traits? Oh, she's a gifted artist. A writer. Resilient. She's gone through hell and somehow has the self-confidence to come back. She's very loyal to friends and family. But she chooses people who tear her down because of her childhood experiences. She's very trusting. Very soft-hearted. Gets herself into situations because of that. She's had her eyes opened a lot in prison.

"During her childhood she was constantly put down by her father and told no man would ever want her. But she's actually worked through that. Women who are abused tend to get into relationships with abusive men. Yet she can always understand and forgive and love these men."

(Carole's family takes issue with Huntsman's statement that Carole was constantly "put down" by her father, observing, "This is not at all true, but of course that seems to be Carole's reality now. Her father was always proud of her achievements and was quick to give praise as he did with the other kids." Carole's family also notes there were times when Carole's actions caused much-deserved consternation and displeasure—she then heard about it from both parents, who presented a united front.)

"Carole is one of my closest friends, even though I don't get to see her very often," Huntsman continues. "The sentence she got wasn't fair. Her lawyer was lazy. Her husband was genuinely going to kill her.

"Carole Alden is an open and honest person. A free spirit. She marched to her own drum. People in this part of the country didn't understand. She thinks and acts like an artist. She doesn't care what other people think. Local townsfolk weren't ready to accept her as one of them. She wasn't LDS [Mormon] and didn't conform in dress and behavior.

"She lived out on a farm and had llamas. Maybe she wasn't the best housekeeper. She was into Native American religion. She wasn't into drinking or taking drugs. She was hippie-like without the drugs. She hasn't channeled her thoughts into any particular religion or belief. But she believes. She has a true belief in God.

"The interesting thing is that she is not naive. She understands. And she forgives."

*   *   *

One story that has passed into local lore since the murder is that of two men professionally connected to the local criminal justice system; the pair happened to stop by Hart's Gas & Food in Delta about two weeks before Marty Sessions's death. Carole's dragon-clad Jeep hove into view, and the men began laughing at her. But one thing led to another, and the pair shortly found themselves in conversation with Carole. Although their work had left them somewhat jaded about people's motives, to their amazement, they discovered that Carole seemed to actually be a nice person.

Climbing into their vehicle after the conversation with Carole, the pair commented on how their prejudice had misled them in their understanding of what kind of person she was. As one put it, "That just goes to show—not everybody's bad. We need to stop judging people like that—they're not all murderers."

CHAPTER 23

THE WAR ROOM

Confidences are strange things. If you listen only to one man, it is possible that he is deceived or mistaken; if you listen to many, they are in a like case; and, generally, you cannot get at the truth at all.

—JOHANN WOLFGANG VON GOETHE,
Maxims and Reflections of Goethe[1]

As far as the prosecution team was concerned, the letter before them might as well have been a grenade.[2] Stephen Golding, a forensic psychologist in the Salt Lake City area, had just weighed in on Carole Alden's suitability for bail:

> She does not have a psychopathic personality structure nor does she have a history of violent behavior (two of the most important predictors of recidivism). In fact, there are no data to support her having been violent in any significant manner in the past. Further, it would

217

appear that the violence that did occur was extremely specific to the situation involving Marty Sessions. Ms. Alden is also quite attached to her younger children . . . and has been actively fighting attempts by her former husband to change custodial arrangements. She is also quite attached to her older daughter, Melloney Bozeman. It is thus unlikely that she would sever ties with them by fleeing. Moreover, she is without any significant financial resources that would enable her to flee. Finally, Ms. Alden is quite committed to defending herself aggressively against the charges and thus she is motivated to "have her day in court," so that others might understand fully what happened on the night of Mr. Sessions' death.[3]

"What do you make of Golding's analysis?" asked Pat Finlinson. Golding was widely known—and well respected—by law enforcement throughout Utah.

"Well, every once in a while, even a master mechanic will misdiagnose a small-block problem," said Jacobson. "She's even got her psychologist fooled."

The prosecution team was set up in the "War Room"—a large room in the basement of the Millard County Sheriff's Office that was notable chiefly for its set of whiteboard walls and dominating table. The room was put to use only in major cases—it was a place where the team could brainstorm, lay out arguments, set up exhibits, decide which witnesses to bring in, and discuss various issues with the evidence.

"But it's not like Alden is really under Golding's care," said Mike Wims, motioning toward the letter. Wims's slow movements bespoke a deliberate nature—as chief of the Special Prosecutions Section of the Criminal Division of the Utah Attorney General's Office, he was lead prosecutor of the case. Wims is a brilliant man—as noted earlier, he had helped steer home the successful prosecution of Ron Lafferty, the polygamous wife-killer described in Jon Krakauer's *Under the Banner of Heaven*, who was also Marty Sessions's former pal and assailant. Both Wims and his colleague, Pat Nolan, an assistant Utah State attorney general, had been brought down to rural Millard County from Salt Lake City because Pat Finlinson had started his deputy county attorney job only a few days before the murder. More than that, though, this murder case was shaping up to be more complex than anyone would have anticipated.

"Golding's not prescribing medication or treating Alden," Wims elaborated. "He was hired to *evaluate* her—to produce a report to be used in litigation. She's his *client*—not his patient."

Wims knew that many clinical psychologists don't check objective collateral sources—that is, other reputable witnesses to a person's claims. After all, it would be difficult to track down who truly said what; for example, when a patient is discussing her childhood arguments with her mother. But psychologists absolutely must check such objective collateral sources when they are serving in a *forensic* role. Golding, Wims knew, was one of the best at this—he lectured nationally on the topic and fairly criticized others for not objectively checking collateral sources. That was why Golding was so well respected.

The real problem was that some things a defendant says, by their nature, are not capable of being confirmed or rebutted by objective sources—things like how the client feels or what the client thinks about something or other. So some things cannot be verified or contradicted.

However, Wims knew that Golding's approach was to *always* suspect malingering from a person he saw in a medico-legal setting, since people in those settings have a strong motive to fabricate. It was therefore very unlikely that Golding was manipulated by anything that could be collaterally checked. However, Golding was free to accept matters that were incapable of being contradicted by collateral evidence.

It seemed clear to the prosecution team that Golding had given too much credence to his client's statements. In fairness, though, all Golding had really said was that Carole Alden wasn't a psychopath and wasn't generally violent. But the general tone of the letter was supportive of the defense. The problem now was to make sure that their prosecution of the case revealed the deception beneath Carole's pose of plausibility.

"Let's think this out," said Jacobson. He thrust back his chair and moved to the whiteboard. "First, she drove 100 miles north to Provo to get money for a gun when she could have gotten money from a bank around here. Maybe it takes longer to get the money in Delta, but the interest rates wouldn't be 400 percent. That tells me Alden needed money *right now*, and maybe she was trying to hide what she was doing."

Jacobson turned to write *100 miles north for money* on the board, his firm hand bending the marker's felt tip.

"The next day, she turns around and drives another eighty miles *south* to Beaver to buy a handgun." Jacobson's eyebrow rose sardonically. "But she could have driven only eight miles instead to buy a gun in Delta, or thirty miles to buy one in Fillmore. She wouldn't have done that unless she didn't want people around here to know she'd bought a gun."

80 miles south for gun

"She's been living with ex-cons for something like ten years. She *knows* she can't have any sort of gun around an ex-con."

No gun ever *allowed around Marty*

"You don't tell the clerk you want to shoot coyotes and then turn around and buy a Smith & Wesson .38 handgun—especially right after the clerk tells you a pistol just isn't right—'you need a rifle for coyotes, lady.'"

Lied about gun

"And you don't go home that evening directly after buying the gun you went through obvious pains to get and shoot your husband in self-defense. Especially not after you went and dragged him home when he was trying to move out. And most especially not after he's charging around the house scaring the hell out of you, threatening to kill you. She says she can't leave because she's afraid he's going to aspirate if he falls down? But she's also willing to shoot him? Twice? *Come on!*"

"Part of the problem is her state of mind when she committed the murder," Pat Nolan pointed out quietly. Nolan didn't say a lot, but when he said something, it was worth listening. Like the others, Nolan was a family man with a natural sense of integrity. The team was a good one—they worked together like a finely tuned engine.

"Every time she explains the story, her state of mind changes,"

Nolan continued, moving past Jacobson to a flip chart. "Let's lay this out methodically." He took up a marker and began writing as the others talked.

"It looks like Slavens is going to claim self-defense and battered woman syndrome," said Wims. "And with Golding's letter giving her a psychological thumbs-up, she may have a good chance at it."

"We don't know that yet for sure. Could be she might try for the delusion defense," said Finlinson. It would be virtually impossible for Carole to plead outright insanity. For her to do so, she would basically have had to have been unsure as to whether she was shooting a human being or a tomato. In any case, all indicators were that Carole Alden was *not* going to plead guilty to murder.

"The problem with that, though," said Nolan, "is Carole's actions up to that point—the point where she fired the second shot—weren't consistent with her being delusional. That's whether she fired the second shot a minute after the first, or two hours after the first. She was just too in control of herself and the situation."

"Well, at least there's no question we've got her on the desecration of a body charge," said Finlinson.

"The body flying around the trailer. The rope. I mean, you can't make this stuff up," added Nolan.

Wims, Finlinson, and Jacobson stared at the exhibits—pictures of Marty's forlorn body, the makeshift grave. They hadn't believed the story *before* they'd gone to witness the crime scene for themselves. Now, even after they'd had a chance to take in the evidence, they still found it hard to believe.

"I'd like to know what she was saying to him before she shot him." The question was rhetorical—it was hard to know who had even mouthed it—but they each had wondered about it. "What got him so mad?"

"We don't know that she was deliberately antagonizing him," said Jacobson, thinking out loud. "Maybe his just waking up to find himself back with her again—especially when he was trying to move out—was enough to set him off."

"That's part of the problem," Nolan said, interrupting his flip chart writing. "There's just no way to sugarcoat Marty's past. The drug use. The criminal history. He clearly was not a sympathetic victim."

Nods all around. Marty Sessions's long prison record and the trail of problems that seemed to follow him were enough to make him walking bad news in the county. In fact, whether the team liked it or not, Sessions's character was one of the most difficult aspects of trying this case. Marty Sessions didn't make for a great victim—if he had just disappeared, there would have been few raised eyebrows.

Nolan cleared his throat, eyes turned to the flip chart, where a breakdown of the charges was neatly outlined:

76-5-203   Murder–1st degree felony (5 to life potential sentence)

To prove it must show

- It was intentionally or knowingly committed (must prove that mental state)
- Caused the death of another

76-5-205   Manslaughter–2nd degree felony (1 to 15 years)

To prove it must show

- Recklessly caused the death of another or/
- Commit a murder but it is reduced (under 203.4) by self-defense
- Commit murder by special mitigation (under 205.5) by delusional thinking

---

"Those are the main charges in a nutshell," said Nolan. "We've either got to prove the murder or the manslaughter charges. We've got to choose which battle we're going to pursue."

The team stared at the board. No question everyone wanted to go for murder—the top charge on the board. (Murder "in the first degree" is television stuff; "murder" in Utah is automatically a first-degree felony.) But how to get them there?

Jacobson hopscotched past Nolan's flip chart to the next space on the whiteboard and wrote: *He was coming straight at me*. He circled it. "That's story number one."

"That's when we pointed out that the bullet was in the back," said Finlinson.

"Yes. So then she changes the story." Jacobson crossed out the circle. "She then says Marty had gone by her in the hallway, heard her, and turned. As he was turning to get her, she shot him. So he was coming toward her, but that's how the bullet ended up in his back."

"Right," said Wims sarcastically.

Jacobson wrote, *He was turning and lunging at me*, and circled it.

"Then for the second shot, she says she was standing above him, about fifteen feet away."

Stood at distance from Marty.

"But that didn't jibe with the forensic evidence—the pillow showed she was right there on top of him, shooting at point-blank range. So she changes her story *again*. This time, she says she kneeled right down by him and fired the *coup de grâce*."

Oops—meant to say I was right by him, Jacobson wrote.

"So then," said Finlinson, once again tackling Carole's twisted logic, "she says she thought for a long time. Eventually, though, she thought she saw him breathing. That's when she shot him again, because she had to go past him to the other end of the house. She had to put the phone there back on the hook and get a dial tone."

Jacobson wrote *Waited for second shot* on the whiteboard and circled it.

"But then it got pointed out to her that it didn't look like it was a 'heat of passion' sort of thing if she waited a long time," said Finlinson.

"Bingo. So she changes the story." Jacobson crossed out the "waited" circle and wrote *Quickly shot again*.

"Then she talks to Slavens and realizes she's got another way out. If she says she was in a trance when she killed him, she can get off via the "murder by special mitigation," 205 sub 5. The delusion claim. So all of a sudden, you see her starting to write her relatives, her supporters, that she was in some kind of trance or dreamlike state. She was in a daze for hours, didn't realize what was going on."

In a trance, Jacobson wrote.

"She says he was lying there with his arms stretched out above his head," said Wims. "But she shoots him again because she's afraid he's going to rise up and grab her. But to shoot him in the head at point-blank range, she had to get right down by his outstretched hands, prop the pillow up there, and pull the trigger. This whole time, she could have easily run out either the front or the back door without having gone near Marty."

"And her daughter said the only place the pillows were stored was in the linen closet or the bedrooms. She would have had to have already *gone past* Marty to have gotten the pillow she popped him through," said Jacobson.

"I think she shot him again because she hated his guts, and this was her big chance to make sure he was dead. Really dead. She wanted to hurt him in the worst way she could. But she didn't want to get dirty. So she stuck the pillow between his pumpkin and the gun. No splatter." It was hard to tell who'd said this—it was something they had all wondered about.

Murder, they felt—no question about it. But practical considerations drew them up short. If they went directly for murder, Golding's letter would make it tougher for them to avoid having the charges reduced to manslaughter by either a self-defense or delusional thinking argument. And there were other concerns. An important one was whether Sessions was even alive when Carole fired the second shot. If he was already dead, she couldn't technically have fired a second, more obviously deliberate kill shot.

This was indeed a case where subtlety underlies subtlety.

Wims began playing devil's advocate: "Melloney said point-blank that Marty Sessions was never physically abusive to Carole. Verbally abusive, but not physically. The kids—Jason and Emily—never saw anything physically abusive, either. But then there's the MP3 recording."

"*That* thing," said Jacobson enigmatically.

Jason had told investigators that he had a recording of Marty threatening to kill Carole if she ever reported anything to the police. But the recording—if indeed it existed—was buried somewhere in hundreds of hours of recordings on two different players. If the case came to trial, they would have to pin this down.

"But look, if Marty was threatening to kill her if she called police, why did she call the police?" said Finlinson. "Not once, not twice, but on a number of occasions? How could it be that she could call dispatch on Sessions for removing a wire from her carburetor, have an officer come out to her house and talk to her *out of Sessions's earshot*, and she still says nothing about any abuse?"

"Then there's her e-mails," said Finlinson. Carole had sent hundreds of graphic, sadomasochistic e-mails to Marty, later explaining them by saying Marty had logged into her account and sent the e-mails to himself; sometimes she said he'd even supervised her writing specific e-mails to him as a sort of insurance policy.

"The bottom line is," said Jacobson, taking up Finlinson's train of thought, "it would have taken Marty more time than he was sober to make up all those e-mails."

On top of all this, Carole Alden was reputedly the queen of sadomasochism of Salt Lake City. She even had her own whip name—and all this had been going on long before she met Marty. Marty himself, on the other hand, had no prior history of involvement in sadomasochism whatsoever. How could they take Carole's own self-serving word, which conveniently distanced her from her past and simultaneously removed her from the responsibility of having written the sordid e-mails that appeared under her name?

"What kind of mother *is* Alden, anyway?" asked Nolan parenthetically. "I mean, what she did to her daughter is . . . I just don't understand this woman. Melloney was *on the phone* with Carole when the first shot was fired. But Carole doesn't tell us that. *Melloney* tells us that. And then Carole told Melloney not to tell police she had heard anything—not the gunshot. Nothing."

"Basically, Carole Alden told her daughter to lie," said Jacobson. "She was setting her daughter up for a jail sentence. All to save her own skin. Because Alden wasn't planning on telling anybody what she'd done to Marty. Except Allen Lake. That was her one miscalculation."

Jacobson paused, collecting his thoughts. "Look at this. First she tells her older daughter and her son that she's going to drive Marty down to Arizona, to the reservation. Now there's no indication that Marty's actually got connections to a reservation, other than maybe what he told her. Or what she told others. Okay, let's let that be. But then when she's interviewed after the killing, she tells Sergeant Burton something different altogether—that she and Marty were going to have a nice weekend together and work on resolving the problems in their marriage. No mention about his leaving.

"And then we learn that Marty himself had told friends he was planning on moving to Ricky Searles's place. He e-mails his daughter to that effect a few days before the murder. No mention of an Indian reservation. Marty had already tried to move out once before, and she'd moved him back. The night of the murder, he was passed out stone-cold drunk in the middle of the road—*and she came and got him.*

"Carole Alden's story was always changing. Always."

"She has to continue with the illusion," said Finlinson.

"It's her third revised version of the truth," said Wims.

"Yes," said Jacobson. "She came and got Marty because she had plans for him. And she wasn't about to let Marty himself screw those plans up. She's a controlling woman—she can't stand to be bested."

"You can see what's going on here," said Wims.

"It's like there's one genus of a story," said Jacobson, "but then there's five species. Ten species, depending on the story. And then there's hybridization." He stared at the board, looking at the circles and crosses, completing the connections mentally. "It's like she thinks about it and thinks about it, and whenever she realizes one story won't work, she tries another. And then another."

He paused, the big picture setting solidly into place. "She never, ever stops."

CHAPTER 24

MARTY'S SECRETS

Too often we underestimate the power of a touch, a smile, a kind word, a listening ear, an honest compliment, or the smallest act of caring, all of which have the potential to turn a life around.
—LEO BUSCAGLIA, *Born for Love*[1]

Part of Marty Sessions's charm—the charm that wooed the many women he happily flirted with in his jail correspondence—was that he was a born storyteller. He liked to tell people, for example, that he was actually the great-grand-nephew of the Apache war chief Geronimo. But, as was often the case with Marty's stories, truth was stranger than fiction. Marty *did* have a Native American heritage, but it certainly wasn't Apache.[2]

Marty's Native American grandmother was around seven years old in 1900—that was about the year she was traded for a mule and two sacks of grain to a Mormon family near Moroni, Utah. The girl came

227

to be called Winona—all she could remember was that before she was traded, she had been walking with her father, mother, and two younger brothers by night for three moons, headed from Idaho toward Mexico. Her tribe's name has been lost in the mists of memory—it was thought to have been either Nez Perce or Blackfoot. Wherever their ultimate destination, trading their little daughter gave Winona's birth family the resources they needed to continue their journey.

Although happy with her new family and Mormon beliefs, Winona tried to keep her heritage alive with occasional furtive smudges and the odd ritual as she grew older. By the time she'd reached her late sixties, when Marty knew her, she was a stern old lady whose demeanor masked a warm and caring heart. Denny, Marty's closest brother, remembers traveling back to Idaho with his grandmother when he was about seven as she fruitlessly searched for her long-lost little brothers—the ones her parents had kept.

Tom, Marty's brilliant, obsessive father, then, was half Native American. In the 1950s, when Marty and Denny were born, a Native American background was nothing to be proud of. This explained why, though Tom's hair was black, he would insist to his sons it was brown. Later, in the 1960s, when an Indian heritage began to become admirable, both Marty and Denny began wearing their own dark hair long, taking pride in their heritage. The two men also had handsome physiques that showcased their inheritance: strong, muscular builds, broad shoulders, wide foreheads, high cheekbones and ready, natural tans.

Marty being Marty, however, a relationship with the illustrious Geronimo wasn't all he made up. To cover for his dozen or so stints in prison, which totaled over two decades altogether, he told people that he had been in the army and had served in Vietnam. In reality, he *had* joined the army—but he'd served only four months, all stateside. Right after basic training he cut off his right ring finger in a hatchet accident and was consequently given a medical discharge. (The finger was sewn back on, leaving others to wonder about what kind of strange axe cut would take off a ring finger.) But Marty embellished his war stories with a slew of realistic certificates and commendations he hauled out to show people, telling them he thought his military years were the best of his life.

The real problem, as Denny later recalled, was not just that Marty Sessions was a chronic storyteller—it was that he believed his own stories. But, as Edee and Anna pointed out, Marty's stories weren't told to hurt anyone or get them in trouble.

Marty Sessions, in short, was the drug-addicted, flawed man whom Carole chose to pursue after having protested that she didn't know what she was getting into with the heroin-addicted Andy Bristow.

But whatever his flaws, Denny insists, Marty never, ever abused women.

*   *   *

Denny has been clean now for seventeen years, and he has done well as the owner of an independent "pilot car" company. He makes it clear he's willing to speak candidly about Marty for one reason, and one reason only—he wants people to know that he's being honest when he says that the stories Carole Alden tells about Marty being a man who abused his wife are very likely not true.

"Marty and I shared a cell in prison," Denny recalls. "But we ran with different crowds. Marty hung out with Andy Bristow—Bristow was a stand-up guy who did drugs and had a little hustle going on the side." Denny was more concerned that Marty also hung out with Dan Lafferty, who was at that time still with the general prison population. (Later, after the publication of Krakauer's *Under the Banner of Heaven*, which describes Lafferty's role in slitting his sister-in-law's and niece's throats, Lafferty would be sent to maximum security.) "I could never understand that—Lafferty was bad news," Denny continues. "Anyway, Lafferty stuck some soap in his sock and beat Marty up in the showers after Marty ripped him off."

While behind bars, Marty also had what amounted to a hobby—corresponding with women. "He must have had eight or ten women he used to correspond with," Denny remembers. "He had beautiful penmanship and a nice way with words. If he wrote you, you'd end up liking him, too." Unlike Denny, who read textbooks for fun, Marty enjoyed reading novels.

"I'll be honest with you: I wouldn't paint a picture of Marty as being Mr. Wonderful. I lived with him. I knew him better than anybody. It's just that he wouldn't hurt a woman. There's a lot of bad you could say about Marty, but *that's just not him.* It made my stomach turn to see the stories Carole Alden had put into the *National Enquirer* about him. Hit her with a two-by-four? Not Marty. Never."

One matter is certain: Marty's many other problems got him in trouble with his family. His father, Tom, was horrified at Marty's deceits and adamantly refused to support his son's drug use. (At the same time, though, Tom was known as an easy touch to all the stray cats in the neighborhood—this love of animals was something he and Marty, not to mention Carole, shared.) To feed his drug habit, Marty sometimes turned to his kindhearted mother Joan, who had much more difficulty saying no to him.

Denny, being a former drug addict himself, was a tough man for Marty to con for drug money. But that didn't stop Marty from simply spinning tales in front of his brother, which Denny generally ignored as innocuous embellishment. Every once in a while, though, Denny would get fed up. At the last major family get-together Marty ever attended, the Thanksgiving turkey and trimmings went airborne during the course of a knock-down drag-out fight involving the menfolk. (As with all of Marty's fights, however, he wasn't the one who threw the first punch—Denny was the hothead in the family.)

It's always tough to know how to handle an addict. Denny tried to introduce Marty to his own support mechanism—AA.[3] But Marty went to a few meetings and decided it wasn't for him. (His choice of religion finally settled on Scientology—not that he practiced its anti-medication tenets.) Indeed, Marty had difficulty seeing his drug or alcohol use as a problem. The Sessions family was happy to see Marty down in the area of Delta, Utah, with Carole Alden—it kept him away from his usual drug haunts in Salt Lake City. The Sessions had always had animals growing up—they'd even kept milk cows for a while, so Marty was in his element with Carole's many creatures. Occasionally, Marty would appear back in Salt Lake City and score hits by showing people where to get drugs. Denny would give Carole gas money to come get Marty and take him back to Delta.

It appears that by 2006, Marty was slowly beginning to get his act together, at least as far as the heroin was concerned. But he still drank, slowly sipping his way through an entire bottle of Captain Morgan every day. Marty had always suffered from pain in his back, but in his last few years—no one quite knows how—he did more serious damage to his spine, so he took heavy doses of methadone, a synthetic opioid, to deal with the pain. According to Denny, Marty also fell and blew out a knee. The doctor ill-advisedly put him on Lortab—another semi-synthetic opioid derived from codeine. Marty's attempts to end his addictions were essentially forms of musical chairs—he always seemed to find another chair when the music stopped.

But there was one definite change Marty wanted to make—he wanted out of his relationship with Carole. A year or two before his death, he'd told his family that he simply wasn't into S&M—it wasn't his thing. But more to the point, a few days before his death, he'd announced that he'd had enough—he was planning to move down to Yuma, to be around Susie's family.

Thus Carole's statements that Marty planned to go to Arizona the weekend he was killed might have had some truth behind them—although, given her interactions with Marty's family members, Carole should have known as well as anyone that Marty had no connections with Indian reservations in that area.

*   *   *

It's worthwhile to know exactly what Carole did accuse Marty of doing and how she saw their relationship. Three years after the homicide, with the benefit of much time to reflect on her story, Carole Alden wrote an extended set of recollections about Marty. If her com-

Carole and Marty together at the wedding of Carole's daughter Melloney in 2003. The pair were themselves married the next year.

mentary does not necessarily offer true insight into the vicissitudes of their relationship, it does show how she wanted the relationship to be perceived by others.[4]

According to Carole, her relationship with Marty first began when he wrote her a letter of condolence from prison after his friend Andy Bristow died. Marty, Carole explained, was one of the few people who reacted sympathetically toward her during her time of grief—others having weighed in (in her retelling, at least) with sentiments of "good riddance to bad rubbish." Marty became a lifeline for Carole—she thought of him as a man filled with "kindness, patience, empathy and a willingness to embrace life." Although she didn't have the feelings for him that she had had for Andy, she felt gratitude coupled with a feeling that she owed him for his kindness in rescuing her at a time when she was emptied of all spirit.

Carole told others about Marty, but because she was fearful of criticism for corresponding with a prisoner, she kept mum about his living arrangements. In retrospect, she concluded that this made it hard for anyone to warn her about what she was getting herself into. But Carole also felt that even if she had been warned, she wouldn't have listened, because she would have allowed Marty the opportunity to explain the admonitions away. In her heart, she was convinced Marty "was a good man with a spiritual agenda"—a man who had been brought low by circumstance. "There but by the grace of God go I," she felt. It was her moral obligation to help, since she knew she had the ability to positively affect his life.

Carole felt it was only her first year with Marty that was a good one, and that was probably a result of the fact that she was still lost in a world of grief. She just didn't have the spirit to argue or notice much of anything. Gradually, as she came out of her fog in the next—and final—four years of her marriage, the situation deteriorated.

In Carole's retelling, she first began noticing something was deeply awry when Marty began covertly hurting her animals: one of her three-month-old baby llamas was allegedly found frozen to the ground, with ligature marks on its neck. Carole then apparently found two strangled alpacas. Although Carole didn't want to believe Marty could have had anything to do with it, what she ostensibly observed next horrified her. From the side door to the garage, Marty tenderly picked up a baby pygmy goat that was a special family favorite, caressed it, and then strangled it. He then threw a sheet of plywood over the body and stood atop the plywood to ensure the baby was dead. Carole was aghast, she said, but she didn't reveal what she'd seen.

Although Marty helped her say prayers over the baby's grave, Carole concluded that it must have been Marty who was responsible for the other inexplicable animal deaths. In her version of the story, at this point she realized that she could never, ever leave her children with Marty—from this time on she always made sure her children went with her, whether to her work at the park, the library— everywhere. She always tried to keep a happy demeanor so as to not make her children afraid, and to also avoid tipping Marty off to the fact she was on to him. This, she felt, would give her time to figure out how to better handle the situation.

According to Carole, Marty had heart-to-heart talks with her in which he expressed chagrin over his inability to work. He felt he was less of a man as a consequence. In Carole's retelling, she reassured him that she didn't gauge him by whether or not he held down a nine-to-five job. Marty pledged to help out by doing laundry and keeping the house clean, taking care of the animals and the lawn, and helping Emily and Jason with their homework.

Carole said she began noticing the animals weren't looking so good. As it turned out, they weren't being fed or watered—responsibilities Marty was supposed to be handling. One day she counted hay bales and was startled to find the same number of bales she'd had the week prior. Even if she got up extra early to give water to the animals, he'd tip the water out as soon as she left. Then he started locking in their two cats and three small dogs. Unable to roam outside to do their business, they left their urine and feces everywhere—spilling garbage while they were at it. The stench was overwhelming. Because Marty was drinking, he'd be in a foul mood—there was no way for her to discuss matters. She was left to simply clean up what she could, galled that, while she was working, he was reneging on his part of the agreement. (Many others have pointed out, however, that virtually every house Carole lived in showed the same pattern of chaotic filth.)

Once, Carole said, she walked up to see Marty burning a nest of baby mice in the yard. He turned to her and said with a grin, "Fire is the easiest way to get rid of babies once their mama disappears." His ensuing laughter gave her to understand that her children were in mortal danger if Marty carried out his threats to kill her.

In fact, Carole noted, he'd made precisely such threats in front of both his drinking buddies and her son Jason—saying that any bitch that called the police on her husband should be stomped until her bones were pulverized, then thrown down a mine shaft while still alive, and finally, set afire. But she also noted that Marty was trying to draw close to Jason, then fourteen, urging him to smoke pot with his group of "reprobate buddies." Carole's statements weren't completely fanciful: police would later say that Marty gave Jason pot as a reward for getting good grades.

Carole claimed that when Marty first started to use sexual abuse as a control mechanism, he ensured her bruises would be in places where she would be too embarrassed to show people. As their home computer system administrator, he also gained access to Carole's e-mail accounts. He would log on as her and send e-mails to his own account begging him to abuse her—on several occasions he actually supervised her in writing e-mails to him. This, she said, was his insurance policy to destroy her credibility and prevent the police from taking her seriously.

If sadomasochistic behavior was the type of treatment she actually enjoyed, she pointed out, why would she kill him over it? In any case, she noted, the sex toys and equipment the police found were items that Marty was trying to sell through an eBay account.

Carole killed Marty, she says, because he was two feet away and he was about to grab her. He had been graphic in his explanation of what he would do to her and how he would kill her children, if he was

Carole and Marty at the Salt Lake Arts Festival, mid-June 2006—
a month before Marty's death. Neither looks happy.

able to get her. She felt there was simply no other option at that critical moment. Up until that point, she thought it would be like all the other previous times, where he'd pass out and wake up remorseful the next day. Carole also worried there was a possibility of more confrontations to come—perhaps also with some of Marty's friends joining in for sadistic entertainment. Surely she had the right to defend herself, since no one else could do it.

Carole gave a number of reasons for later changing her story about Marty and the shooting. First, she said the police never asked for details of her and Marty's relationship before the killing. She also still had feelings of loyalty toward her husband and didn't want others— particularly his two daughters—to be exposed to the ugly details of his behavior. Marty was basically a good person, she felt; it was the drugs that induced the dementia. Carole was also concerned about further traumatizing her own children. Perhaps worst of all, she was embarrassed that others would talk about how idiotic she was to have remained with him. She said people just didn't realize the leverage he had, threatening to help her ex-husband by telling the court that she was an unfit mother. She could lose not only her house but her children. In fact, the second time she called the cops, Marty had contacted her ex-husband Brian and told him she was acting erratically and that the children should remain with him at his house. Marty's actions in threatening to have her children removed from her, Carole felt, crossed the line into utterly unforgivable behavior—it was at this point, in fact, that she realized she was emotionally finished with him and angry to the core.

At the same time, in Carole's retelling, because Marty's actions were a consequence of the drugs, alcohol, and mental illness, she felt he was a victim who still deserved her sympathy. Thus, for the first eight months she was in jail, she kept many of the details of Marty's behavior to herself, defending Marty and trying to preserve his daughters' good memories of their father.

While in jail, Carole was presented with hundreds of e-mails between Marty and another woman. Marty, as it turned out, had been laying on plans to, as she put it, "part her from her assets." (One prosecutorial source, however, questions what assets Carole could have been talking about.) Carole felt the fool for having been suckered into believing that Marty had actually loved her. Even now, after therapy, she writes that she finds it difficult to feel anger for him—she still misses him and pushes the fearful parts of her memories from her mind. This is a source of anxiety for her—it means she can't trust herself to stay away from people who might hurt her. By Carole's account, she has been confused to find herself wanting to forgive Marty. At the same time, however, she doesn't think she'll ever be able to forgive her ex-husband Brian, who she feels is an "obstruction to any sort of normality" between her two youngest children and herself. No one gets between her and her kids, she asserts repeatedly.

Carole presents her relationship with Marty as having gone from being rescued, to being a caretaker, to feeling petrified with terror. In her account, she never wanted him to be arrested when she called the police, because she knew he'd have his pain medications withheld, which would cause him to suffer. When she called police, it was simply as a wakeup call, to try to prod him into either fixing his attitude or leaving. She states that she wanted *him* to make the decision to leave her; in that way, she figured, he wouldn't feel rejected.

Carole claims that her perspective on Marty hasn't changed so much as her perspective on herself. Marty, she says, was looking for a gullible mark from the get-go, and Carole failed to recognize the deception as a consequence of her feelings of guilt, low self-esteem, and sense of wanting to feel needed. According to Carole, her gut sense is that love fixes everything, and she notes that no matter how many times she's seen that belief proven wrong, she still can't change her feelings. She does feel, however, that she's finally become aware of what a mess of her life she's made by trying to fix others. She's come to the point, she says, at which she acknowledges what she terms Marty's "disgustingly evil qualities," even while noting that she still loves him anyway.

Carole also maintains that Marty's abuse didn't end when she took his life. Her life, after all, is now taken away from her, day by day, with the government's blessing. She declares that she has always been perfectly capable of admitting anything she's ever done wrong. If she was honest about killing Marty, she points out, why would she not be honest about lesser mistakes? Though trapped in dysfunctional patterns of pathological altruism, and also physically imprisoned, she is nonetheless, she maintains, psychologically free—able to face the truth about herself and others. She is bitter, though, about the sharp contrast between the supreme importance the truth has had in her own life and the trivial status it has been accorded in the public disposition of her case. The only way she's able to keep going is to remind herself that if she weren't in prison, she'd be dead. She'd never have known what Marty would have done to her children when they returned the next day. The horror of that thought, she says, is the reason she shot Marty.

*   *   *

We can never know for certain the intimate details of the relationship between Marty and Carole. One of the only two key witnesses to that relationship is now dead. But we do have the statements of the other closest witnesses: According to police, Carole Alden's children stated unequivocally that they had never seen Marty Sessions become physically violent with Carole Alden. None had ever—*ever*—seen him hit her or hurt her in any physical way.

CHAPTER 25

MEDIA MAESTRO

Trial by media has become a phrase that is familiar to many lawyers. It pits competing constitutional principles against each other: freedom of the press, the right to a fair trial and the right to a public trial. Trial by media can cut both ways. It can result in the public condemnation of a seemingly guilty (but a yet untried) defendant—or it can result in the public's perceiving that a defendant is being "railroaded" (before the prosecution has presented any evidence).

—MICHAEL WIMS,
*How to Prepare and Try a Murder Case:
Prosecution and Defense Perspectives*[1]

Т
he Millard County Jail is set on the open slopes of the Pahvant Valley, where stretches of sagebrush run up against fenced pas-

241

tures filled with dark-brown mixed-breed cattle—the result of local cattlemen breeding their local herds away from the classic red and white Hereford toward leaner Black Angus. Close as the cattle were to the jail, Carole's life inside was sharply separate from the animals she loved. Her daily rhythm settled into a monotonous, tightly circumscribed routine.

Still, Carole kept herself busy by organizing a mass publicity campaign in her defense. She sent slews of letters to media outlets and also asked her children to act on her behalf. One early payoff for these efforts was a March 26, 2007, article in the British version of the *National Enquirer*: "Wife Kills 'Depraved' Hubby Who Made Her Wear Chastity Belt,"[2] with a tag line insinuating the title was actually a quote from the police. The article began boldly: "Artist Carole Alden endured living hell at the hands of her sadistic husband—including drunken rages, beatings and the indignity of a chastity belt—until she couldn't take it anymore and shot him dead, cops say."[3] The rest of the article consisted of a more straightforward version of the killing.

Carole's letters to the press and to sympathetic outsiders displayed an exquisite sense for the kind of underdog story that might strike an editor's fancy, describing Carole's plight as she imagined it—a gutsy, truth-speaking woman who, despite her molestation as a child and horrific abuse in her marriage, dared to stand up against "the man." Carole portrayed herself as a free-thinking flower child, an independent feminist in a group of lockstep, chauvinistic Mormons behind the "Zion curtain."[4]

A year and a half after the homicide, Carole's twenty-one-year-old daughter Krystal used the same approach—her words being quoted in provocatively titled articles that shaped a sympathetic storyline. "Forced to Wear a Chastity Belt!" appeared in the British tabloid *Pick Me Up*,[5] and in a major PR coup, the American *National Enquirer* ran "Woman Marries for Love—THEN KILLS FOR SURVIVAL: 'Loving ex-con turned into ABUSIVE MONSTER who got physical *once too often*.'"[6] This was a shorter version of the *Pick Me Up* article. Marty was portrayed as a straggly-haired, tattooed monster who cast a spell on kindly Carole, who thought her love was enough to fix him. He was timing Carole's jaunts to neighbors and the store, obsessed with the crazy idea she was cheating on him. Worst of all, Krystal said, was that Marty had "pierced Mum's genitals and forced her to wear a chastity belt so she couldn't sleep with other men. . . . It was like something from the Dark Ages. The pain must have been horrific. And the mental anguish of being abused like that, utterly degrading."[7]

In the aftermath of the homicide, Carole had written Krystal a letter from prison, thanking her for standing by her and apologizing for being an embarrassment. "She could never be that," Krystal wrote, adding poignantly: "I pray her parole board sees she killed Sessions because he was killing her, and releases her early. After years of torment, she deserves to be free."[8]

SHAPING THE BRAIN

It makes perfect sense that a child's story would support that of a parent's, even if there is evidence to the contrary. This is the result of a process that starts early and can last all through the maturation process. Scientists have found astonishing resonances and synchronizations between a mother and her baby, as if at some deep level, the pair form a single creature. This mother-baby creature shares sleep patterns, brain patterns, heart rhythms, direction of gaze, facial expressions, and speech.[9] Mothers can excite or soothe their babies through their voice alone, or by jostling, or in a myriad of other warm and comforting ways.

Baby's brains take a long time to develop. The limbic areas dealing with emotion develop early on, but the prefrontal cortex—the part of the brain that deals with rational thinking and control of our emotions—develops much more slowly. (This is why babies and toddlers throw temper tantrums so easily.)

To support the methodical but slow development of a baby's brain, the mother's prefrontal cortex initially pulls double duty and also serves as the *baby's* prefrontal cortex. At least, it does so until the baby's own prefrontal cortex is developed enough to slip into gear.[10] As the infant matures, the parents' interests and ways of looking at the world shape what the infant and child focus on, and in this way amplifies some neuronal activities even as other neuronal activities are diminished.[11]

But what this also means is that adults—particularly the child's mother—have an extraordinary influence on how a child's brain develops. As Yale professor of psychiatry Bruce Wexler observes: "Thus, from a very early age, social interaction with adults shapes the mechanisms that underlie social interaction, externally influences the direction and manner in which the infant's attention is deployed, and shapes the development of the self-regulatory mechanisms that direct attention throughout the individual's adult life."[12]

As always, the brain's two hemispheres focus on different aspects of interacting with the world as the child develops. Where the left hemisphere, rather slow to pick up steam, focuses on analyzing bits and pieces of what is sent to it by the right hemisphere, the right hemisphere itself is experiencing the richness of the world in context. Indeed, the right hemisphere can be thought of as the bridge to emotions—it is connected more strongly with the evolutionarily ancient limbic system and is more strongly focused on interacting with others.

Carolyn Zahn-Waxler, using the research skills she'd honed as one of the National Institute of Mental Health's top developmental psychologists, found that sensitive children can be swept into a disturbing role-reversal situation, in which the "parent looks to a child to meet a parent's need for comfort, parenting, intimacy or play, and the child attempts to meet those needs."[13] This promotes an "empathic over-arousal" as the child tries to help and care for a parent even as the child begins to suppress his or her own needs.

According to family friends, Krystal has served as her mother's confidante since she was a child. Even when she was visiting family in other parts of the country, Krystal would be caught up in hours of lengthy "compulsive care-giving" telephone conversations with

Carole back in Utah, helping her mother sort out whatever crisis was at hand for the day. This use of the children as witnesses and coconspirators in Carole's dramas surpassed normal bounds. For example, Carole invited Krystal, then in her mid-teens, to watch the cremation of Andy Bristow's body. Krystal later described how she watched the body burn through a little window as layers flaked off.

Krystal was taught early on who was worthy of focused care and compassion—and who wasn't. Any hint of criticism toward her mother, for example, seems to arouse instantaneous feelings of aversion. In some sense, this is understandable—who wouldn't react to criticism of one's mother? But when that mother is Carole Alden, well, a dollop of dispassion couldn't hurt. One can't help but wonder what years of entanglement in Carole's never-ending misfortunes have done to her children. "Empathic overarousal," notes Zahn-Waxler, "can begin in the first years of life when children try to help and care for their parents. . . . This 'grown-up' behavior likely masks insecurities as children begin to suppress their own needs. Patterns of codependency between parent and child can develop."[14]

*   *   *

Melloney, Carole's oldest daughter, is also in thrall to her mother. According to Carole and other family members, Melloney, a kindhearted young woman who is a marvelously caring mother, dutifully visits Carole at every opportunity—although it is more difficult now that Carole is nearly one hundred and fifty miles away, in the Utah State Prison in Draper, near Salt Lake City. Carole writes that Melloney also puts money in Carole's prison account and accepts weekly phone calls. Once she is paroled, Carole notes, Melloney plans to have her move in with her family.[15]

It is always hard to know the real motivations underlying any relationship, whether mother-daughter or husband-wife. Melloney told an acquaintance that Carole got so used to persuading everybody else to believe her lies about Marty that she started believing them herself.

Melloney reported that Carole really loved Marty, too, and love can be quite blind.

Another family friend goes deeper.

> To some extent, all of the children do understand there is something terribly wrong with their mother. But it is too painful for them to believe that Carole could be totally responsible for herself—that she has had the same opportunities as everyone else to create the life she wanted. Her eviction from home after home because she didn't pay rent wasn't because she didn't have money. She *did* have money—child support, welfare, help from family. But she always blames her problems on the situation, or the guy she's with, or what-have-you. She's learned to make a living out of being a victim.

And yet another friend adds, "The children all know, but they don't know. They don't want to know. Because if they faced the truth, they'd have to admit that everything they believed growing up—*everything*—was a lie."

CHAPTER 26

PRELIMINARY HEARING— THE GRAND FINALE

If two things don't fit, but you believe both of them,
thinking that somewhere, hidden, there must be a
third thing that connects them, that's credulity.

—UMBERTO ECO, *Foucault's Pendulum*[1]

Michael Wims, the lead prosecutor on the Carole Alden case, is a very careful man. When he pronounces the word *mountain*, for example, his tongue taps out the *t* clearly, as if he has a special affection for the subtle sounds overlooked by others. He's also fond of strictly correct use of grammar and logical constructions. Wims's wife, Pam, knows better than to ask him whether he would like apple pie or cherry pie. His answer would be *yes*.[2]

A good attorney never asks a question with two options. The answer lacks rigor.

Wims was born and raised in England, arriving in the States when he was fifteen, which perhaps accounted for others' perceptions of him during his high school years as being somewhat aloof. But there is another side to his character: Wims chose the University of North Texas for his undergraduate studies because it was rated the number-two party school in the country that year by *Playboy* magazine. (The number one school, unfortunately, was a private one out of his price range.) Once he received his law degree from the University of Texas in Austin, Wims flew all over the world in his work for the military, which culminated in his becoming a chief circuit prosecutor and eventually the chief of the Military Justice Division in Washington, DC. Wims is also a fountain of historical knowledge. He doesn't just know the year of any given historical event, such as the signing of the Magna Carta—he can tell you the precise date: June 15, 1215. Asked whether Wims has a photographic memory, Pam shrugs and answers, "He's got

Michael Wims stands before the Peter and Paul Fortress in St. Petersburg, Russia, August 2010. He finished his collaborative opus *How to Prepare and Try a Murder Case: Prosecution and Defense Perspectives* for the American Bar Association the day before leaving for the trip.

more stuff up there than he should have room for."[3] Wims himself demurs: "I'm not any smarter than anyone else," he points out, alluding to Thomas Edison's quote about genius being 1 percent inspiration and 99 percent perspiration. "But they can't outwork me."

Wims has literally written the book for the American Bar Association on how to try homicide cases.[4] He has a single, ironclad, all-important rule in the courtroom: *Never let them see you sweat.* Never make anything the other side does look important. And never, ever, *ever* make it look like the other side has scored points. If the other side "annoys" him (and "annoys" is in quotation marks because it's virtually impossible to annoy this even-tempered man), Wims never changes his expression. Even if the other counsel is rude, Wims never retaliates or becomes in any way upset. He simply out-polites and out-nices the other person. If another counsel is rude to him in front of the jury, he believes the jury will penalize that person for being rude. If anything, when the other side is doing something—anything—Wims stands by looking politely bored. He may occasionally politely stifle a yawn or glance at his wristwatch.

Michael Wims was born for the challenge of the courtroom. "It is," he observes, "as intricate as a game of chess—but playing hardball for keepsies." He pauses, reflecting on his own reflections. "But you can never reject empathy. You must understand the feelings of the victim's families. You have to understand the jury. But you must not get so emotionally involved as to lose your objectivity. And then, too, you need to understand the state of mind of the defendant. See it from his or her point of view, take account of that, put it before the jury, but then also encompass it within a state of mind that embodies the norms of the group with which the jury identifies." Wims does this all as naturally as breathing.

With his unique, contrapuntal juxtaposition of traits, Michael Wims is one of the best prosecutors in the State of Utah.

*   *   *

Mr. Wims: "We are prepared to proceed to summation."[5]

Judge Eyre: "You may argue."

Mr. Wims: "Thank you. Your Honor, count one is domestic violence: murder. The elements of the offense starting with the first one are that the Defendant did on or about July the 28th or 29th of last year, element No. 1, cause the death of Martin Sessions.

"The evidence you have heard today is that the Defendant said she killed Martin Sessions, her husband, because she was afraid of him. She explained that he came down the hall while she was concealed in the laundry room just off of the hall. And while hiding in the laundry room she got the gun, which she had bought earlier that same day, and which she had secreted in the laundry room. According to the Defendant, as Martin walked down the hall and passed the laundry room, he turned and raised his fist. That is when she shot him the first time. She described where she shot him as being in the left ribs.

Wims pointedly made a gesture toward his *front* left ribs. Carole's initial statements to police, before her story had begun its back-tracking, circuitous path, had indicated she'd shot Marty from the front—not the back. Wims continued his methodical encapsulation of the crime:

Mr. Wims: "The autopsy report is not consistent with this explanation of the first shot. He was in fact shot in the back, and the exit wound is on the right front side of his body. However, the first shot, as you heard from the doctor, was likely not fatal.

"The Defendant's explanation of the second shot is while Martin was lying prone on his face about five minutes after she heard him fall, she wanted to walk past him in order to place a phone call to her daughter. Consequently, she went and got a pillow, put it over his head, aimed at the pillow and fired a shot through the pillow, putting a bullet in his head. The second shot was highly likely to be the fatal shot—the doctor, of course, called it a *coup de grâce*. The second element is that she killed him knowingly. The evidence you have heard on that element is that the Defendant knew she shot Martin—twice. She said so.

She intended to shoot him the first time and she offered a self-serving explanation for her so-called motive.

"Incidentally, of course, as you well know, motive is not an element of the offense, but it is evidence in this case of intentionality. The fatal shot, the second shot, was intentionally inflicted, and since she told Officer Burton about it, she knew she was shooting the victim in the head. A bullet through the brains is almost certain to cause death. That's fairly common knowledge.

"The angle of the shot and the entrance of the wound on the crown of the head and exit wound between the chin and throat is consistent to the gun being parallel to the floor, which is where the victim fell the first time. So that's a bullet in the brain of a man that is lying down, not moving. The second shot can fairly well be inferred to be an intentional execution shot.

"Count two is obstruction of justice. The first element of that charge, Your Honor, is that the Defendant did, on or about the 28th or 29th of July, 2006, alter, destroy, or conceal or remove anything. The Defendant acknowledged she removed the clothing she had worn when killing her husband. She also removed any trace evidence by hosing herself off prior to dressing in different clothing. She acknowledged that she removed the pillow which had a bullet hole and blood on it, along with the body of her victim. All of these were taken from the crime scene.

"The second element is that she did this with the intent to hinder, delay, or prevent the investigation, the apprehension, the prosecution, conviction, or punishment of any person regarding conduct that constitutes a first degree felony, to wit: murder. The clearest indication of her intent regarding this is her digging of a hole to conceal the evidence. She dug a grave in the back of her house and dragged the body and pillow back there, obviously to place them in the ground to put dirt on top. Nobody else got invited to any graveside services. One may infer that such was because she wanted to stick the body and the pillow in the hole in the back of the house and make sure the hole was beneath the pond, making it less likely to be discovered.

"Further, the fact that she chose not to call 911 until the next day further evidences her intent to at least delay the investigation. Because this didn't occur until after she had that conversation with Lake, who told her to turn herself in. If the standard is whether or not Your Honor should issue an arrest warrant for this, the amount of evidence you have heard today is about 20,000 leagues beyond that. I don't have anything else on this, unless Your Honor does have any questions."

Judge Eyre: "No, Mr. Wims."

Mr. Wims: "Thank you."

Judge Eyre: "Mr. Slavens?"

Mr. Slavens: "Well, I want to point out initially in this matter, Your Honor, that I don't think the State has allowed any presumptions from this Court to take it out of manslaughter to the first degree. I think that they've only established that she recklessly caused the death of another."

Judge Eyre: "You don't think shooting somebody in the head, point-blank, is an intentional act?"

Mr. Slavens: "That complicates things. I understand that, and I think my argument would be better if it was just the first shot."

Judge Eyre: "Thank you. Mr. Wims?"

Mr. Wims: "Very briefly, Your Honor—if you want to go with the self-defense theory, her first shot self-defensed him in the back, and her second shot self-defensed him through the brains."

*   *   *

Judge Eyre: "The Court does find, based upon the evidence, that there is some believable evidence to the level of probable cause as currently established by our Supreme Court, that definition for bindover, that the Defendant, Ms. Alden, did cause the death of Martin Sessions. There's no question about that. And that the Court does find that there is credible evidence that she did so intentionally or knowingly, or did so acting under circumstances that was clearly dangerous to human life, that being that she did shoot him twice, and either shot could eventually have caused the death. As to counts two and three, there is clearly evidence as to the obstruction of justice charge, that she did remove certain items of evidence: the pillow is the main thing I see."

Mr. Slavens: "So that's what it's bound over on—the pillow?"

Judge Eyre: "Well, the pillow, and also that she tried to conceal the body, and she cleaned herself up—she removed her clothing and hosed herself down. Those are all basis for obstruction of justice. And there is evidence, believable evidence, that she did move the body—disturbing it. And therefore it binds all three charges over for arraignment. Though the other things you raise, Mr. Slavens, are in my belief rightfully for the trier of fact to make those determinations, not for the magistrate at the time of the bindover. I think that at least in my mind as to the evidence that I've heard, there is sufficient evidence to bind it over. So is it the desire of your client to be arraigned at this time?"

Mr. Slavens: "May I have a moment with my client? . . . She's prepared to be arraigned today, Your Honor."

*   *   *

The preliminary hearing was over.

Now the real decisions would begin.

But as the smoke cleared from the courtroom battle, one thing became painfully clear. Carole's cries of helplessness while she made it nearly impossible to help her were beginning to drive everyone crazy.

One never-ending problem involved James Slavens, the glassy-eyed local defense attorney who had been appointed as Carole's public defender. Slavens made his living handling divorce, family law, adoption, and criminal defense cases. His contract with the County meant he was required to represent the County's indigent defendants—which included, in this case, Carole Alden.

But in an ironic twist, Slavens had previously defended another indigent client for the County—Marty Sessions. In fact, Slavens had defended Marty *against Carole.*

This created a set of possibly mixed loyalties for James Slavens, which in turn posed an important legal question that ultimately went all the way up to the Utah State Supreme Court. Could a defense attorney fairly represent a client when he had previously opposed her in court? More ticklish still, could he fairly represent her when he had previously opposed her while defending the very client she ended up killing?

Carole, for one, told supporters in no uncertain terms that she was adamantly opposed to having Slavens represent her. It was, she stated, a "clear cut conflict of interest."[6]

But the record shows that it was not Carole who was attempting to get Slavens off the case. It was her *adversaries*—the prosecutors. Slavens, prosecutors felt, could have inside knowledge of Marty Sessions that he'd gained during the domestic violence proceedings. This could give Carole an advantage if the case were to come to trial. It could also be grounds for challenge on appeal. After all, if Alden were convicted, then she could complain that Slavens should have been kicked off the case because he had conflicting loyalties and duties to Marty, his earlier client. Or she could complain that Slavens had knowledge from Marty that could have been used on cross-examination but wasn't because he received the knowledge in confidentiality during the attorney-client relationship with Marty. Slavens himself notes that, in all honesty, he didn't have inside knowledge about Marty Sessions—in fact, he couldn't even remember whether he'd had direct contact with Marty, since the plea in abeyance had been handled through intermediaries. But what Slavens *did* have was an insider's knowledge of Millard County—he could have been counted on to nudge the jury selection process in favor of jurors who might be more sympathetic to Carole. And by virtue of his previous work in his court-room adversary's position as local prosecutor, and his own inimitable courtroom technique, Slavens was more formidable as an opponent than most outsiders realized. But whatever the State's objections, machinations related to the prosecutors' losing battle to remove Slavens delayed the trial for months.[7]

All this could have been avoided if Carole had simply waived the conflict of interest, or, contrarily, if she'd firmly stated she thought there *was* a conflict of interest. In her many letters to supporters, Carole complained bitterly and continuously about her lawyer.[8] (One retains the impression that anyone, had he or she been Carole's lawyer, would have been equally maligned.) She wrote that she felt "victimized all over again" by the justice system.[9] But in court, she'd refuse to answer either way about whether she wanted Slavens to represent her. When asked to answer a point-blank question from Judge Eyre about whether she felt a conflict existed in Slavens's representation of her, Carole replied, "I see no conflict from my end of things." She then continued, "I understand your concerns about other people might— seeing it as a conflict. So I'm kind of open minded about the whole thing, as far as what the Court decides is best."[10]

Carole thus neatly preserved her ability to complain after the fact, on appeal, that she never really waived the conflict. Prosecutor Mike Wims would later say, "She was essentially trying to have the truth about her lawyer both ways, depending on who she was talking to and what day it was. There was a time when Pat Nolan and I told the judge about it in chambers, but the judge said he wouldn't do anything about it."[11]

CHAPTER 27

MARTY'S GOOD SIDE

**It is not just that what we find determines the
nature of the attention we accord to it, but that
the attention we pay to anything also determines
what it is we find.**

—IAIN MCGILCHRIST, *The Master and His Emissary*[1]

Surprisingly, among those who refuse to malign Carole Alden is
Anna Ruttenbur—Marty Sessions's oldest daughter.[2] She quietly
asserts: "I don't want to say Carole's a bad person. That's not my style.
My dad wouldn't have wanted us to be hateful towards her. He wasn't
that way himself. He would have wanted us to forgive her."

Unlike Carole's children, who apparently based affection for their
parent or stepparent on Carole's own vacillating moods, Marty's children look back dispassionately on their father's relationships. Both of
Marty's daughters were happy for him when he found Carole. The
relationship seemed a little odd in that they thought Carole wasn't

really Marty's type—her earth-mother, aging hippie demeanor was very different from that of other women Marty admired, dated, or, for that matter, married. "She was different," noted Edee, "but she was nice." Although Edee liked Carole, she remembers being flummoxed during her first visit to Marty and Carole's house. Beside the front door was a dead goat under a tarp. Edee was surprised at the house's lack of cleanliness—Marty had never lived in such disarray or filth. Edee was even more surprised when, heading to the bathroom for the first time, she discovered a baby goat being housed there. (The mother goat had had complications while giving birth, Carole told her, so she'd had to put it to sleep.) But to Edee, the household seemed a happy one. Edee's sister Anna also liked Carole—she allowed "Whooshy," her then five-year-old daughter, to spend a week with Grandpa and his wife. Whooshy loved her time there and begged to go back.

"Anybody who knew my Dad liked him," says Anna. "He was outgoing, soft-spoken, friendly, kind-hearted, very smart. . . . His biggest downfall was his addiction. *Everything* would have been different if it wasn't for that. He knew that, too. He was a genuinely good human being—his addiction didn't make him into a bad person."

Indeed, odd as it may seem, given Marty's very real flaws, it's difficult to find any person who actually knew Marty, save Carole and her offspring, who has anything bad to say about him. Travis Jones, for example, owned a picture-framing and sign shop in Delta where Marty used to work. Jones told the *Tribune* reporter that Marty "was a great guy. He was one of those guys who had finally learned all of his lessons."[3] Similarly, a nineteen-year-old coworker of Marty's, Jessie Coons, viewed him as "a 'really cool' man, one to whom he looked as a grandfather." According to Coons, Marty "was distressed about his relationship with Carole, who he believed was seeing someone else. He was really in love with Carole and wanted to work it out."[4]

*   *   *

Russ Crook, a lanky, longtime Millard County resident, had met Marty and Carole a number of times while working at the livestock auction. He recalls:

> Marty seemed like a nice guy. He was polite. Everybody liked to visit with him. He was quite serious, though, and good with livestock. I've never seen him abusive. Marty and Carole bought sheep and goats—he knew how to handle 'em. If you abuse sheep they'll run together and put their heads together. I never saw any evidence that Marty's sheep were abused.
>
> People often don't know how to unload sheep. It's kind of funny how you do it—you have to crawl in on your hands and knees and pant like a dog. The sheep get scared and get off the truck, but you haven't hurt 'em. Marty knew how to do that—he handled animals real well. She was good with animals, too.
>
> They came to auction together all the time. They'd sit in front so they could see what they were buying. They'd bring fat lambs back and sell them here.[5]

*   *   *

Joe Trujillo, now in his mid-seventies, lives in the oldest house in the valley, about three-quarters of a mile from where Marty and Carole lived.[6] In sparsely populated South Tract, this made the Trujillos virtually Marty and Carole's next-door neighbors. Joe had noticed Carole and Marty when they were first moving in and had gladly lent a hand. The appreciative Marty offered to help Joe with his computer needs. A friendship was born. Joe gave Carole some chickens and peacocks and helped them out on occasion with hay. "She had lots and *lots* of animals," he says. "Too many. But they were well cared for." As an old-timer, Joe was shocked to see that Carole had tattoos. "Guys have tattoos—that's pretty common. But it's strange to see a gal with tattoos all over her body. Maybe it was okay—just stood out as unusual." Joe was referring to Carole's large "Andy Bristow" tattoo, some two inches tall, which ran from shoulder to shoulder on her upper back. A second tattoo was a large, ornate symbol on her deltoid. A third, smaller tattoo on her breast—the name of a friend—was one she'd done herself as a teenager in New Zealand.

Joe's own spread was a large one, and he went out to check on his cows around six to seven times a day, even late at night. Moreover, Joe's house overlooked the road from the Sessions house to the town of Delta. So Joe, perhaps more than anyone, had a sense of the comings and goings of the Sessions household. Carole, Joe noticed, came and went as she pleased—often making two to three trips a day to town in her red Jeep. Marty, on the other hand, was home most of the time, since he had no driver's license and no car. Marty didn't let that make him a shut-in, though—every few days Marty would get out his bicycle and ride the ten miles to town to get his cigarettes and Captain Morgan.

Joe often offered Marty a ride when passing on the way to town, and Marty would regale him with stories of his proud Native American heritage. Joe had an army background himself, but he doesn't recall Marty ever talking about the military. Marty "liked to take a nip or two. He'd offer it to me, but I told him my drinking days were done. He never acted drunk, though."

One odd incident remained in Joe's memory. That year's hunting season was fast approaching, and Joe had suddenly realized that he had to apply for an elk license that day or he'd miss the deadline. So Joe came over to his friend Marty's house, and the pair sat together at a computer in the master bedroom as Marty pulled up the web page. As the two were talking, the phone rang. Marty answered it—and the caller's response was to hang up.

At that point, Joe recalls, Marty hung up and stared at the phone. He shook his head, as if he wanted to say something, but he also didn't want to. Finally, he turned to Joe and said, "Joe, I think this wife of mine is out gallivanting around with another man."

"What do you mean? No way! You're just listening to gossip," Joe replied. "Who'd you hear that from?"

"Oh, no—it's not gossip. She told me so herself."

"No—that can't be!"

"She showed me the key to his apartment. She says she goes there to wash his dishes and clean his sheets."

As the pair sat, thinking things over and finally getting back to the business at hand—the elk permit—the phone rang again. Again, there was no one on the other end of the line.

Marty shook his head—Joe could see that he was thinking about whether to say something. "Ever heard of a guy named Allen Lake?" Marty finally asked.

Joe says he remembers thinking: "Well, of course. I've known Allen since he was a kid. *Allen Lake?* It didn't make sense. But later I realized that I'd been seeing Allen around my land, out in the fields. I'd thought he was hunting rabbit or pheasant or something. But maybe he had other reasons to be around here. Allen came by to visit me a couple days after the killing—a friend dropped him off. It was cold, but Allen was in his bare feet. Allen told me the night of the killing, he'd woken up with a hangover, come out to get something to drink, and found Carole on his couch. He was pretty surprised."

Some in Delta thought something was going on between Carole and Allen Lake, although Carole herself would deny any relationship. But there is no denying the note that Carole Alden left on Allen Lake's table the morning after she shot Marty Sessions.

You can call . . . anytime now without anyone getting uptight. He's gone. I really need a friend I can trust right now.[7]

Allen's shocked reaction, of course, had been to instantly call the police.

Joe himself was also shocked when the killing occurred. "Marty was a good guy. To get herself out of the hole, Carole lied and lied."

"Marty be mean to Carole? Oh, God, no." Joe says emphatically to the question.

*   *   *

Even Carole's family had nice things to say about Marty. One relative recalls camping with Jason and Emily at a lovely KOA Campground in Fillmore.[8] Carole and Marty came to the campsite to have supper. Jason was exploring in a nearby field and brought back a rock. Marty calmly and gently explained that if one took something from the earth one must then give something back. He was a gentleman toward Carole's parents, who by all accounts liked him, finding something spiritual about his way of talking and thinking.

Marty's stepsister Rosemary Salyer has fond memories of her big brother, the son of a man Rosemary's mother had married. Marty was some twenty years older than her, but the two kept in contact—visiting on occasion and exchanging e-mails. Rosemary had e-mailed Marty just a few days before he died; she had been hoping they'd be able to get together for dinner, since Marty had mentioned he was moving out of Carole's house.

Rosemary has a clear-eyed perspective on her brother's drug-addicted faults, but she also knew him to be a caring and warm man. In court, Salyer had referred to the callous shooting of her brother as "cold-blooded" and said the victims included Sessions's two daughters and nine grandchildren.[9] "There's a thing called divorce that you can easily go get," Salyer told a reporter.[10]

At it turned out, the twenty-fifth of July—three days before Marty was killed—was Edee Sessions's birthday. Edee was disheartened when her father didn't call, so her husband e-mailed Marty explaining how disappointed she was.[11] Two days later, on July 27, Marty responded. He was very sorry he hadn't contacted Edee, he wrote, but he had bigger problems: Carole was doing a lot of lying to him, he explained, and he thought she was seeing someone else. Marty mentioned that he had moved out of Carole's house and was living with a friend.

Two days later, Marty was killed. Edee immediately turned the e-mail her husband had received over to police. But meanwhile, both Anna and Edee were shocked—their father's death seemed an out-of-the-blue repetition of Susie Sessions's horrific murder. What was just as shocking was learning how Carole was beginning to portray their father. Constantly angry? Violent toward her? Sexually abusive? This just *wasn't* their dad. At least not the person they knew before he lived with Carole.

"He didn't *have* anger problems, not that I ever knew of," says Edee Sessions. And indeed, the police themselves, with their understanding of Marty's lengthy criminal history, said that Marty "wasn't violent—he was never a fisticuffs kind of guy." When asked about Carole's accusations of Marty's torture and abuse, Edee answers,

> I just don't believe it. I don't believe my dad laid a hand on her. I understand he could have raised his voice and mentally abused her—but really, I can't even say that's true, because he never did that to us kids, nor did I ever see him do that to any of his wives. I mean, even with my step-mom, they never fought, ever. If they argued, they'd go in the bedroom and argue. You'd never see it happen in front of us kids.
>
> I know Carole and my dad had issues with her kids—they argued about that. My dad was big on chores, or if you walked out of a room, he was like "turn the light off." But I don't believe he hit her, that he abused her like she says. No way. For as big a prison record as my dad had, there was no violence and no abuse. You won't find it there if you look. That just wasn't my dad's style.

Anna adds: "My dad loved Carole's kids—he was good to them."

The couple also took issue in that Marty had *always* loved animals. Even as a young man, he'd refused to go out trapping coyotes with the others, despite the fact that there was good money in it, because he couldn't stand to see the animals in pain. Like his father, Marty had a special love of cats; he'd spend hours high on *chiva* playing with his cat, Booper. "I cannot see my brother ever hurting an animal," says Denny. "I just can't imagine him changing—suddenly revealing a different side. That just wasn't him *at all*."[12]

Both Edee and Denny spoke with Marty's third wife, Debbie McClain, to try to see whether she'd ever experienced hidden abuse at Marty's hands. "She said my dad was a lot of things," noted Edee. "But he wasn't a wife beater. Ever. If he had been, she wouldn't have married him." Debbie had known Marty for years—in fact, she had been best friends with Marty's first wife. Perhaps predictably, despite his promises, after Debbie and Marty married, Marty resumed his drug use. In an effort to help him, Debbie turned Marty in to the parole board several times. Although he was returned to prison as a consequence, Debbie told Denny that Marty had never threatened her because of what she'd done—in fact, he'd never laid a hand on her. Although the pair divorced as a result of Marty's drug use, they remained friends. (Debbie herself died a year after Marty's death.)

"There was a time when Slavens—Carole's lawyer—and Carole were coming around trying to get my dad's records, saying he was a bad person and maybe this should have happened to him," says Edee. "But the judge threw that out. Regardless of my dad's past and regardless of what happened between him and Carole, he didn't deserve to die. He was a human being, too."

"I *never* heard my dad raise his voice in front of my step-mom," echoes Anna. "That's the thing that's hardest for me to accept. Abuse doesn't just happen. People don't just turn into monsters when they've never showed that kind of behavior before in their lives. Carole is not the victim she paints herself as. My dad's life was not only taken—he was cheated. Nobody ever heard about the good things. My dad was a good person—he had a huge heart." Anna's voice breaks as she remembers, "He was so happy when I told him I was pregnant. 'I'm gonna be a grandpa,' he said. Then he started to cry. *That* was the person he was—not the monster that Carole has made him out to be."

Denny concludes, "On March 8, 1994, I last stepped out of prison. I made myself a vow that I would never, ever come back. But next year, I am going to break that vow. I'm going to make myself go stand in front of that parole board. I want to make sure they understand that Carole Alden got away with murder. I don't believe in the death penalty—neither did Marty. But I think she should do every day of the time she got. And I'm going back to prison one more time to help make sure that happens." He chuckles, acknowledging his uncanny resemblance to his brother. "I hope she thinks I'm his ghost."[13]

*   *   *

Perhaps most interesting of all are the assault and domestic violence charges Slavens had defended Marty against some six months before his death. Distraught after yet another argument, Marty was ultimately charged for throwing an object at Carole as she and the children were leaving the house. Carole had driven away afterward and called 911 from a nursing home.

When deputies arrived at the house, Marty was gone, leaving a note: "I'm tired of the cheatin' wife who wants more than she is willing to put forth and doesn't have the courage to tell me she doesn't want me because I'm disabled. I have no choice but to end it NOW!"[14]

The object Marty threw, as it turned out, was a pillow.

CHAPTER 28

HOW LITTLE
WE KNOW ABOUT
PSYCHIATRIC DISORDERS

**Believe more deeply. Hold your face up to the
light, even though for the moment you do not see.**

—BILL WILSON,
cofounder Alcoholics Anonymous[1]

Few laypeople realize how little we actually know about the underpinnings of psychiatric disorders, writes Daniel Carlat, MD, in *Unhinged: The Trouble with Psychiatry—A Doctor's Revelations about a Profession in Crisis.*[2] Carlat, who trained at Harvard Medical School and is currently on the faculty of Tufts University, has been a practicing psychiatrist for fifteen years.

He notes: "In virtually all of the psychiatric disorders—including depression, schizophrenia, bipolar disorder, and anxiety disorders—the shadow of our ignorance overwhelms the few dim lights of our knowledge."[3]

We do know that certain neurological conditions carry with them a propensity for deceit. Psychopaths, for example, have a glib ability to lie that is somehow part and parcel of their strangely different neurological makeup.[4] (Psychopaths seem to have notable deficits in the right side of the brain—the side that allows for empathy.)[5] Those with borderline personality disorder share this deceitfulness and also have an uncanny ability to manipulate.[6] This latter disorder is known to be a disorder of "attachment"—that is, a failure to form an effective connection with caregivers in early childhood.[7] Borderline personality disorder, too, is thought to be a disorder of the empathetic right hemisphere.[8]

The problem with antisocial and borderline syndromes is that embedded within the dysfunction is the conviction that "nothing's wrong with *me*—it's everyone else who's crazy!" This belief, especially when held by those who show more extreme traits of narcissism, makes it difficult to be open to psychological help. Even if forcibly placed in front of a psychiatrist—in a prison setting, for example—people with these disorders will naturally dissemble, projecting their own faults onto everyone but themselves.

Carole, for example, still insists that when someone is outright abusive in how he treats her—for example, even if he rapes her in a drunken stupor—her first instinct is always to attempt to help that person. She gets closer so as to assist him; if she doesn't, she feels great guilt. In many of her other observations, Carole often alludes to her sense that her problem has always been that she's just too nice. However, many who know Carole well are extraordinarily fearful of her, citing her propensity for publicly smearing those who offend her, her tendency to involve the police or child services in any matter that doesn't go her way, her vitriolic temper when crossed, and of course, her ability to turn her children against others.

In Carole's case, people often found that what she said at any given time seemed to make sense. It was only later, after reflection, that a person might realize something was odd—things didn't add up. For example, Richard Senft, Carole's first husband, explained that it wasn't until the marriage broke up that he realized the extent to which he'd been lied to and manipulated. "It may be that her radar for prospective long-term mates guided her not just to men who were basically decent but also to men who were particularly obtuse about pathological behavior, men who just couldn't imagine it and thus had no defenses against it," notes Joe Carroll, Curators' Professor of English at the University of Missouri, St. Louis.[9] "They were like the birds on remote islands, never before visited by humans, who could be knocked over by hand, since they had no instinctive fear of sailors out for an easy meal."[10]

In their classic book on borderline personality disorder, *Stop Walking on Eggshells*, Randi Kreger and Paul Mason describe a similar reaction—it is the "light bulb effect," when deceit and manipulation finally make sense because they are suddenly seen as purposeful activity propelled by an underlying personality disorder.[11] But Carole may well have not been alone in her misbehavior. Marty Sessions's addictions had caused problems in all of his marriages, even though Susie Sessions had clearly found in him the love of her life. Carole Alden and Marty Sessions may well have one-upped each other in their interactions—each feeling justified for the pain inflicted by virtue of the previous pain inflicted by the other.

In any case, one person who has suffered from decades of Carole's manipulations says: "It's not like Carole gets up one morning and says to herself, 'I need $100, so I'm going to go con some kindhearted Mormon.' It's much more complex than that. Carole's got a very rational intelligence that rides hand-in-hand with a deeply emotional irrationality. Unfortunately, the rational part of her brain is subservient to the nutty part. The nutty part makes a decision, and then the rational part says, 'How can I make this happen?'"

*   *   *

Carole's claim that Marty had pierced her genitals took her case to a new, lurid level—as evinced by the "Wife Kills 'Depraved' Hubby Who Made Her Wear Chastity Belt" *National Enquirer* headline.[12] Carole's theatrics—lowering her head to the defense table and sobbing

Carole Alden lowered her head to the defense table and
sobbed at the mention of Marty's intentions involving the
chastity belt. But this only set the stage for a further bombshell.

in the courtroom at mention of Marty's intentions involving a chastity
belt—took the tale even further over the top.[13]

Although Carole said she'd soft-pedaled her accusations against
Marty in the days immediately following his death, the stories she ultimately told diverged from known facts and also would have required
superhuman abilities on her part. For example, Carole had pointed out
to Deputy Josie Greathouse a total of four genital piercings, two on
each side of her labia. At that time, Carole had said that Marty had
intended to put a chastity belt through the holes, but he had never done
so. In a later retelling of the story, however, she claimed to have twelve
piercings (six on each side of her labia), all slowly done by Marty over
a period of six hours, with her passing out multiple times from the pain
and Marty shocking her back awake with alligator clips attached to her
sensitive parts.[14] She was then sewn completely shut for weeks,
almost dying of septicemia.

Such confabulation is typically seen in personality-disordered individuals—most prominently, those with antisocial and borderline personality disorders.[15] Whether sadomasochists show higher rates of personality disorders is hotly debated—a vocal group protests inclusion of such atypical sexual behavior in the psychologists' catalog of mental disorders (the *DSM*), saying that it discriminates against those who practice alternative sexual lifestyles.[16] (Despite or because of its clear association with forensic populations, the study of those who practice sadomasochism has long been hampered by advocacy groups who seek to destigmatize the practices.)

But is it instead, as one study perceptively asks, that those who "misbehave" sexually are simply *generally* misbehaving people whose misbehavior also shows up in the sexual domain?[17] There is little question that among prison populations, sexual sadism and related behaviors are found in far higher percentages than in the normal population. But the jury is still out. In any case, although nobody's quite been able to deduce a "distinct neurobiological substrate or correlate of sexual deviancy," quirky brain function is definitely affiliated with a higher incidence of deviant sexual behaviors.[18] Clearly neurotransmitters and sex hormones will play an important role in clarifying our understanding of sadomasochistic tendencies.[19] (A 2006 study came to the surprising conclusion that power—not the giving and receiving of pain—lies at the core of sadomasochism.)[20]

In regard to Carole's sadomasochistic tendencies, there was another bombshell in the case—one that never exploded. A local man eventually admitted that Carole had proudly showed him her genital piercings, and a second local man was also thought to have seen similar behavior. This exhibitionism, far from the sobbing, ashamed demeanor that Carole showed in court, demonstrated that Carole was hardly the unwilling victim she made herself out to be and also provided clues as to her manipulative side. If prosecutors had learned of this development, they could have used this knowledge to devastate a key element of Carole's defense.

But prosecutors remained unaware of this fact.

*   *   *

So how does this all relate to Carole Alden's seemingly formative crisis—her possible molestation by her father?

Carole's old confidante, Penny Packer, would later say: "Carole never said anything about her father molesting her when I knew her, when she was in junior high school. And I think she would have told me. She didn't mention anything about it until she was a full adult. She never came out and said in black and white what he did—it was always left up to the conjecture of the person she was telling. She'd use subtle innuendo to insinuate he'd been sexually abusive, but she'd never come right out and say. Same as at the massage parlor. I've known Carole's parents and friends. I just can't see it happening."[21]

One person who knew Carole well when she was in her late teens and early twenties said she made vague accusations of abuse about her father even then, never supplying any details. At first Carole was believable, he said, but gradually, during the course of getting to know the Alden family, he began to doubt her story.

It is important to note, however, that sexual abuse during childhood may lead to borderline personality disorder—"the more severe the abuse was, the more repeatedly it occurred, the closer the person was to the victim, and the more they were threatened to be 'silent,' the sicker they are," writes Blaise Aguirre, a psychiatrist who specializes in understanding borderline personality disorder in adolescents.[22] But on the other side of the equation, those with borderline personality disorder commonly make false allegations of abuse. Emotional needs—and the resulting revenge when such needs are not being met—are common motives in such cases. Forensic psychiatrist Richard Hall notes that such false allegations "occur with some regularity," particularly from those with substantial traits of borderline personality disorder.[23] Hall urges investigators to consider whether the accuser exhibits a pattern of making other false accusations; if such a pattern is present, the allegation is more difficult to take seriously. The mix of victims and those only crying wolf can make it very hard to respond sensitively and accurately in this realm.

Randi Kreger, author of *The Essential Family Guide to Borderline Personality Disorder*, cautions, however, that the behavior of those with borderline personality disorder varies so much that generalizations should be avoided. Kreger notes that the word *abuse* is vague, and that those with borderline personality disorder may be "splitting and seeing their childhood and parents as all bad."[24] While those with borderline personality disorder do outright lie, their "mental and emotional disturbances can also give them firm beliefs about things that may not really be true."[25]

When false allegations are made against virtually all available evidence, we swing back again to ideas related to left-hemisphere dominance—the resolute insistence in one's own version of a story, facts be damned.

Carole began sharing her vague insinuations about her father with family members when she was in her late twenties and thirties—often at times when she was at her angriest and most vengeful. Recollections of her subtle innuendos still leave a sense of frustration among the other Aldens. How do you talk with someone who makes such an insinuation, however faint, and then refuses to speak further about it—shrugs it away with a "just kidding" sort of air?

Both Carole's parents remained close to their other children, none of whom showed Carole's over-the-top teenage angst. Her parents couldn't help but hope that once Carole passed into her twenties, she would level off and become like her siblings. But Carole's antagonism for her father simply intensified, sometimes reaching irrational levels.

For example, not long after Carole's first marriage, women with babies who could not tolerate cow's milk would sometimes stop by to see if they could obtain milk from Carole's little goat herd, which was clearly visible from the highway. But rather than discuss whether goat's milk was available, Carole would sometimes take the opportunity to inappropriately change the topic of conversation to describe to these strangers what a jerk her father was.

This type of irrational "splitting" behavior is yet another aspect of borderline personality disorder. With splitting, another person is seen as either all good or all bad, with nothing in between. In the case of her father, Carole frequently painted him as all bad. Indeed, this type of black-and-white thinking pervaded many of her interactions. Carole's husbands and lovers were all good, at least until they disapproved of some aspect of Carole's behavior—at which point they became all bad.

By the time of Carole's marriage to Marty, her relationship with her father had settled into an uneasy truce. Their conversations were kept to a minimum—if Carole called home and her father picked up, for example, he'd say hello and then pass the phone immediately to her mother. At the time of Marty's homicide, her father was recovering from a bout of cancer, which had arrived like an anvil falling from the sky onto this virile, healthy outdoorsman.

Marty's killing upset the silent truce between father and daughter. They began to have heated phone conversations—the substance of the conversation apparently surrounding Carole's intention to tell the court that she had been molested as a child. Carole's father was devastated. Within two months he was dead—not of cancer, but of a stroke. Within three days of his death, Carole had created an intricate fabric rainbow trout in his honor.

And she charged ahead with her plans to accuse her father. Carole's mother, weighed down with grief at the loss of her husband of forty-eight years, was blindsided. She could see no reason for Carole to go on with her accusations. Her father could not defend himself—what would be the point? Carole replied to the effect that the judge might be more favorable to her if these accusations were made. She never explained exactly what her accusations were or what she was going to say, but she vowed her charges were true. Later Carole would vilify her family for their lack of support, telling others that her family had actually denied to investigators that anything had happened. Of course, from her family's perspective, there was good reason for the denial.

One investigator who has heard the tapes of Carole's external phone messages simply shakes his head. "To listen to all those phone

calls and to hear how everything was always someone else's fault. . . .
She always made everything all about her, her loss." Another officer
says: "I was stunned. Just stunned. In the first phone call Carole had
with her family after her father's death, there was not one word about
her father, or a single question about how the family was holding up.
It was always *me*, *me*, *me*. That was the way all her phone calls were.
Her plight. *Her* future. Nothing else mattered to her. The inhumanity
of it wouldn't go out of me for days."

Square at the crossing of the most pernicious of personality disorders—borderline and antisocial—lies narcissism, that most insidious
and least understood of traits.

LEAPFROGGING LOGIC

At the National Institutes of Health, Carolyn Zahn-Waxler has spent
decades researching questions that focus on environmental factors and
characteristics of children that lead to anxiety, depression, and aggression. She has worked to understand characteristics such as a difficult
temperament or personality, impulsivity, and negative emotionality;
she has also studied the effect of emotional factors such as harsh discipline and parental rejection. She conducts longitudinal research, following families over time. This makes it possible to learn how a
child's inborn personality traits interweave with parental treatment to
influence how problems develop. To do this, she compares children
from high-risk environments (for example, children with depressed
mothers) to those in low-risk environments (children whose mothers
are psychologically healthy). She has a good understanding of the
methodology necessary to gain a scientifically grounded perspective.
Her experience could prove useful in establishing more solid science
to help us understand the environmental factors and characteristics of
people that eventually lead to domestic violence.

The best way to truly sort out the problem of understanding battered women, Carolyn Zahn-Waxler suggests, would involve con-

structing a long-term study of women who vary in risk for being battered.[26] (Technically, this would be known as a "longitudinal pre-post design" study.) Researchers would assess the preexisting characteristics of the women in the study, including any penchant for deception or violence as well as their personality traits and problems. It would also include similar assessments of their partners. These assessments would be done both *before* and *after* the battering or family violence situation. In theory, this method would allow everyone to gain a clear understanding of battered women. Unfortunately, such an exercise could be done only as a thought experiment. Unlike in Zahn-Waxler's research with children, the women and men who would be involved in this study would already have had such diverse life experiences that it would be impossible to obtain adequate measures of what the women (and men) were like prior to their relationship with a violent partner.

What researchers could do instead, Zahn-Waxler observes, is an in-depth study of women who have been battered to examine the ways in which they compare and differ from one another. This should be done in conjunction with a comparison group whose members have never experienced battering. (There are also battered men, so genders could be reversed in this discussion.)

Once an in-depth study was done, the women could be sorted into different groups depending on their circumstances and psychological functioning. These classifications would not be based solely on self-reports but would include direct observations and assessments by others who know the women—both clinicians and family members. Poring over the results, researchers could then make a reasoned estimate of the proportion of women prone to victimization as a consequence of the qualities they themselves brought into the situation. This would be the golden stage—the time when an in-depth understanding of the full range of battered women could be developed. What accounts for who puts themselves in this situation and who doesn't? What is the difference between women who experience violence but do not strike back with violence and women who do?

As Lenore Walker has implied, some of these women would be

normal people who simply made an unlucky choice. Others would not initially have seen problematic traits in their partners because of qualities they themselves valued that also helped them meet their own needs. (They might, for example, have been attracted to a person who is dominant, assertive, and liked to be in charge. These positive-sounding traits can become aversive as a couple gets to know each other better and the violent partner becomes more domineering and controlling.) There are probably important variations within this latter group, which might include women who are normal but who are not good at reading others' emotions, as well as women who are immature; those who don't want to see what is clear to others; and those with mild personality problems.

Then there would be a group whose members are victim-prone because of preexisting personality problems that encourage violent partners to engage in aggression. Among this group would be women who would trigger abuse via their own antisocial behavior toward their partner. There may be women who actually make things up to explain their own violence. We might not like to admit that such women (or men) could exist, because it could stigmatize the many innocent women who unwittingly find themselves in a battering situation. But to truly comprehend battering in an objective manner, it's important to understand the people involved in situations where battering is claimed. As Linda Mills points out in her masterful *Violent Partners*: "The popular conception of domestic violence, in which the female victim lives in terror of her controlling abuser, only represents a small fraction of the American couples struggling with violence today."[27]

The supreme importance of all of this research is in how it could help women understand their own inclinations, as well as those of their partner, and thus help alert them to danger before they get into an abusive situation. Moreover, it could help women see that they don't have to repeat bad choices once they have been in one of these relationships. Far from being research that "blamed the victim," it would instead be helping women to avoid becoming a victim in the first place. No longer viewed as hapless victims, women could ask themselves those vital questions: "What parts do you have control over? What can you become more aware of so as not to choose, or continue to participate in, this?"

As it stands now, battered woman syndrome has leapfrogged its lack of scientific underpinnings and is ensconced in laws in most states, including Utah, where it may be used as a defense in court cases in which women have assaulted or murdered male partners. Use of this defense implies that the defendant is a "normal" woman whose problems were created solely by her violent male partner—the defense says it is these partner-induced problems that led the woman to injure or kill her partner in self-defense. But in all probability, many situations are far more complicated or nuanced than that simple defense implies. In fact, not only might Carole and Marty's situation be full of shades of gray, but it may well be that Carole Alden's preexisting personality traits played a role in her killing her husband.[28]

David Faigman, John F. Digardi Distinguished Professor of Law and director of the University of California Hastings Consortium on Law, Science, and Health Policy, could have been describing the Carole Alden case when he summarized the situation with battered woman syndrome:

> The amount of research that actually exists to back the claims of expert witnesses who testify on the battered woman syndrome makes cold fusion look as solid as the second law of thermodynamics. . . . At the start . . . the hypothesis had little more support than the clinical impressions of a single researcher. Five years later, Walker published a second book that promised a more thorough investigation of the hypothesis.[29] In fact, however, this book was little more than a patchwork of pseudoscientific methods employed to confirm a hypothesis that the researchers never seriously doubted.[30] Indeed, the 1984 book would provide an excellent case study for psychology graduate students on how *not* to do empirical research. Yet, either because they shared the researchers' political agenda or did not look at or understand the science, judges welcomed the battered woman syndrome into their courts. Increasingly, however, legal commentators are real-

izing that this original conception was without empirical foundation and, perhaps more troubling, inimical to the political ideology originally supporting it. In short, in the law's effort to use science to make good policy, it is now obvious that the battered woman syndrome provides neither good science nor good policy. . . .

[B]ecause the syndrome has no empirical basis and thus might apply in any case, many defendants claim it when the facts of their cases fall well outside any reasonable conception of self-defense. For example, Lenore Walker sought to testify when a defendant hired a hit man for $10,000 to kill her husband. These abuses cast long shadows and undermine the effort to make the law more responsive to the true challenges of domestic violence.[31]

Faigman wrote those words in 1999, but as Linda Mills notes in the introduction to *Violent Partners*, as the decade has passed, the situation hasn't changed.

In 2008, if a woman is hit by her husband and calls 911, the police arrive promptly and take the incident seriously. The officer doesn't suggest that his time is being wasted, and he doesn't suggest that the man step outside to cool off. Instead, he handcuffs the perpetrator and takes him to the police station, where he will be booked and jailed, while another officer offers to escort the wife and her children to a shelter. Violence against a woman in her home is now defined as a crime by our society, and the criminal justice system treats it as such.

But has this enormous revolution in both public perception and public policy made America less violent? Are there fewer batterers than before? Are batterers learning to take responsibility for their behavior? Are women safer or more in control of their own lives? Unfortunately, after years of researching this social problem, I can't answer any of these questions with a resounding yes. What's more, the ideology and rhetoric of the anti-domestic violence movement have become so rigid that they have created a new set of myths—or, at the very least, a new set of highly partial truths—that can be as pernicious as those we fought to dispel years ago.[32]

Feminists may understandably take issue with criticism of Walker, noting that it is Walker's work that has jumpstarted research and advocacy for battered women. This, precisely, is the crux of the problem. Just because someone means well doesn't mean they don't have to play by the rules; Walker's work should have been the beginning of an important study, not the end of it. Is it justified for good intentions to mask bad science—especially when it is to the ultimate detriment of many?

Both Lenore Walker and Carole Alden could serve as exemplars in seeking answers to that question.

ACCEPTING THAT GOOD PARENTS MAY PLANT BAD SEEDS— BUT THERE IS A DEEPER TRUTH

One thing that science is becoming clearer about is that good parents can sometimes, for whatever reason, have a child who has real difficulties grappling with life, or who even turns out badly. Perhaps such behavior could be due to a high fever in utero from chicken pox that sends a few critical cells offtrack, or inadvertent exposure to diethylstilbestrol, or any number of other unfortunate environmental influences. Or, such children might simply have been afflicted with an ill-fated confluence of genes, as with the probable partial role of genetics in predisposing Marty Sessions and his siblings to their addictions. "Accepting That Good Parents May Plant Bad Seeds" is the title of a recent *New York Times* article by psychiatrist Richard Friedman. In the article, Friedman's colleague, Dr. Theodore Shapiro, a child psychiatrist at Weill Cornell Medical College, points out: "The central pitch of any child psychiatrist now is that the illness is often in the child and that the family responses may aggravate the scene but not wholly create it. . . . The era of 'there are no bad children, only bad parents' is gone."[33]

∗   ∗   ∗

Conner Rusek, Carole's oldest son, inherited a mix of features from both sides of the family—he has dark-blond hair that might be wavy if he were to let it grow, a husky build, and a deceptively unhurried demeanor that belies his intellectual horsepower—he shares with his father the distinction of being a "brainiac." Despite his early hop-scotching around the country, the intellectually advanced Conner was accepted into a high school gifted and talented program. Unfortu-nately, this program required that Conner go to school on certain days to "check in," after which he was supposed to work at home on self-directed projects. But Conner already had his hands full at home—other family members observed that Conner's chief duty often seemed to be babysitting his younger half-siblings, Jason and Emily. Without support, the gifted young man's education floundered. He began to experiment with drugs and alcohol.

Brian Poulson, Carole's second husband, was very different from Richard, her first. Brian allowed himself to be drawn into Carole's dramas—the two would become involved in lengthy scream-fests observed by the children. Carole always had the advantage in these battles, since her five offspring had been trained to come down on her side no matter what happened. Conner was just one among many in the audience, cheering Carole on. One evening, the drunken Conner, then in his late teens, was pulled in as a collaborator in Carole's fight with Brian, during the course of which Conner took an ax to his step-father's possessions.

But Carole's response to Conner's violent action on her behalf was not only unexpected; it turned Conner's world upside down.

The frightened Carole called the police. Conner was arrested and jailed. In the resulting legal proceedings, the cost of Brian's destroyed belongings was estimated to be high enough that it changed the nature of the crime—turning it into a felony. Conner ended up in prison.

Even after what his mother had done to him, Conner still attempted to build bridges—to reestablish contact with Carole once he'd finished his stint in prison. However, the counseling he received while in a halfway house helped him put his mother's behavior in perspective. Thus, to Conner's credit, when Carole reacted to him with the same entrenched patterns, he decided to break off contact rather than getting sucked back into the same dysfunctional interactions. Conner's continuing positive relationships with both his father and, perhaps surprisingly, his stepfather Brian, have helped him. Neither Richard nor Brian, Conner noted, ever asked him to choose between them and his mother. With Carole, however, you were either with her or against her. There was no middle ground.

Conner's sister Melloney had seen what happened to Conner when he had upset his mother. It is a tribute to Melloney's integrity, and her concern for her own children, that, in the case of Marty's killing, she defied her mother and told the truth to police—she admitted that her mother had asked her to lie.

One official who listened in on telephone conversations between the imprisoned Carole and her son Conner observed that Conner was legitimately appalled at his mother for the position in which she'd placed Melloney in, after the killing, even as Carole professed to being seriously concerned for her oldest daughter. "The phone call between Conner and his mother, ironically enough," noted the listener, "was probably one of the few moments in observing the case from outside where I realized I was listening to someone become flat-out disgusted with Carole's behavior through just plain decency and common sense. I know that probably does not make sense to anyone but me."

The abrupt jolt of being pulled as a collaborator into his mother's fight and then betrayed by her was the major shock Conner needed to break the spell of such an expert manipulator. To his great credit, Conner has moved beyond his traumatic early experiences and profound betrayal. He is happily married now. Entirely self-taught, he has become a highly skilled web designer. With the template of victimization he was raised on, his life could have easily gone in a different direction. But Conner took the reins of his life firmly in hand and steered toward sunlight.

CHAPTER 29

THE DEAL

. . . we must be aware of the dangers which lie in our most generous wishes. Some paradox of our natures leads us, when once we have made our fellow men the objects of our enlightened interest, to go on to make them the objects of our pity, then of our wisdom, ultimately of our coercion.

—LIONEL TRILLING, *The Liberal Imagination*[1]

Tucked like an oversize shoe-box behind the Fillmore, Utah, Texaco station was the nameless motel housing James Slavens's offices (*Please ring both bells for service. Legal Office & Rooms 1–6*). Slavens, Carole's public defender, didn't have the luxury of a whiteboard-walled War Room in the basement of the sheriff's office. Instead, he laid his file folders out on the polyester bedspread over a queen-sized mattress, just down the hall from the solitary Coke machine manning the lobby.

The prosecution, on the other hand, not only had the benefit of the capacious War Room, it also had the advantage of being helmed by two of the state's most brilliant and accomplished prosecutors. Michael Wims and Pat Nolan each had extraordinary expertise honed through years of practice on some of the state's most difficult cases.

The best Slavens could do to simulate a defense team was to look in the mirror over the scratched top of the motel's bedroom bureau. But Slavens was himself a factor that had to be contended with by the prosecutors. He had decades of experience that provided an uncanny ability to sniff out weaknesses in the prosecution. Worse yet, he was like grit in a bearing—there was just no way to expect him to do *anything* reasonable. Unlike other defense attorneys, for example, who could be counted on to stipulate obvious factors, Slavens would agree to nothing, obvious or not. Like a dog with an itch, he could be counted on to scratch relentlessly, no matter how obnoxious the itching might appear to others.

In fact, unlikely though it might seem, the wily Slavens, through his sheer, intractable, and ultimately insufferable manner, found a hole in the prosecution's strategy. And Slavens, the lone defense attorney with almost no resources, a man reviled by many—even his own indigent client—went at that hole with the enthusiasm of a terrier going after a gopher just out of his reach.

CODEPENDENCY, BATTERED WOMEN, AND THE SANCTITY OF THE VICTIM

Our knowledge of codependency, of women who truly are battered, and of women who merely claim to be battered, is currently in a primitive state. The various criteria researchers have proposed for codependency aren't based on solid scientific studies, and the criteria overlap with many other disorders. But *many* disorders in the *Diagnostic and Statistical Manual of Mental Disorders* have overlapping symptoms and little if any scientific basis (as UCLA's Robert Bilder, with his outlines of neuropsychiatric phenomics, has shown).[2]

There is a clear history of institutionalized sexism in medical research.[3] This makes it easy to suppose researchers may be avoiding the careful analysis of codependency for sexist reasons. But it is equally likely, however, that researchers steer clear of research in this vital area because of the hallowed status of the sanctity of the victim. Who wants to be the villain who puts blame on victims?

*   *   *

To examine the viability of his proposed mental defense, Slavens had firmly insisted that Carole Alden be examined by a psychologist, with the results accepted by both prosecutors and the defense. As noted, there was one superb psychologist whom both sides could agree would provide fair results—Stephen Golding. For most professionals, the bespectacled Golding was the nearest thing to "walks on water" there was.

Although it was something of a nuisance (as usual), Slavens's request wasn't out of line. And given the wealth of information that prosecutors, detectives, and officers were uncovering about Carole's manipulative abilities, it seemed logical that Golding would sniff out Carole Alden in the same way they had.

Slavens's motivations, on the other hand—well, it was tough for prosecutors to know what Slavens was thinking.

After the preliminary hearing drew to a close, Slavens attempted a covert coup in arguments with Wims before Judge Eyre. Carole was a clean offender, Slavens insisted: a simple battered wife. Because of her lack of previous criminal involvement, it would be unduly harsh to convict her in the first degree. She should have a reduced sentence under section 76-3-402—conviction of a lower degree of offense as a result of mitigating circumstances.

But Judge Eyre—as conscientious and widely respected a judge as Golding was a psychologist—upheld the prosecution's perspective.

Golding's evaluation, though, was Slavens's ace in the hole. It weakened the State's position in that it implicitly strengthened Carole's case as an abused woman.

Creighton Horton, the State's leading expert in mental defenses and chief of the Criminal Division in the Attorney General's Office, began to analyze the prosecution's options. The bottom line, in the collective experience of the State's prosecutorial experts, was that whenever there was only one survivor to a domestic homicide—as with Carole—and there was evidence that the "bad guy" was to some degree culpable—as it appeared Marty Sessions might have been—a jury generally agreed to convict of a charge that was one degree less than that originally requested.

Carol's original charges were ten years to life for first-degree murder with a firearm, one to fifteen years for obstruction of justice, and zero to five for desecration of a body, plus a handgun-domestic violence enhancement. (Because she had killed her husband, Carole was deemed to occupy a "position of trust" under that section of Utah law; and, therefore, both the sentencing court [for sentencing purposes] and the Board of Pardons [for purposes of determining her length of imprisonment] would consider that status to be an aggravating factor in coming to that decision. Hence the domestic violence enhancement.) Essentially, Carole was looking at the possibility of a twenty-to-life sentence. Even if she did the bottom end of around twenty-five years, she would most likely die in prison.

There was a convoluted range of possible outcomes if the proceedings went on to a jury trial. For Carole to walk free, she'd need a unanimous decision of "not guilty" by the jury. Less than a unanimous verdict of either "guilty" or "not guilty" would mean a hung jury—which could mean a retrial. Usually, however, a hung jury resulted in both prosecution and defense having a real incentive to agree to a disposition—a final negotiated settling of the matter—since a retrial might result in the unpalatable possibility of one's own side losing. So after a hung jury, both sides would reengage in disposition discussions and would probably arrive at an agreed disposition.

The upshot of all this for both the defense and the prosecution was to have a go at making an agreement right from the start. This avoided the egg-in-the-face risky situation of being on the losing side of jury unanimity in the first trial.

Risky business indeed. Slavens knew that convincing a psychologist of Carole's sincerity for the brief duration of an analysis was one thing. But was Carole good enough to convince a jury of her peers? A real jury of peers was a myth, anyway, but if the jury members were anything like her neighbor Joe Trujillo, or her coworkers for the City of Delta, Carole's proverbial goose would be charcoal.

All indications were that Carole was *not* going to plead guilty.

After lengthy discussion at the highest levels of the State's Attorney General's office, Creighton Horton and Pat Nolan went to work on Slavens. Looking logically at potential outcomes, the principal charge Carole would likely be found guilty of would be manslaughter (as Utah law had no choice of "second-degree murder"). If Carole agreed to a plea of manslaughter now, it would mean she would avoid the risk of being found guilty of murder, with its ten-years-to-life sentence. Suggesting such a plea offer was something prosecutors did with clenched teeth: they'd be giving up the very charge—murder—they felt Carole was guilty of. But if both sides could agree on manslaughter, they would avoid the anguish, the risk, and the expense of a full trial even while achieving what in all probability would have been the outcome anyway, and they would also avoid the risk of a walk-out-of-the courtroom acquittal. It was a reasonable compromise that had something good and bad for everyone. In such a disposition, Carole would, after all, become a felon convicted of the homicide. Slavens worked to remove the one-year mandatory extension of Carole's sentence for using a gun, and the State agreed.

Slavens then presented the options to his client. Shortly thereafter, Carole indicated her willingness to accept an agreed plea disposition for an indeterminate sentence of one to fifteen years. In essence, the parole board would be determining her sentence.

Pactum factum, as lead prosecutor Michael Wims would say. A done deal.

*   *   *

Later, Carole said she accepted the agreed plea disposition for the sake of her daughter, Melloney, who Carole insisted had been threatened with potential prosecution for obstruction of justice. Mike Wims, with his broad expertise gained from decades of experience, recoils at the very idea, noting

> It is unusual for law enforcement to "threaten" witnesses, because it calls into question everything they tell you after being threatened. It's about as useful as a confession beaten out of somebody. In other words I don't want to ever have to put a threatened witness on the stand and then have such a witness (who probably doesn't like the prosecution anyway) get to be "cross-examined" by a defense attorney they like, about how they were *threatened* by the authorities and "made" to tell the story they just told. So, in sum, unless there is a law enforcement officer willing to come forward and say "I threatened her" I don't buy into the proposition that she was threatened.[4]

*   *   *

"We were happy with her sentence," says Detective Jacobson, sitting with Deputy Attorney Pat Finlinson on the back patio of the sheriff's office.[5] Both are using their lunchtime to reflect on the case.

Jacobson continues: "It's always tough in these kinds of situations to know what the outcome will be before a jury. She's got kids—and Marty wasn't a very good victim. You know what I mean. People are not going to be real sympathetic to his case, just because of his past. That's the tough part in all this," Jacobson says, his compassion glimmering despite his efforts to keep it under wraps. "Our hearts go out to both Martin's and Carole's families. *They* are the collateral damage in all of this."

Finlinson interjects with an important point: "We figured if we could just get her in prison for a year—just one year—that would be enough for them to see how manipulative she really is."

As far as the prosecution went, in fact, there had been a single deal breaker. Carole Alden *had* to go to the state prison. None of this business of a year in the county jail and then she's out on probation.

Utah has an unusual, open-ended sentencing format for those con-victed of a crime. It seems unfair to some, because this system basi-cally leaves the sentencing up to the Board of Pardons and Parole. But viewed from another perspective, such a system is eminently fair. It separates the verdict from the actual sentencing, makes it more dis-passionate, and also makes for a more centralized method of handing out the sentence ultimately received, so that people can expect more uniformity from the various counties in Utah. There would be similar sentences, in other words, for similar crimes, although backgrounds and behavior in prison would also be taken into account. From the prosecutors' perspective, once Carole showed her true manipulative colors in prison, she'd be in for a goodly stretch—more toward the fifteen-year mark of her one- to fifteen-year sentence.

"What do I believe?" asks Jacobson, shaking his head. "I believe Carole Alden is a devious, ill-designing, selfish woman. And I believe that if Marty Sessions had disappeared one hot summer day in July, not a soul would have been able to make much of his absence. It was very nearly the perfect crime. She's an extraordinarily clever woman who made only one tiny mistake."

Jacobson leans back, savoring the recollection. "Allen Lake. *He* was her mistake." Jacobson collects his thoughts. "Carole Alden's grooming abilities begin at first sight and first speak. Her victims, or those who fall into her web, are there by her design. With Allen Lake, I think she thought *I'm going to need that some day*. That allegiance was poorly bargained. She counted on an allegiance that wasn't there when she needed it."

A question arises: *But do you think that Carole counted on Allen because she really did have feelings for him? That whatever her feel-ings might have later changed to after Allen would have fallen off the pedestal, right then, she really did care about Allen? And that's why she called him?*

Jacobson squints toward the sky, reflecting. "Maybe. Could have been."

Brent Turvey could have been describing Jacobson when he wrote that "the forensic victimologist is best conceived as an objective, dis-passionate, and above all scientific examiner."[6]

Jacobson concludes: "I feel so badly for her kids. I think when you grow up around someone like that—when that person is your mother—she can twist how you view everything. Carole's a very, very smart woman—a sheer genius at manipulation. Think about what you would feel if you'd grown up with those tentacles in you. Even if you caught her in a flat-out lie, she'd tell you she'd been lying *for you*. To help you. And she'd make you believe it."

*   *   *

Carole Alden writes that she signed her plea offer on her birthday, March 11, and that she'd been awakened at 3:00 a.m. that morning listening to the feet of a young man in the next cell beating against the wall as he hanged himself and died. However, the court records show her as having signed her plea in mid-June, and there's no record of any young man who hanged himself in the adjacent cell of the Millard County Jail.

Folks think it was about time I cracked and murdered him after everything he'd done to me, Carole Alden writes. *But it wasn't like that at all. He was still the love of my life.*[7]

The State's brilliant prosecution team believed that modern science and psychology could illuminate Carole Alden's true character and motives. But Slavens, for the defense, figured psychologists would be lost in the labyrinth of Carole Alden's personality.

People in the know say Slavens got Carole Alden a good deal.

CHAPTER 30

CLOSURE

**I have elsewhere given the name of moral realism
to the perceptions of the dangers of the moral life
itself. Perhaps at no other time has the enterprise
of moral realism ever been so much needed, for at
no other time have so many people committed
themselves to moral righteousness. We have the
books that point out the bad conditions, that
praise us for taking progressive attitudes. We have
no books that raise questions in our minds not
only about conditions but about ourselves, that
lead us to refine our motives and ask what might
lie behind our good impulses.**

—LIONEL TRILLING, *The Liberal Imagination*[1]

I have long been fascinated by kindness and feelings of compassion. But after publication of my last book, the tongue-in-cheek-titled but seriously researched *Evil Genes: Why Rome Fell, Hitler Rose, Enron Failed, and My Sister Stole My Mother's Boyfriend*, a perverse curiosity began to arise. Could our own feelings of kindness lead us astray? Could people do bad things because they thought they were doing good?

I took on *Cold-Blooded Kindness* after I happened across the *National Enquirer*'s luridly titled article "Woman Marries for Love—Then Kills for Survival."[2] The title said it all—if true, I thought, this seemed a story tailor-made to illustrate how our feelings of kindness can backfire and even endanger us. This was worth looking into. Besides, after *Evil Genes*, I was looking forward to the opportunity to write about someone *nice* for a change.

By contacting some of Carole's supporters—people who had been movingly quoted in newspaper articles about her case—I began to learn of Marty Sessions's sinister reputation in the community. I learned how Carole, through her profound desire to help others, became ensnared in a relationship from which she could not escape. I began a lengthy correspondence with Carole, and her letters evinced a profound love of her children and for art. The writing was by turns playful and moving as it described the unjust treatment Carole felt she had received throughout her life—from her family, her relationships, and her legal defense.

Here was a caring, loving mother of five who was unfairly incarcerated because she was trying to protect her young children from a crazed psychopath. What better story could there be to illustrate the dangers of misplaced kindness?

It was when I met Carole in the Utah State Penitentiary that the picture began to tilt.

I was sitting in the visiting room facing the door from which the prisoners emerged. Just when I was about to give up hope of seeing her—the visiting room had filled up fast with pensive, wistfully smiling female prisoners—Carole emerged. There was no mistaking her tiny figure. Her long, free-flowing gray locks gave her the aura of a hippie despite her prison garb.

We began chatting, each obviously trying to get a feel for the other. I had a long mental list of questions I'd prepared. Why did she get into, and remain enmeshed in, the relationship with Marty, despite the obvious possibility of harm to her children? Could there have been something about her own behavior that had led to the crime, and to her incarceration? What were her feelings about her father and the alleged molestation?

There is something about watching a person's face when asking difficult questions that can provide far more insight than pen and paper ever can.

Carole began answering my questions with understandable sadness. She spoke of missing her children, of her lack of art supplies, of the sheer inanity of prison regulations.

To my surprise, just as I began to move into some of my deeper questions, Carole's mother and younger sister arrived in the waiting room. They'd been delayed in traffic, but they were visiting near Salt Lake City that day and made a point of going to the prison while they were there.

There were hugs and introductions all around. Carole's mother was obviously overjoyed to see her daughter; her sister was more subdued but clearly happy to see Carole.

But Carole's reaction was quite different. As I watched, it almost seemed as if she were disconcerted to see her mother and sister—somehow uneasy in their presence. She glanced from her relatives to me, her previously open, caring demeanor changing before my eyes. Perhaps, I thought, her demeanor was changing because of what her family had done to her—abandoning her in her moment of need, ignoring signs of abuse from her father.

But her mother and sister were there visiting—they were clearly both supportive and loving. This wasn't making sense. An unwanted thought popped to mind: "Perhaps Carole's demeanor is changing because she can't tell me the stories she's been planning to tell me. *Because those stories don't jibe with what she's told her relatives.*

A feeling is one thing, but facts are another. I put the thought aside and listened to the halting conversation, feeling very much the third wheel. It didn't take me long to realize that *everyone* felt like a third wheel. It's hard enough to carry on a routine conversation in a prison. But to carry on a routine conversation with a complete stranger sitting beside you, listening in? I was stuck, though. There was no way I could gracefully get out of the situation, other than to simply excuse myself then and there. But I'd come too many miles for that.

So I thought, what the hell—why don't I go ahead anyway? I asked everyone whether it was all right to broach my planned questions. The eager nods in response helped launch me.

Why did you stay with Marty, even if he was dangerous? Didn't you consider your kids when you moved Marty into your house?

Carole answered at length, going on about her misplaced love for Marty, how he'd fooled and hurt her, and how her fear for her children kept her his slave. Glancing over, I realized Carole's mother and sister were listening intently. To my surprise, I realized that they themselves had never had the opportunity to hear these questions asked or answered.

Did your father really molest you?

I watched Carole carefully. Carole's mother and sister leaned forward expectantly. Only later would I realize the amorphous nature of Carole's accusations—that she'd never really told anyone connected with the family exactly what her father had supposedly done.

This was Carole's big opportunity to lay her cards on the table— to explain to her mother and sister what had been done to her—when and where, with credible details to back her up. To help them understand why she had made the accusations.

Carole looked toward her relatives, taking in their focused, pained looks. She stared down at the floor. Then she changed the subject.

After my prison visit, I began to carefully dig into the evidence, interviewing dozens of people affiliated with the case, reading court transcripts, visiting the scene of the crime, the trial, talking to locals and in general trying to get a good commonsense view of what had happened.

I also undertook to learn everything I could about empathy, how empathy might go awry, and how altruism itself can become pernicious. To that end, while researching and writing this book, I simultaneously put together an edited volume for Oxford University Press— *Pathological Altruism*—that featured chapters by experts ranging from the neuroscience of empathy to the psychology of suicide bombers. Exploring a nonfiction, true-crime story while editing such a volume is the ne plus ultra of nonfiction writing.[3] Can't find good scientific research about codependency? Ha! Ask one of the most thoughtful, independent-minded researchers in the field—psychiatrist Mike McGrath—to look into it and write about it. Having trouble understanding why children of troubled parents might end up being too kind themselves? Get in touch with distinguished developmental psychologist Carolyn Zahn-Waxler. What about animal hoarding—can that give us any clues as to why someone would behave in a seemingly altruistic manner that worsens the very situation it is meant to help? Contact veterinarian Gary Patronek and his social work colleague Jane Nathanson to learn the latest. Does altruism have a cultural basis? Nudge anthropologist John Traphagan, with his extraordinary understanding of Asian cultures, to see what he thinks. What do we know of certitude and self-righteousness? Neurologist Robert Burton and science fiction writer David Brin share their wisdom in relation to this little-studied area. Do helpful people become more readily victimized? Robert Homant and Dan Kennedy have ready insight into the question. What about evolution itself—does that give us an overarching perspective? Indeed, David Sloan Wilson, Satoshi Kanazawa, and Joachim Krueger have profoundly helpful approaches.

Dispassionate, sincere researchers like these, who allow the facts to lead them to new frontiers of knowledge, have my profound admiration and respect. I couldn't have written this book without them.

One contributor to *Pathological Altruism*, however—star Harvard researcher Marc Hauser—gave me pause. Hauser's research, and his well-received 2006 book, *Moral Minds*, placed him in the forefront of neuroscientific researchers on human morality.[4] But Harvard University found Hauser solely responsible for eight significant instances of scientific misconduct. Hauser in turn acknowledged making "significant mistakes" regarding his research.[5] Hauser himself is now on leave from Harvard, teaching a course in critical thinking and reasoning to some of the highest-risk delinquents in the country. It's an experience he characterizes as amazing, even as he observes that his own situation pales in comparison with that of his charges. Even Hauser, that all-too-human expert on morality, finds himself reflecting with surprise on the truth of the oft-repeated adage that helping others is somehow uplifting when one's own life is down in the pits.[6] (From Hauser's perspective, media coverage of his case was "completely slanted and one sided"—he refrains from further explanation, noting the situation is too complex.)[7]

Preeminent literary theorist Joseph Carroll has an expertise with sophistry in literary and cultural theory that lends him unique insight to the moral issues at hand. "Could it be the case," Carroll muses, "that Hauser, concentrating on the 'moral' implications of his own work, was willing to sacrifice means to ends, perhaps even unconsciously, or not quite consciously, aligning data with conclusions that, in his own mind, contribute to the greater good? Without venturing to read Hauser's mind, we can say confidently that some such cognitive process is often at work in intellectual life. It is at work, for instance, in the case of Lenore Walker, and in the case of the many passionately committed people who have defended her. Whenever a scientist sacrifices objectivity, accuracy, or honesty for the sake of some 'altruistic' end, that altruism can reasonably be designated pathological."[8] This happens in research far, far more often than we might think. "[S]elective reporting is everywhere in science," notes Richard Palmer, a biologist at the University of Alberta who has been surprised by his own findings.[9] Neuroscientist Jonah Lehrer adds that "scientists find ways to confirm their preferred hypothesis, disregarding what they don't want to see. Our beliefs are a form of blindness."[10] Lehrer continues:

> Such anomalies demonstrate the slipperiness of empiricism. Although many scientific ideas generate conflicting results and suffer from falling effect sizes [in other words, the original findings decline in size and significance], they continue to get cited in the

textbooks and drive standard medical practice. Why? Because these ideas seem true. Because they make sense. Because we can't bear to let them go. And this is why the decline effect is so troubling. Not because it reveals the human fallibility of science, in which data are tweaked and beliefs shape perceptions. (Such shortcomings aren't surprising, at least for scientists.) And not because it reveals that many of our most exciting theories are fleeting fads and will soon be rejected. (That idea has been around since Thomas Kuhn.) The decline effect is troubling because it reminds us how difficult it is to prove anything. We like to pretend that our experiments define the truth for us. But that's often not the case. Just because an idea is true doesn't mean it can be proved. And just because an idea can be proved doesn't mean it's true. When the experiments are done, we still have to choose what to believe.[11]

If this is true for scientific findings, which can be empirically tested, what does it mean for disciplines such as social psychology, where theories float far removed from biological or physical underpinnings?[12]

Indeed, perhaps the concept of pathological altruism, and empathy gone awry, can help build rapprochement—a scientific bridge of sorts—between liberals and conservatives.[13]

*   *   *

One day, right in the middle of writing this book and working on the *Pathological Altruism* project, I was surprised to learn that I had been accepted into the New York Academy of Medicine. A wonderfully altruistic friend had nominated me.

That friend and I met near the south end of Central Park in New York City and traveled up to the corner of Fifth Avenue and 103rd Street, where the academy is located. Here I was, a lowly engineer from flyover country, in one of the most prestigious halls of medicine. I felt like a bacon burger at a vegetarian banquet. During the actual award ceremony, I was introduced as being from Minnesota rather than Michigan. The announcer corrected himself, adding in that wonderfully New York–centric way—"Who cares what's west of the Hudson, anyway?"

After the ceremonies, my friend introduced me to some of the players in the academy. One of them, whom I'll call John, was a former academy president. John had made a deep impression on me during his after-dinner speech with his eloquent words of praise for his colleagues and their support of the academy and its mission. In fact, John's caring tribute to his coworkers was one of the nicest I'd ever heard—it made me look forward to meeting him. As I was introduced, my friend added—"and she's editing a book called *Pathological Altruism.*"

John's demeanor changed in a wink from saintly to sour. "*Pathological* altruism?" he spat. "Altruism can never, ever be pathological. See that man there?" John pointed toward a neurasthenic-looking fellow standing near the *hors d'œuvres.* "That man is one of the most altruistic people I've ever met. He gives and gives—you could never call him pathological."

I turned to the man in question. I'd never made the (retrospectively obvious) connection before that even simple volunteerism might, like virtually anything done to excess, become pathological. But in that moment, it *did* occur to me that the more this man might have helped John, the less likely John would be to call it pathological. In fact, the more this man helped, the more likely John was to consider such a person as almost holy.

Before I could even open my mouth to say a word, John gave a derisive snort of disgust and marched with his entourage off toward the exit. I wanted to say, "Wait! Stop! Really, altruism *can* be pathological!" But it was clear that I'd already been relegated to the crackpot bin. This brilliant man would never give me a chance to explain myself, because his mind was already made up. *Altruism is always good.*

This episode changed my perspective about altruism. I began to see that not only can altruism have a seamy side, but that seamy side is studiously—almost religiously—ignored by researchers. It was almost as if, by studying the dark flip side of altruism, researchers were afraid they'd come across findings that would discourage what they perceived as the most sacred of human traits.

As I was to discover, would-be contributors to *Pathological Altruism* who were affiliated with "altruism studies" programs often seemed to have the most difficulty grappling with altruism's darker side. It was as if the sun never set on the world of happy helping, so they were left groping when they tried to walk into the darkness. The chapters these individuals ultimately submitted were often simple paeans to altruism with nary a wink about altruism's possible harm. It was a painful irony indeed to have to gently reject them.

All scientists know there is real research and then there is "research"—specious findings that make it into the media largely because they sound good, and no one wants to tie their career knickers in a knot rebutting what "everybody knows" is "true." I believe this dubious research often shares an underlying theme—it grows out of pathological altruism. Such investigations are epitomized by people like Lenore Walker, who, it seems, truly believe they are doing the right thing. This self-righteousness is so profound that such researchers find ways to attack those who attempt legitimate scientific scrutiny and criticism of their work. Marc Hauser, for example, purportedly bullied his students into accepting his version of events, while Lenore Walker implies her critics are against abused women. Sometimes I suspect that the more over-the-top self-righteous researchers themselves realize that criticism of their work is well-founded. But they've gone so far out on the research limb they'd grown for themselves that if they gave credence to the criticism, they'd chop off their life's work. Few people, even scientists, have the ability to take an ax to their livelihood in this fashion.

On the other hand, occasionally a well-grounded, commonsense researcher like Murray Straus (or Harvard's venerable E. O. Wilson, for that matter),[14] is willing to suffer outrageous ignominy and calumny from fellow researchers in the simple pursuit of truth—a truth that others, with their devotion to dogma, are unwilling to acknowledge (shades of the stroke patient's left hemisphere deliberately hiding his hand, the better to insist it isn't there). I can't help but wonder whether Straus and Wilson's "costly punisher" critics (Wilson, for example, was publicly doused with a pitcher of water) might best be termed "malevolent altruists."

While working on the two projects, I reflected what I was learning from science and research onto what I was learning about the story of Carole Alden. The picture emerging from many different sources— from Carole's closest relatives to the police and prosecutors who dealt with her and tracked her every move once the homicide had occurred—was the opposite of everything I had hoped to write about. Carole Alden, rather than being a victim of her own empathy, was instead something different altogether. After much searching, it seemed that the best I could make of her peculiar constellation of traits was to call her a professional victim. She is a practiced master at eliciting—and abusing—the kindness of others. My book was inverted.

This book isn't really about gullible Carole. It's about gullible us.

As I discovered, Carole has a sophisticated ability to manipulate family, friends, acquaintances, and the media by pulling at our natural sympathies for victims. In particular, Carole is a ready comrade to anyone who lends a sympathetic, nonjudgmental ear. But life, particularly when small children are involved, is about more than sympathy, creativity, and following a dark muse wherever it might lead you. The life of a parent—a truly loving parent—involves responsibility and foresight. It involves the ability, for example, to prioritize a child's profound needs over those of an endless line of adult, drug-abusing convicts and ex-convicts with imagined depths of golden, latent traits.

Coming from this perspective, society's buy-in to Carole Alden's manipulations—that is, our resolute idealization of the sanctity of the victim—is *not* a victimless crime. Neither is it a necessary lesser evil to be endured for the greater good of the many true victims. People like Carole Alden *create* true victims, like an ambulance sent to rescue that instead plows into a crowd.

When I first began corresponding with Carole, I warned her that I was sympathetic but that I would follow the facts where they led me. In the nearly one hundred pages of letters she subsequently sent me, I found that what she wrote often diverged from the facts in self-serving fashion. One of the most interesting letters, however, was one she wrote to her family after she began realizing that the author (me) on whom she had unleashed her story of helpless abuse was spinning out of her control. *Don't worry*, she reassured her family—*I haven't told the author anything about the family.*

Considering the brutal criticism of her family in her letters to me—criticism that ran counter to much of what I have been able to determine—I found Carole's statement to be sad, at the very least.

Some feminists who have read this book have expressed concern that having a better scientific understanding of battered women could play into the hands of unscrupulous prosecutors. But to repress scientific study of this phenomenon means that we take information from *scrupulous* prosecutors—information that is vital in protecting the interests of children. Is it worth that trade-off?

One real surprise for me is that my feminist friends would often turn to me after reading this book and say, by way of final comment, "You know, the one thing though, Carole Alden is not a very good example of a pathological altruist." *But*, I explain gently, *Carole Alden is not meant to be an example of a pathological altruist.*

*   *   *

All things considered, this extraordinary story is a tribute to humanity's best traits. Frankly, given what happened, things don't get much better than how they actually turned out. Except for Marty Sessions.

Richard Senft, Carole's first husband—against whom she so masterfully made accusations of abuse in order to keep the children—is now on the twentieth year of his happy second marriage. Richard and his second wife have walked the tightrope of love, offering Carole's older children glimpses of a stable home life during their summer visits to Pennsylvania. It is these glimpses, I'm convinced, along with the material support they have provided, that have helped the youngsters edge toward a normal life despite Carole's never-ending efforts to keep them within the maelstrom of her orbit.

In some sense, the children were raised in the Cult of Carole. The cult's ostensive First Law is the importance of helping others—particularly the poor and wretched. The children were raised, in other words, to believe in the sanctity of the victim and in the overwhelming importance of their own role in selfless service to those victims.

Carole's children, in other words, were raised to feed Carole's primal needs.

Underlying the First Law is an essential corollary: "The children must instantly reject any criticism of Carole—and as importantly, they must reject any*one* who dares criticize Carole." This insidious corollary has kept Carole's children in her ruinous vortex—it is the dangling Sword of Damocles around which dance all who love Carole's children. Richard Senft's children with Carole have meant everything to him, and his resolute personal rule to never use the children as pawns has meant that he has shouldered silence in the face of unending deceit and calumny as the painful price of that love. His second wife's own love for the children has meant that she, too, has paid that price—a price many stepmothers would never willingly pay.

Brian Poulson, Carole's second husband, and his wife have shouldered similar burdens on behalf of Carole's younger children. And indeed, perhaps the most fortunate aspect of Carole's incarceration is that her two youngest children were removed from her care. (At the very least, Carole's incarceration has prevented her tiresome trick of calling child services to report as abusive or neglectful whichever husband her children happened to be visiting.) Despite the difficulties of adjusting to a new home with a stepparent, Jason and Emily have blossomed. In prison, though, Carole has turned herself into the ultimate victim-martyr. She has turned a special focus on Emily, the youngest, an empathetic and caring youngster who shares Carole's creative drive. Emily, in return, is beginning to idealize her mother.

One family member muses: "I don't think she will ever change.

There's just no remorse there. None at all. Never has been." Another sadly adds, "There seem to be so many convincing people in the world that I am becoming a skeptic in my old age. It was such a comfort being naive!"

We will never know the actual psychiatric diagnosis Carole Alden was given when she received her court-ordered psychological analysis. Borderline personality disorder? Bipolar disorder? An inchoate mixture of syndromes? Carole Alden's specialty is manipulative deception, wrapped in the guise of the sanctity of the victim. Perhaps, then, she was perceived as being psychologically normal. In any case, whatever the diagnosis, or lack thereof, most who truly know Carole would admit she needs help. The sad fact is, however, that medical science is simply not advanced enough at present to truly help her. So that brings us again to the best of all possible outcomes. If Carole isn't getting the help she needs because we don't know enough yet about the brain to give that help, at least she's being kept away from those whose love for her would bring them into harm's way.

After Carole's sentencing in Fillmore, two of the judge's assistants, whose job was to do interviews for the judge in relation to the case, came and kindly embraced members of the Alden family, asking them to please not take what had happened personally. This is typical of the graciousness of those who serve the people of Millard County. Throughout the course of working on this book, I've interviewed law enforcement officers, detectives, and prosecuting attorneys involved in the case at length, including "Jake" Jacobson, Mike Wims, Pat Nolan, and Pat Finlinson. Frankly, society's sentinels don't come better than these fine men. It would have been easy for these individuals to have stonewalled an outside writer—and it's a tribute to their passion for following the facts and making the world a better place that they were willing to take the time to explain, warts and all, what the evidence revealed. Sadly, I was never able to interview Officer Josie Greathouse, who did the initial "dressing down" search of Carole Alden. Josie was killed by one of the drug dealers who are the bane of rural Utah's existence. Guarding society has a cost.

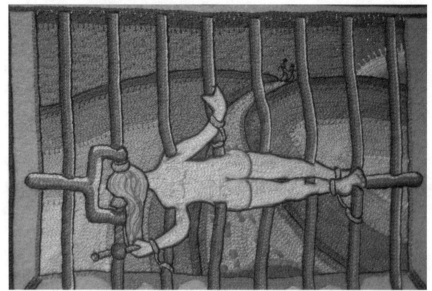

While in the Millard County Jail, Carole drew a picture, titled "Limbo," of a naked woman skewered on cell bars, watching her children disappear into the distance. This picture was re-created later with felt, embroidery thread, and an illicit sewing needle. Artist Sheryl Gillilan interviewed Carole in prison and wrote: "When I ask how she got access to the needle, Carole smiles and says, 'Well, there's always a way around everything. The guys in State custody [at the jail] could have needles, so I would draw them soft-core 50's style porn and they would send me over some needles tucked inside the mop bucket.'"[15] The original color image shows what appears to be bright red blood that has pooled on the ground below the figure's genitals. The children appear to have walked through the pool, leaving a path marked with bloody footsteps as they walk into the distance.

As I found while researching this book, our one-size-fits-all approach to males as being the primary source of problems in relationships does a disservice not only to our idealized sense of fairness but also to real people. It is telling that one of the unsung heroes of this story, Allen Lake, had the wit and wherewithal to do the right thing when tested. If not for Allen, Marty's family would likely have suffered heartache for decades—ever wondering what had become of him.

As it was, though, Marty Sessions's daughters, having lost their mother to AIDS and their stepmother and stepbrother to horrific murders that dragged the family into the courts again and again, were once more pushed to the brink with their father's brutal slaying. This time, if the girls were to see true justice done with a full-jury trial, they would have had to watch their father be branded everything he was not—a sadist and a monster—even while his parade of venial sins would also be trotted out for the world to see. As it was, it was heartbreaking for Edee and Anna to view a picture of their father in the *National Enquirer*, the words "ABUSIVE MONSTER" next to an arrow pointing toward their father's sad face.[16]

Marty Sessions was a man. A very imperfect man, but a person who was still much loved by his children, grandchildren, siblings, and parents. A man whom Susie Sessions loved with all her heart. A man who reached out to help his neighbors, a man who had friends, and a man who was trying, even if imperfectly, to climb out of the hole he'd made in his life.

*   *   *

In prison, Carole has become involved in new relationships with needy fellow convicts, both male and female, and was caught exchanging love letters and plans to meet up and live together on the outside. Taking up with a fellow ex-con is strictly verboten, but this sordid repetition of the "I've got to fix them to fix me" behavior that had led her to prison in the first place showed that Jacobson and Wims were right. Carole's manipulative side would, and did, manifest itself. This will probably lead to a longer prison sentence—something that is likely the best thing that can happen for the children who still idealize her. Carole's offspring are being given the opportunity, sad as it may feel to them and to Carole, to grow up away from her.

Meanwhile, Carole is also busy with her art, which provides opportunities to offer up her story to the public. *15 Bytes: Utah's Art Magazine* features a recent article titled "There's Always a Way: Carole Alden Continues the Artistic Life behind Bars."

Carole says, "I want to take the materials we're restricted to here and make something really amazing out of them. I want to do pieces that really show the complexities of drug abuse, poverty and domestic violence that shape women's lives. Much of it will be disturbing for people to view, but I think it's an important message to communicate on a visceral level. Only then will some people grasp the terror and despondency that pervades so many lives in secret."[17]

Similarly, a recent *Salt Lake Tribune* piece, "Utah Inmates Escape through Art," features a large picture of Carole accompanied by one of her crocheted creations (she taught herself to crochet in prison).[18] Carole is also now involved in silk-screening—the pieces she produces have the elegant, sometimes savage beauty of all her art. Carole's family can't help but point toward her extraordinary ability to manage under the worst of circumstances: "When thrown up, she lands on her feet like a cat!"

Carole is also busy in a new campaign, writing the publisher of *Cold-Blooded Kindness* to tell them that the substance of this book has been largely fabricated by a twisted imagination for shock value—stitched together by interviewing people who didn't have any real involvement in her life, topped off with threats of blackmail against her and her children.[19] Overlooking the fact that, according to police, she herself helped spoon-feed a lurid version of her story to the *National Enquirer*, she states that this book has been made out to be at the level of "the worst sort of *National Enquirer* tripe available."[20] Carole says she finds the whole tawdry enterprise extraordinarily disrespectful not only to her own family but to the family of her departed husband (the very family who had to endure seeing pictures of Marty labeled an abusive monster from stories Carole helped seed in the *National Enquirer*).

How can we know who Carole is and why she does what she does? Rebecca Smith, the local artist and arts administrator who has followed Carole's work for many years, muses:

I don't know how to describe it, but Carole's brain just works differently than most artists I know. Unfortunately for her, however, I think she also got the "crazy" part of genius artist.

Most artists can easily separate their art from who they are, even though they're totally interrelated, but Carole just IS her art. That probably isn't healthy, frankly, but it might explain why she thinks her dragon is a self-portrait. As a comparison, if I made a dragon, I would say, "This is a dragon I made. It looks really scary and I feel that way sometimes, so I got it out of my system by making this dragon." But, Carole says, "This is me." Whoa—that gives me pause. And maybe that's where the "crazy" genius part comes in— she can't separate herself from her creations. (Which, as a weird aside, makes me wonder about how this relates to her children as her "creations"?)

Even though Carole is really disdainful of people she doesn't think are as smart as she is, in a lot of respects she's just like the rest of us: We all have our own truths about ourselves and other people. The difference with Carole and others like her might be that she is unable to incorporate other people's truths into her own persona. I, of course, have truths about myself, and when they don't jibe with other people's truths about me, it immediately causes discomfort. Then I go on a self-reflection binge and try to meld the two images. Generally, I think I have a pretty good idea of how I function in the world, but of course there are moments when I am taken aback. The difference may be that I am able to hear other people's truths and can incorporate their meanings without disintegrating—or vilifying them because they don't agree with me. It seems Carole is unable to do that.

That's the interesting thing to me about Carole. She doesn't believe she is lying. Her truth is flexible and tends to mold itself the way she wants it to, just like her art. Maybe she believes the truth is like her fabric—she can cut it and sew it to match the image in her mind. That could explain why she thinks your book is tripe and lies. I wouldn't imagine she could incorporate your complex and critical analysis of her psyche into who she believes she really is.

So, is all of this genius? Beats me. Far greater people than I have pondered this question!

One can't help but reflect on Carole's art with regard to hemispheric theories of the brain. As Iain McGilchrist notes, the left hemisphere is interested in what it has *made*; it "is more at home dealing with distorted, non-realistic, fantastic—ultimately artificial—images. This may be because they invite analysis by parts, rather than as a whole. But it does appear that the left hemisphere has a positive bias toward whatever is bizarre, meaningless or nonpersistent."[21] Would a healthy, balanced brain mean that Carole would lose interest in her art? Or would her drive for art remain but somehow be shifted in focus?

Does Carole's art grow like poisoned fruit from the source of her dysfunction? Or does it spring from something altogether different—perhaps instead forming an unrelenting effort to heal herself? Might it be both at once—a Janus-headed coin?

The brain has two ways of seeking truth. For the left brain, truth is *correctness*—static and unchanging. For the right brain, truth is an unveiling. And any unveiling of some truth inevitably veils another.[22]

Carole's adult daughters, meanwhile, are continuing their support. Melloney, ever in thrall to her mother, wrote the author directly to threaten legal action, asserting this book doesn't have the right to say that Carole doesn't love her children, because she does, very deeply. The author of this book, Melloney notes, should look in the mirror to find the real liar. (Melloney, Krystal, and Conner all refused the author's many requests to make corrections and provide additional insight.)

Krystal Rusek, also a willing supporter of her mother's enterprises, complained to Oakland University (the author's home institution) that Krystal and her family had been forced to participate as subjects of the author's research, which should have been approved before it was started by the Institutional Review Board. This prompted a comprehensive review of *Cold-Blooded Kindness*, as well as careful consideration of the definition of research with the Office of Human Research Protections in Washington, DC. The book was cleared.

Krystal complains that I have unfairly portrayed Carole Alden as a "neurotic, cold blooded, professional victim," and that her mother is not the "menace to society" that I seem to believe.[23]

That remains to be seen.

One investigator who has been deeply involved in the case ever since the shooting of Marty Sessions has been curious not only about Andy Bristow's mysterious death, but also about the eerily similar death of another of Carole's acquaintances that apparently took place in Ohio during her brief sojourn there with "Brutus from Cleveland." Unfortunately, limited police resources meant the investigation swirling in the wake of the 2006 homicide had to remain focused on the killing of Marty Sessions, where the facts and evidence were relatively clear. Meanwhile, in the Millard County Jail, Carole apparently reveled in her nickname: *Killer.* The question will forever haunt: is Carole Alden actually a serial killer?

One who knows Carole intimately—too well to reveal his name—says there is only one reason Carole's first two husbands, as opposed to Marty, are still alive. Brian and Richard paid child support. Marty didn't. One starts to ask not "What must the brutal Marty Sessions have done to poor Carole to make her shoot him?" but rather "Marty may not have been an angel, but what kind of person did he unwittingly become entangled with when he hooked up with Carole Alden?"

Investigators privy to Carole Alden's correspondence are disgusted by Carole's claim that Marty Sessions forced piercings on her and compelled her to write sadomasochistic e-mails. This disgust went beyond the many drawings Carole made before the time she claimed Marty had pierced her, all of which indicated that she had a fixation with such piercings. In fact, one repeated criticism seen in Carole's communications with others prior to the homicide involved her complaints about Marty's unwillingness to physically abuse her—she taunted him for it. Carole's correspondence both before and after the homicide with others—many others, even including her children—has sometimes been so appallingly graphic and twisted in nature that investigators have found it impossible to put into words. "No one," says one who has seen the voluminous correspondence, "should write about those things to anyone, much less their own children." (Investigators, in fact, show deep concern for Carole's gifted, good-hearted children, whom they couldn't help but come to admire over the years.)

Closer to home, one family member weighed in with the following.

> I still find the whole story a bit surreal and can't believe this happened in our family. Trust me, I do know it happened and know it is real—but wish it wasn't. . . . I have always known that the line between truth and fiction with [Carole] was blurred. That blurred line has become wider as we have become older. She has lived within the blurry zone for so long now—I don't even know if she would recognize or acknowledge the truth if it was standing in front of her in complete clarity. It may be all too painful to confront—therefore staying in that zone . . . it's like being medicated. This book brings some perspective—which I imagine she will discard. Instead of seeking and embracing truth in order to be truly free, I believe she will use the book to continue to build her victim identity.
>
> In this sense, she is her own prisoner. That is a life sentence.

Ultimately, the brain is capable of enormous change. To be able to make these changes, however, we must be capable of understanding that there is something that needs to be changed. Sometimes, it seems, we get a bad shake from life—our natural disposition is such that the hurdle of change is just too high for us to leap. For others, the mental patterns they've grown up with have solidified. They have the mental flexibility to change, but as with animals kept penned all their life, when choices confront them, they are unable to conceive of different thoughts.

Kindness is one of our most triumphant human characteristics. But our empathetic care for others, our altruism, and our loving concern can also inadvertently become the strongest of all psychological tethers. Ultimately, our underlying feelings of passion and compassion must be brought into the light of reason.

In truth, there are times when loosening the bonds of kindness can be the kindest act of all.

ACKNOWLEDGMENTS

I owe a great debt to the law enforcement officers, detectives, and prosecuting attorneys of Millard County, particularly Detective Richard "Jake" Jacobson and Deputy Attorney Pat Finlinson. Two minutes after Pat and I met, we were deep in conversation about the relevance of Thomas Kuhn's *Structures of Scientific Revolutions* to the Alden case. And Jake Jacobson? He's an extraordinary scientist lurking under the guise of a provincial detective. Anyone who might think that Millard County is too rural to hold onto its talented progeny would be sadly mistaken. Michael Wims's ability to grapple with complex issues is awe-inspiring. This book is far the better for Mike's perceptive eye. Patrick Nolan is one of the most dedicated and talented public servants I have had the good luck to meet—Utah is a fortunate state indeed to have him.

Marty Sessions's daughters, Edee Sessions and Anna Ruttenbur, and his stepsister Rosemary Salyer, have taken the time to fill the portrait of Marty Sessions as a full, vibrant man who is sorely missed.

Revisiting Marty's death has been painful for these fine women—I greatly appreciate their efforts. Dennis Sessions has perhaps the most complete picture of his brother Marty of anyone living—I deeply appreciate his candor and gracious recounting of his wild younger years.

I am especially grateful to the many members of Carole Alden's family who have taken the time and care to explain their experiences over the years. In this regard, I must reiterate that any errors of fact or interpretation remain my own. I salute Richard Senft in particular for his willingness to speak publicly about his experiences. Many people are understandably fearful to speak on the record about Carole Alden, so I extend a special thank-you to those who cannot be thanked by name.

Michael McGrath and Carolyn Zahn-Waxler earned my respect for their outstanding contributions to *Pathological Altruism*. Their willingness to open themselves up for a more extensive examination of their research and beliefs is even more admirable. This book could not have been written without them, and it is far the better for their cogent insights. Murray Straus has served as a beacon of bravery in the face of those who would intimidate. I also greatly appreciate Lynn O'Connor's nuanced perspectives, which allowed me to better understand my own.

Irene Scott has been a gem of a resource in helping me to better understand the history of Millard County; Leonard Hardy, Randy Morris, and Scott Ross are among the nicest people I've never met—their willingness to share their experiences is very much appreciated. I also appreciate Allen Lake's willingness to share his experiences.

Sheryl Gillilan's guidance in the world of art is much appreciated, as are Rebecca Smith's insights.

I would also like to thank Kevin Avery; Augustine Brannigan; Joanne Cantor; Russell Crook; Margaret Cochran, PhD; Howard Ditkoff; Shelly Dutson; Don Fullmer; Sander Greenland; Jeremy Harmen; Victor Harris; Cheryl Jones; Olga Klimecki; Randi Kreger; Mandy Law; Michael Lubin, MD; Jerry Oppenheimer; "Penny Packer"; Deputy Sheriff Tony Pedersen; Sheriff Ed Phillips; Josh

Poulsen; Lisa Sewell; Tania Singer; Jean Smith; Brent Turvey; Joe Trujillo; James Vanden Bosch; and Ruth Waytz.

Amy Alkon, my writing buddy, has been a terrific inspiration, along with her special guy, Gregg Sutter. Life is all the better for having wonderful friends like these. I also very much appreciate Lowell Cauffiel's willingness to walk me through the ropes of true crime. Daphne Gray-Grant is an expert at pulling prose out of writers in even the toughest of circumstances—her wisdom even from afar has been very helpful indeed. Virginia Postrel's work, particularly *The Future and Its Enemies: The Growing Conflict over Creativity, Enterprise, and Progress*, has been particularly important in shaping my overall thinking. So also has psychologist Mark Blumberg's body of work, including his subtle masterpiece *Freaks of Nature: What Anomalies Tell Us about Development and Evolution.* (I especially appreciate Mark's correction of several inadvertent deterministically oriented genetic faux pas in the manuscript. Truly, nature and nurture combine in extraordinarily complex ways.) Finally, Dr. Helen Smith has led the way in showing me how a psychologist can perhaps best make new contributions to the field by avoiding the abyss of dogma.

Joseph Carroll's insights have helped take this book to a higher level. As an evolutionary literary theorist, Joe has been making profoundly important efforts to shift the very foundations of literary study. It has been my great good fortune to have him for a mentor.

Audrey Perkins is not only a terrific editor—she's a friend who has an uncanny intuition for what I really should have been writing. Her innate human decency is reflected throughout this book.

I have been very fortunate to work with Linda Greenspan Regan, senior acquisitions editor at Prometheus Books twice now. Also at Prometheus, Chris Kramer in production has been sine qua non, and Catherine Roberts-Abel later took up the production banner with ability. Grace Zilsberger's cover design catches austere danger with élan. Julia DeGraf's skill, patience, and good humor involving the copyediting are very much appreciated, as is Jennifer Kovach's highly effective work in publicity. Will DeRooy's detailed final edits were well above the call of duty and made this a far better book. Editor in chief Steven L. Mitchell's dedicated efforts in ensuring integrity regarding every jot and tittle of this work are deeply appreciated. (Any errors, of course, remain my own.)

My publisher, Prometheus Books, is that rare publishing house that makes a point of publishing extraordinarily important, yet highly controversial material that others won't touch. It is an honor and a privilege as an author to be associated with them. My special appreciation in this regard goes to Jonathan Kurtz, the president of Prometheus Books.

My agent, Rita Rosenkranz, is a one-woman literary powerhouse. Her dedication, intuition, ethics, and meticulous attention to detail are awesome to behold—I count myself lucky to be one of her authors. My longtime friend Guruprasad Madhavan has made both this book and my life by far the richer for his insights. Cormac McCarthy's encouragement has meant more to me than I can ever say.

Truly my family is my lodestone—Rachel and Rosie Oakley have held down the home fort for us while we were traveling and made every day at home while I was working on this book a joy. Bafti Baftiu has been off holding down a more important fort in Iraq. Kevin Mendez-Aracena's work on illustrations is deeply appreciated.

My husband, Philip Oakley, is the love of my life. This book could not have been born but for his ready willingness to spend months driving us around Utah, and his acumen (and patience) as a sounding board. He makes every day a thrill to be alive.

NOTES

CHAPTER 1: A KILLING IN MILLARD COUNTY, UTAH

1. Anthony St. Peter, *The Greatest Quotations of All-Time* (Xlibris, 2010), p. 212.

2. Alois Pichler and Herbert Hrachovec, eds., *Wittgenstein and the Philosophy of Information: Proceedings of the 29th International Ludwig Wittgenstein-Symposium 2006* (Frankfurt am Main: Ontos Verlag, 2008), p. 140.

3. Recent research has shown that the pits near snakes' noses ("pit organs") contain special protein channels that react to the infrared given off as heat by mammalian prey. In humans, these protein channels are also known as wasabi receptors—they are the same molecules that allow humans to enjoy the pungent accompaniment to sushi. Who knew? Janet Fang, "Snake Infrared Detection Unravelled," *NatureNews*, March 14, 2010, http://www.nature.com/news/2010/100314/full/news.2010.122.html (accessed August 11, 2010).

Chapter 2: Mike McGrath's Disturbing Revelation

1. Melody Beattie, *Codependent No More: How to Stop Controlling Others and Start Caring for Yourself*, 2nd ed. (Center City, MN: Hazelden, 1986), p. 32.

2. These quotes and reminiscences, unless otherwise noted, are from e-mail correspondence between Michael McGrath and the author during 2010.

3. Michael McGrath, "Codependency and Pathological Altruism," in *Pathological Altruism*, edited by B. Oakley et al. (New York: Oxford University Press, in press).

4. P. Mellody, A. W. Miller, and K. Miller, *Facing Codependence: What It Is, Where It Comes from, How It Sabotages Our Lives* (HarperOne, 1989).

5. A reviewer on Amazon's page for the book; the review is titled "I'm Finally Understanding Quirks About Myself," Amazon.com, 2000, http://www.amazon.com/Facing-Codependence-Where-Comes-Sabo-tages/dp/0062505890 (accessed November 22, 2009).

6. S. J. Katz and A. Liu, *The Codependency Conspiracy: How to Break the Recovery Habit and Take Charge of Your Life* (Grand Central Publishing, 1991).

7. R. Subby, *Lost in the Shuffle: The Co-Dependent Reality* (Health Communications, 1987).

8. Benjamin James Kaplan, Virginia Alcott Sadock, and Pedro Ruiz, eds., *Kaplan & Sadock's Comprehensive Textbook of Psychiatry*, 9th ed. (Philadelphia: Lippincott Williams & Wilkins, 2009), p. 1264.

9. McGrath, "Codependency and Pathological Altruism."

10. Ibid.

11. L. L. Stafford, "Is Codependency a Meaningful Concept?" *Issues in Mental Health Nursing* 22, no. 3 (2001): 273–86; J. P. Morgan, "What Is Codependency?" *Journal of Clinical Psychology* 47, no. 5 (1991): 720–29.

12. Dana N. Jackson, "Admissibility of Evidence of Battered Woman's Syndrome Evidence on Issue of Self-Defense," Georgia State University "Research Guides" website, http://libguides.law.gsu.edu/content.php?pid =110018&sid=829255 (accessed August 28, 2010); David L. Faigman, *Legal Alchemy: The Use and Misuse of Science in the Law* (New York: W. H. Freeman, 1999), p. 72.

CHAPTER 3: MAYBERRY WITH AN EDGE

1. Stella H. Day and Sebrina C. Ekins, *Milestones of Millard: A Century of History of Millard County, 1851–1951* (Art City Publishing Company, 1951), p. 598.

2. Ibid., p. viii.

CHAPTER 4: TOUGH LOVE

1. Ambrose Bierce, *The Devil's Dictionary* (Plain Label Books, 1925), p. 125.

2. What follows is based on Sergeant Morris Burton's and Josie Greathouse's testimonies, as recorded in the Fourth Judicial District Court, in and for Millard County, State of Utah, *State of Utah, Plaintiff, v. Carole Alden Sessions, Defendant*, Case No. 061700168, before the Honorable Donald J. Eyre, Fourth District Court, 765 South Highway 99, Fillmore, Utah 84631, transcript, preliminary hearing, January 8, 2007.

CHAPTER 5: MIKE MCGRATH'S DISTURBING REVELATION, CONTINUED

1. Sander Greenland and Charles Poole, "Problems in Common Interpretations of Statistics in Scientific Articles, Expert Reports, and Testimony," *Jurimetrics* (in press).

2. These quotes and reminiscences, unless otherwise noted, are from e-mail correspondence between Michael McGrath and the author during 2010.

3. S. F. Brosnan, "Nonhuman Species' Reactions to Inequity and Their Implications for Fairness," *Social Justice Research* 19, no. 2 (2006): 153–85; ibid.; M. D. Hauser et al., "Food-Elicited Calls in Chimpanzees: Effects of Food Quantity and Divisibility," *Animal Behaviour* 45, no. 4 (1993): 817–19.

4. Iain McGilchrist, *The Master and His Emissary: The Divided Brain and the Making of the Modern World* (New Haven, CT: Yale University Press, 2010), p. 86.

5. Linda G. Mills, *Violent Partners: A Breakthrough Plan for Ending the Cycle of Abuse* (New York: Basic Books, 2008), p. xi.

6. Lenore E. A. Walker, *The Battered Woman Syndrome*, 3rd ed. (New York: Springer, 2009), p. 42.

7. Ibid., specifically, Walker notes: "After analyzing reported details about past and present feelings, thoughts, and actions of the women and the violent and nonviolent men, the data led me to conclude that there are no specific personality traits that would suggest a victim-prone personality for the women (see also Brown, 1992; Root, 1992), although there may be an identifiable violence-prone personality for the abusive men . . ." And on page 6: "Although there are 'risk-markers' for both men and women, increasing the probability of each group becoming involved in a violent relationship, the most common risk-marker is still the same one that the battered woman syndrome research study found; for men it is the exposure to violence in their childhood home (Hotaling & Sugarman, 1986) and for women, it is simply being a woman (APA, 196a). Other studies have found that poverty, immigration status, and prior abuse, are also risk factors for women to become battered, although they are not predictive (Walker, 1994)." Page 15: "Although certain childhood experiences seemed to leave the woman with a potential to be susceptible to experiencing the maximum effects from a violent relationship, this did not necessarily affect areas of the battered women's lives other than her family life. Most of the women interviewed were intelligent, well-educated, competent people who held responsible jobs."

8. Purists may be concerned about the use of the term "control group" when "comparison group" would actually be the proper term here. But as epidemiologist and statistician Sander Greenland (see more specifics as to his bona fides below) points out, "In all health-science (and for that matter, social-science) research I know, over the past 40 or so years the term 'control group' has become watered down to mean the same as comparison group. That usage is what you'll find in scores of textbooks (including for example all the best-sellers in research methodology in health sciences, such as *Modern Epidemiology* by Rothman, Greenland, and Lash). Modern usage, it should be noted, no longer means the investigator is controlling anything (at least in a valid or physical sense), and so the comparison may be providing little information about the effect under study." E-mail communication, August 28, 2010.

9. Walker's preface to the third edition of her book begins:

When I wrote the first edition of *The Battered Woman Syndrome* in the early 1980s there were very few articles and no books that described empirical data about conducting research with battered women. There was a great deal of interest in learning more about domestic violence and although some were interested in the psychological theories, more wanted to hear directly from the women themselves. Our original research team had learned a lot about how to obtain reliable and valid data from the women and I wrote the first edition to share our knowledge. For example, we chose to ask both open-ended as well as forced-choice questions. These women had a lot to say and we wanted to capture it all in this first exploratory study. Over 4000 variables later, we learned an enormous amount of information about what living in a battering relationship was like for the women. We emphasized the areas that the original 400 women had in common and shared the numerous descriptive statistics to demonstrate what they said to compare them with each other. As we understood it would be as difficult for other researchers to obtain a matched sample of non-battered women as a control group, we explained how we solved that problem by using each woman who also had a non-violent relationship to be her own control and used statistical techniques to manipulate the many variables that would help us develop those important comparisons. This turned out to be over half of the sample. At the time, this was considered innovative research methodology but today, holding variables constant with various statistical techniques is much more commonly used with large samples.

Fifteen years later, I wrote the second edition of the book, after there was much new research that supported our original conclusions. I used the same categories as in the first edition but integrated the newer data into the sections. I also demonstrated that scientific support continued to exist for the theories I proposed earlier. (Walker, *The Battered Woman Syndrome*, pp. xv–xvi)

However, Sander Greenland, professor of epidemiology, UCLA School of Public Health, and professor of statistics, UCLA College of Letters and Science, a leading authority on quantitative methods and statistical theory in epidemiology, notes the following:

First: "At the time, this was considered innovative research methodology but today, holding variables constant with various statistical techniques is much more commonly used with large samples."

This doesn't sound right. "Holding variables constant with various statistical techniques" was well under development by the 1960s and prevalent by the 1970s, so if there was anything innovative about her research methodology it isn't that. And by the 1970s expressions of concern about the outputs of these methods were starting to appear, which became a groundswell in the 1980s. Since then, innumerable pitfalls in the methodology have been discovered and elaborated, and most apply even in large samples. (This topic is one of my specialties and I've lectured about it all over the world.)

Second, one of the biggest concerns of critics is that all techniques available in standard software before very recently would start to break down without warning as the number of variables increases, gradually producing more and more misleading results. That breakdown can set in with just a few ill-chosen variables and is virtually guaranteed to be well underway when the number of variables becomes an appreciable fraction of the number of subjects. She stated "Over 4000 variables later, we learned an enormous amount of information about what living in a battering relationship was like for the women." While I have no doubt there was some worthwhile information in there, with 4000 variables—ten times the number of subjects—I have no idea what techniques she was using to guard against these problems. But I do know that there were no valid techniques known at the time that could assuredly work well in such a situation. Even today, certain problems (like misreporting) have no general solution and can throw results off tremendously.

Third, and most candidly, my alarm went off when I read

"given the finite resources available, it was decided to sacrifice the traditional empirical experimental model, with a control group, for the quasiexperimental model using survey-type data collection. It was seen as more important to compare battered women to themselves than to a nonbattered control group. Comparing battered and nonbattered women implies looking for some deficit in the battered group, which can be interpreted as a perpetuation of the victim-blaming model."

Sounded like use of ideology to shore up weak arguments for not collecting potentially important information. I see much of this sort of rationalization for weak research, especially in psychosocial areas where ideology becomes most intrusive.

Everyone has finite resources. Say you go to your HMO doctor concerned about a suspicious lump you found in your breast, and she gives you two aspirin with instructions to take them and come back in a year if the lump isn't gone. You question this prescription and she responds, "Well I know a biopsy would be better, but we have finite resources." While we are always limited by resources, sometimes the argument is used as an excuse to do something that is hardly better than nothing. That something is often proposed in the misguided notion that doing something is better than doing nothing. Well, it is if you are trying to dodge the unpleasant reality that to make any further progress on a topic, something else much more expensive will be needed. I doubt her case is this extreme, but she does seem to be trying [to] rationalize not obtaining half the data she would need to convince moderate skeptics.

Of course her underlying methods and rationale may be stronger than it looks in these quotes. I am only saying that the passages you cited set off a three-alarm warning for me. Close study of her actual work might reveal them to be false alarms, or at least not as serious as they look at first glance.

See also S. Greenland, "The Need for Critical Appraisal of Expert Witnesses in Epidemiology and Statistics," *Wake Forest Law Review* 39, no. 2 (2004): 291–310; Greenland and Poole, "Problems in Common Interpretations of Statistics in Scientific Articles."

10. Lenore E. A. Walker, *The Battered Woman Syndrome*, 2nd ed. (Springer, 1999), p. 146.

11. J. W. Dixon and K. E. Dixon, "Gender-Specific Clinical Syndromes and Their Admissibility under the Federal Rules of Evidence," *American Journal of Trial Advocacy* 27 (2003): 25; M. McMahon, "Battered Women and Bad Science: The Limited Validity and Utility of Battered Woman Syndrome," *Psychiatry, Psychology and Law* 6, no. 1 (1999): 23–49.

12. Walker herself noted that because of the high percentage of abused females, it would be too demanding to do a controlled experiment that matched four hundred battered women with four hundred non-battered women. Personal communication with the author, September 22, 2009.

CHAPTER 6: A COMPULSION TO CARE

1. Stella H. Day, *Builders of Early Millard: Biographies of Pioneers of Millard County 1850 to 1875* (Art City Publishing; repr. 1998 by J. Mart Publishing, Spanish Fork, UT, 1979), p. 451.

2. These quotes and reminiscences are from a personal interview with "Penny Packer" (a pseudonym), June 2009.

3. Cornelia deBruin, "Bad Taste? Critics Say Art Gives Wrong View of Utah Women," *Salt Lake Tribune*, January 5, 1993.

4. Jean Decety, Philip L. Jackson, and Eric Brunet, "The Cognitive Neuropsychology of Empathy," in *Empathy in Mental Illness*, edited by Tom F. D. Farrow and Peter W. R. Woodruff (New York: Cambridge University Press, 2007).

5. Y. Cheng et al., "Expertise Modulates the Perception of Pain in Others," *Current Biology* 17, no. 19 (2007): 1708–13. The discerning critic might wonder whether the acupuncture experts reacted differently because they had naturally different reactions to watching others experience pain. But Decety provides convincing evidence that was not the case. The hypothesized timing of the sequence described here is currently under study.

6. J. Decety and J. A. Sommerville, "Shared Representations between Self and Other: A Social Cognitive Neuroscience View," *Trends in Cognitive Sciences* 7, no. 12 (2003): 527–33.

7. J. L. Goetz, D. Keltner, and E. Simon-Thomas, "Compassion: An Evolutionary Analysis and Empirical Review," *Psychological Bulletin* 136, no. 3: 351–74.

8. L. Rueckert and N. Naybar, "Gender Differences in Empathy: The Role of the Right Hemisphere," *Brain and Cognition* 67, no. 2 (2008): 162–67.

9. Melody Beattie, *Codependent No More: How to Stop Controlling Others and Start Caring for Yourself*, 2nd ed. (Center City, MN: Hazelden, 1986), p. 29.

CHAPTER 7: EMPATHY'S ECHOES

1. Iain McGilchrist, *The Master and His Emissary: The Divided Brain and the Making of the Modern World* (New Haven, CT: Yale University Press, 2010), p. 86, citing *King Lear*, act 3, scene 5, lines 34–35.

2. Unless otherwise noted, all quotes from Carolyn Zahn-Waxler are from Carolyn Zahn-Waxler, "The Legacy of Loss: Depression as a Family Affair," in *Breaking the Silence: Mental Health Professionals Disclose Their Personal and Family Experiences of Mental Illness*, edited by Stephen P. Hinshaw (New York: Oxford University Press, 2008).

3. A recent book, *Delusions of Gender*, by Cordelia Fine, ostensibly "debunks the myth of hardwired differences between men's and women's brains, unraveling the evidence behind such claims as men's brains aren't wired for empathy and women's brains aren't made to fix cars." Fine does a good job at poking holes in problematic research, although her one-sided reading of the research literature and condescension for those who disagree with her thesis is troubling. The real story is far more complex than her presentation would make it appear.

For example, David Reimer was a boy who, because of a horrific accident during circumcision, was raised as a girl following the advice of Dr. John Money, a well-known Johns Hopkins psychologist. Money subsequently claimed that the treatment was highly successful, which implied that the differences between the sexes must be primarily cultural in origin.

Nothing could have been further from the truth, as John Colapinto relayed in his book *As Nature Made Him: The Boy Who Was Raised as a Girl*. Rather than the effortless transformation claimed by Dr. Money, David did everything he could as a child to fight the gender reassignment—tearing off frilly dresses, beating up his brother and taking his toy guns, rolling in the mud with the other boys, stomping on the dolls he had been given, complaining to his parents and teachers that he felt like a boy—and all this without ever having been informed of his biological sexual identity. David's identical twin, Brian, noted that his brother "walked like a guy. Sat with her legs apart. She talked about guy things, didn't give a crap about cleaning house, getting married, wearing makeup. We both wanted to play with guys, build forts and have snowball fights and play army. She'd get a skipping rope for a gift, and the only thing we'd use that for was to tie people up, whip people with it. She played with my toys: Tinkertoys, dump trucks. This toy sewing machine she got just sat. [Until, because she] loved to take things apart to see how they worked, [she] sneaked a screwdriver from her dad's tool kit and dismantled the toy."

As one reviewer, Jill Lightner, commented: "Reading over interviews and reports of decisions made by [Dr. John Money], it's difficult to contain anger at the widespread results of his insistence that natural-born gender can be altered with little more than willpower and hormone treatments." Dr. Milton Diamond, the prescient psychologist who exposed Dr. Money's misleading account of the gender change, concluded that "if all these combined medical, surgical, and social efforts could not succeed in making that child accept a female gender identity, then maybe we really have to think that there is something important in the individual's biological makeup; that we don't come to this world neutral; that we come to this world with some degree of maleness and femaleness which will transcend whatever the society wants to put into it."

Neuroscientist Lise Eliot, on the other hand, points out that the David Reimer case is in some ways quite weak, since Reimer wasn't converted to a girl until nearly two years old, when children already have a pretty sophisticated understanding of gender. Also, Reimer's tight bond with his identical twin brother would have complicated matters. Other cases of boys raised as girls (due to cloacal exstrophy) show more successful conversion, especially if it begins at birth. And girls with CAH (congenital adrenal hyperplasia), exposed to extremely high androgen levels before birth, are generally happy with their female gender identity. As Eliot cogently summarizes in *Pink Brain, Blue Brain*, "So it's all biology, whether the cause is nature or nurture. Sex differences in behavior *must* be reflected as sex differences in the brain, but the older children are, the less confidently their differences can be ascribed exclusively to genes and hormones. There are, to be sure, a few truly innate differences between the sexes—in maturation rate, sensory processing, activity level [and] fussiness . . .

"However, the male-female differences that have the most impact—cognitive skills, such as speaking, reading, math, and mechanical ability; and interpersonal skills, such as aggression, empathy, risk taking, and competitiveness—are heavily shaped by learning. Yes, they germinate from basic instincts and initial biases in brain function, but each of these traits is massively amplified by the different sorts of practice, role models, and reinforcement that boys and girls are exposed to from birth onward."

It's notable that Fine seems to play some of the same games noted by

Murray A. Straus in "Processes Explaining the Concealment and Distortion of Evidence on Gender Symmetry in Partner Violence," *European Journal on Criminal Policy and Research* 13 (2007): 227–32, to wit, creating "evidence" through citations that don't actually support the assertion. For example, on page 263 of *Delusions of Gender*, Fine notes that "the use of the digit ratio as a marker of prenatal testosterone exposure is controversial and lacks clear empirical support. For review see (McIntyre, 2006)." But McIntyre's review concludes "The validity of digit ratios as markers for perinatal androgen action is supported by a number of lines of recently reported evidence, but further support is needed." In other words, Fine implies that McIntyre is supporting her conclusion that the digit ratio is very problematic, when that's not what he concludes at all. See endnote 22, chapter 16, p. 353 for more discussion of Straus's findings regarding concealment and distortion in research literature. J. Colapinto, *As Nature Made Him* (New York: HarperCollins, 2000), pp. 57–58, 174–75. C. Fine, *Delusions of Gender: How Our Minds, Society, and Neurosexism Create Difference* (W. W. Norton & Company, 2010). Jill Lightner was a reviewer for Amazon.com. Lise Eliot, *Pink Brain, Blue Brain: How Small Differences Grow into Troublesome Gaps—and What We Can Do about It* (Houghton Mifflin Harcourt [HMH], 2009).

4. Carolyn Zahn-Waxler and Carole Van Hulle, "Empathy, Guilt, and Depression: When Caring for Others Becomes Costly to Children," in *Pathological Altruism*, edited by Barbara Oakley et al. (New York: Oxford University Press, in press).

5. The author's husband, Philip, for one. He's also a master mechanic. In other words, Philip is both an empathizer *and* a systemizer. There's a reason she likes to point out that she went to the end of the earth to meet that man. (They met at the South Pole Station in Antarctica.)

6. S. Baron-Cohen, *The Essential Difference* (New York: Basic Books, 2004); Simon Baron-Cohen, "Autism, Empathizing-Systemizing (ES) Theory, and Pathological Altruism," in *Pathological Altruism*, edited by B. Oakley et al.

7. It can actually get more complicated. (Can't it always?) For example, there are various ways that tissue can be more sensitive to testosterone rather than there simply *being* more testosterone. Underlying Baron-Cohen's *E-S* theory is another, perhaps deeper one—that "the human brain makes a fundamental distinction between the living and non-living world, and that distinct cognitive networks and rule systems operate when processing subjects and objects. . . . [In Baron-Cohen's formulation, e]mpathiz-

ing refers to the psychological processes involved in making sense of the living world, most notably other human beings (e.g. mentalizing, empathy, sympathy). Systemizing refers to the understanding of mostly non-social systems governed by orderly input-operation-output relationships." As Baron-Cohen explains, one "advantage of the *E-S* theory is that it can explain what is sometimes seen as an 'inability to generalise' in autism spectrum conditions. . . . According to the *E-S* theory, this is exactly what you would expect if the person is trying to understand each system as a unique system." S. Baron-Cohen, "Autism: The Empathizing-Systemizing (*E-S*) Theory," *Annals of the New York Academy of Sciences* 1156 (March), *The Year in Cognitive Neuroscience 2009* (2009): 68–80. For dissenting views about Baron-Cohen's work, see, for example, J. Andrew and M. Cooke, "The Relationship between Empathy and Machiavellianism: An Alternative to Empathizing-Systemizing Theory," *Personality and Individual Differences* 44, no. 5 (2008): 1203–11, and E. Pellicano et al., "Children with Autism Are Neither Systemic nor Optimal Foragers," *PNAS* 109, no. 1 (2011): 421–26.

8. The theory was kicked off by the father of American behavioral neurology—brilliant, charismatic Norman Geschwind (1926–1984)—and Albert Galaburda, as described in detail in Norman Geschwind and Albert Galaburda, *Cerebral Lateralization: Biological Mechanisms, Associations, and Pathology* (Cambridge, MA: MIT Press, 1986). See also W. H. James, "Further Evidence That Some Male-Based Neurodevelopmental Disorders Are Associated with High Intrauterine Testosterone Concentrations," *Developmental Medicine & Child Neurology* 50, no. 1 (2008): 15–18, and references therein.

9. See C. Zahn-Waxler et al., "The Origins and Development of Psychopathology in Females and Males," *Development and Psychopathology* 1 (2006): 76, wherein it is noted:

> Beginning in adolescence, females are two to three times more likely than males to experience unipolar depressive disorders, as seen [in] both community-based and clinically-referred samples (Kessler, McGonagle, Swartz, Blazer, & Nelson, 1993; Nolen-Hoeksema, 1990; Weissman & Klerman, 1977; Weissman, Leaf, Bruce, & Florio, 1988). It is also present whether depression is diagnosed as a disorder or measured along a continuum of symptom severity.
>
>   . . .
>
> After puberty, the lifetime prevalence in females is twice that of

males (Lewinsohn, et al., 1993). Comorbidity of depressive and anxiety disorders is much more common in girls than boys (Lewinsohn, et al., 1995b); moreover depression that is comorbid with more than one anxiety disorder is virtually exclusive to females (Lewinsohn, Zinbarg, Seeley, Lewinsohn, & Sack, 1997). Female gender and presence of a coexisting anxiety disorder are also related to severity of initial depression (McCauley, et al., 1993). Co-occurrence of symptoms is even higher when subclinical levels also are considered. Although depression and anxiety can be clearly differentiated at biological, cognitive, behavioral, and affective levels, the extent to which they overlap and cooccur suggests that the combination represents a unique but common form of depression, particularly in females.

Females show a different constellation of depressive symptoms than males, notably more anxiety, more somatic symptoms, hypersomnia, weight gain, increased appetite, fatigue, psychomotor retardation, and body image disturbance (see review by Zahn-Waxler, et al., in press). Increased appetite and weight gain seem to be the most distinct symptoms in women and adolescent girls. Higher rates of crying, sadness, and negative self-concept have been noted for school-age and adolescent girls.

In research by Gjerde and Block (1995), dysphoric males often expressed their unhappiness directly and without hesitation, by acting on the world in an aggressive, hostile manner. Dysphoric symptoms in female adolescents, in contrast, were characterized by introspection, absence of open hostility, and a mostly hidden preoccupation with self. As early as age 7, boys who later showed dysthymia were aggressive, self-aggrandizing, and undercontrolled, whereas dysthymic girls were intropunitive, oversocialized, overcontrolled, anxious and introspective (Block, Gjerde, & Block, 1991). Young girls who later became depressed also had close relationships. The sadness and anxiety in depressed girls and hostility in depressed boys can be seen as exaggerations of normative sex differences. These studies focus on subclinical depression. Further studies of males and females with clinical depression are needed to determine whether their symptomatology shows a similar pattern. Other research suggests that young, depressed boys show a pattern of acting out (Kovacs 1996). In a recent observational study of young children, boys, but not girls, with both subclinical and clinical depression were likely to show anger relative to controls (Luby et al., 2005).

Genetic/Biological Explanations. Some studies report similar heritability estimates for depressive disorders in males and females, several others find differences (e.g. Bierut, et al., 1999; Jacobson & Rowe, 1999; Kendler, Gardner, Neale, & Prescott, 2001a; Tambs, Harris, & Magnus, 1995). Kendler, et al. (2001) suggest that in genetic linkage studies, the impact of some loci on risk for major depression will vary in men and women. Genetics are also involved in the etiology of depression through their effect on sensitivity to environmental events. Silberg, Rutter, Neale, & Eaves (2001) found that genetics had a larger effect on the development of depression in adolescent girls who had experienced a negative event in the previous year than on those who did not. Kendler and colleagues (Kendler, 1998; Kendler, et al., 1995) found that persons at greater genetic risk were twice as likely to develop major depression in response to severe stress than those at lower genetic risk. Genetic risk also altered sensitivity to the environment for women only (Kendler, et al., 1995a). At puberty, girls' negative life events and stability of depression over time are more genetically mediated than for boys (Silberg et al., 1999).

See also C. Zahn-Waxler, E. A. Shirtcliff, and K. Marceau, "Disorders of Childhood and Adolescence: Gender and Psychopathology," *Annual Review of Clinical Psychology* 4 (2008): 275–303. This paper, as Zahn-Waxler points out, "is about the origins of sex differences in different forms of psychopathology in males and females. Internalizing problems (anxiety and depression) are much more common in females than males and externalizing problems (Conduct problems, ADHD, etc.) are much more common in males than females. These differences hold across cultures, though the relative differences may vary." (E-mail communication with the author, August 27, 2010.)

Also see C. Zahn-Waxler, E. Race, and S. Duggal, "Mood Disorders and Symptoms in Girls," in *Handbook of Behavioral and Emotional Problems in Girls*, edited by Debora J. Bell, Sharon L. Foster, and Eric J. Mash (New York: Kluwer Academic/Plenum, 2005), which notes:

The rates of depression in childhood are comparable for boys and girls (with boys showing slightly higher rates), but while the rates dramatically increase around puberty for girls, they remain the same for boys or increase to a lesser extent (Anderson, Williams, McGee, and Silva, 1987; Angold and Rutter, 1992). Studies based both on diagnostic interviews and standardized self-reports indicate that this change in prevalence rates begins around ages 13–15 (Angold, Costello, and Worthman, 1998; Ge, Lorenz, Conger, Elder, et al., 1994; Petersen, Sargiani, Kennedy, 1991; Wichstrom, 1999). There is a 4–23% increase in diagnosed depression in adolescents between the ages of 15 to 18 (Hankin, Abramson, Moffitt, Silva, & McGee (1998). After puberty, the lifetime prevalence of depression in females is two times that of adolescent males, and one-year first incidence of depression is 1.6% greater for females than males (Lewinsohn, et al., 1993). Sex differences in depression are found consistently across cultures within the United States and the world, controlling for income, education, and occupation (McGrath, Keita, Strickland, & Russo, 1990; Weissman, Bland, Canino, Faravelli, et al., 1996).

See also M. Altemus and L. Epstein, "Sex Differences in Anxiety Disorders," in *Sex Differences in the Brain: From Genes to Behavior*, edited by Jill B. Becker et al. (New York: Oxford University Press, 2008); M. H. J. Bekker and J. van Mens-Verhulst, "Anxiety Disorders: Sex Differences in Prevalence, Degree, and Background, but Gender-Neutral Treatment," *Gender Medicine* 4 (2007): S178–S193; M. Altemus, "Sex Differences in Depression and Anxiety Disorders: Potential Biological Determinants," *Hormones and Behavior* 50, no. 4 (2006): 534–38; K. McRae et al., "Gender Differences in Emotion Regulation: An fMRI Study of Cognitive Reappraisal," *Group Processes & Intergroup Relations* 11, no. 2 (2008): 143–62; I. Esther, T. W. Fop Verheij, and F. F. Robert, "Differences in Finger Length Ratio between Males with Autism, Pervasive Developmental Disorder-Not Otherwise Specified, ADHD, and Anxiety Disorders," *Developmental Medicine & Child Neurology* 48, no. 12 (2006): 962–65; H. W. Hoek and D. van Hoeken, "Review of the Prevalence and Incidence of Eating Disorders," *International Journal of Eating Disorders* 34, no. 4 (2003): 383–96.

10. A. Von Horn et al., "Empathizing, Systemizing and Finger Length Ratio in a Swedish Sample," *Scandinavian Journal of Psychology* 51, no. 1 (2009): 31–37. Citing E. Herrmann et al., "Humans Have Evolved Specialized Skills of Social Cognition: The Cultural Intelligence Hypothesis," *Sci-*

ence 317, no. 5843 (2007): 1360. M. H. McIntyre, "The Use of Digit Ratios as Markers for Perinatal Androgen Action," *Reproductive Biology and Endocrinology* 4, no. 10 (2006): 1–9; Baron-Cohen, "*E-S* Theory." But see S. A. Berenbaum et al., "Fingers as a Marker of Prenatal Androgen Exposure," *Endocrinology* 150, no. 11 (2009): 5119.

A quick way to tell how much testosterone someone was exposed to in the womb is by looking at the right hand. The longer the ring finger in comparison with the index finger, the more testosterone. Although this technique seems like it should be about as accurate as palm reading, the science underlying the digit-ratio phenomenon is real and well studied—although still highly controversial. See John Manning's *Digit Ratio: A Pointer to Fertility, Behavior, and Health* (Rutgers University Press, 2002).

11. E-mail communication with the author, May 1, 2010.

12. McGilchrist, *The Master and His Emissary*. It is worthwhile to note that Baron-Cohen attributes systemizing thinking to the right side of the brain, and empathizing to the left. See S. Baron-Cohen, *The Essential Difference* (New York: Basic Books, 2004); McGilchrist makes a far better case for the converse: systemizing is on the left, while empathizing is on the right. In support of this latter thesis, see also L. Shlain, *The Alphabet Versus the Goddess: The Conflict between Word and Image* (Penguin, 1999). E. Goldberg, *The New Executive Brain: Frontal Lobes in a Complex World* (Oxford University Press, 2009).

13. Helen Thomson, "We Feel Your Pain: Extreme Empaths," *New Scientist* no. 2751 (March 15, 2010).

14. R. Bachner-Melman et al., "The Relationship between Selflessness Levels and the Severity of Anorexia Nervosa Symptomatology," *European Eating Disorders Review* 15, no. 3 (2007).

15. E. Bachar et al., "Selflessness and Perfectionism as Predictors of Pathological Eating Attitudes and Disorders: A Longitudinal Study," *European Eating Disorders Review* 18, no. 6 (November–December 2010): 496–506.

16. Rachel Bachner-Melman, "The Relevance of Pathological Altruism to Eating Disorders," in *Pathological Altruism*, edited by B. Oakley et al.

17. Ibid.

18. Lynn E. O'Connor et al., "Empathy-Based Pathogenic Guilt, Pathological Altruism, and Psychopathology," in *Pathological Altruism*, edited by Barbara Oakley et al.

19. Zahn-Waxler and Van Hulle, "Empathy, Guilt, and Depression."

20. The thoughts in this paragraph are slightly paraphrased from e-mail correspondence from Joseph Carroll, Curators' Professor of English, University of Missouri, St. Louis, August 28, 2010.

21. Olga Klimecki and Tania Singer, "Empathic Distress Fatigue Rather Than Compassion Fatigue?—Integrating Findings from Empathy Research in Psychology and Social Neuroscience," in *Pathological Altruism*, edited by Barbara Oakley et al. Klimecki and Singer's work is based on developmental theories of Dan Batson and Nancy Eisenberg. See C. D. Batson, "Empathy-Induced Altruistic Motivation," in *Prosocial Motives, Emotions, and Behavior*, edited by M. Mikulincer and P. R. Shaver (Washington, DC: American Psychological Association, 2009); C. D. Batson, "These Things Called Empathy: Eight Related but Distinct Phenomena," in *The Social Neuroscience of Empathy*, edited by J. Decety and W. Ickes (Cambrdige: MIT Press, 2009); C. D. Batson et al., "Is Empathic Emotion a Source of Altruistic Motivation?" *Journal of Personality and Social Psychology* 40, no. (1981): 290–302; C. Daniel Batson et al., "Influence of Self-Reported Distress and Empathy on Egoistic Versus Altruistic Motivation to Help," *Journal of Personality and Social Psychology* 45, no. 3 (1983): 706–718; C. D. Batson, J. Fultz, and P. A. Schoenrade, "Distress and Empathy: Two Qualitatively Distinct Vicarious Emotions with Different Motivational Consequences," *Journal of Personality* 55, no. 1 (1987): 19–39; N. Eisenberg, "Emotion, Regulation, and Moral Development," *Annual Review of Psychology* 51, no. 1 (2000): 665–97; N. Eisenberg et al., "Relation of Sympathy and Personal Distress to Prosocial Behavior: A Multimethod Study," *Journal of Personality and Social Psychology* 57, no. 1 (1989): 55–66.

22. L. W. McCray et al., "Resident Physician Burnout: Is There Hope?" *Family Medicine* 40, no. 9 (2008): 626–32.

23. Matthieu Ricard, a monk who collaborates with Tania Singer and Olga Klimecki, gave a short interview in which he talks about the distinction between empathic distress and compassion: http://www.huffingtonpost.com/matthieu-ricard/could-compassion-meditati_b_751566.html. (The quotes in the figure caption are from the video accompanying this story.)

24. Madeline Li and Gary Rodin, "Altruism and Suffering in the Context of Cancer Caregiving: Implications of a Relational Paradigm," in *Pathological Altruism*, edited by Barbara Oakley et al.; Klimecki and Singer, "Empathic Distress Fatigue Rather Than Compassion Fatigue?" in *Patholog-*

ical Altruism, edited by Barbara Oakley et al.; M. Paris and M. A. Hoge, "Burnout in the Mental Health Workforce: A Review," *Journal of Behavioral Health Services and Research* 37, no. 4 (2009): 519–28; D. Edwards et al., "Stress and Burnout in Community Mental Health Nursing: A Review of the Literature," *Journal of Psychiatric and Mental Health Nursing* 7, no. 1 (2000): 7–14; L. W. McCray et al., "Resident Physician Burnout: Is There Hope?" *Family Medicine* 40, no. 9 (2008): 626–32.

25. Klimecki and Singer, "Empathic Distress Fatigue Rather Than Compassion Fatigue?" citing T. D. Shanafelt et al., "Burnout and Self-Reported Patient Care in an Internal Medicine Residency Program," *Annals of Internal Medicine* 136, no. 5 (2002): 358; J. J. Hillhouse, C. M. Adler, and D. N. Walters, "A Simple Model of Stress, Burnout and Symptomatology in Medical Residents: A Longitudinal Study," *Psychology, Health & Medicine* 5, no. 1 (2000): 63–73; C. P. West et al., "Association of Perceived Medical Errors with Resident Distress and Empathy: A Prospective Longitudinal Study," *JAMA* 296, no. 9 (2006): 1071; C. R. Figley, "Compassion Fatigue: Psychotherapists' Chronic Lack of Self Care," *Journal of Clinical Psychology* 58, no. 11 (2002): 1433–41.

26. Klimecki and Singer, "Empathic Distress Fatigue Rather Than Compassion Fatigue?" citing R. Schulz et al., "Patient Suffering and Caregiver Compassion: New Opportunities for Research, Practice, and Policy," *Gerontologist* 47 (2007): 4–13.

27. E-mail communication between Margaret Cochran and the author, February 8, 2010.

28. Ibid.

29. Zahn-Waxler, "The Legacy of Loss: Depression as a Family Affair."

30. See Barbara Oakley, Ariel Knafo, and Michael McGrath, "Pathological Altruism—an Introduction," in *Pathological Altruism*, edited by B. Oakley et al., which notes: "Pathological altruism—in the sense of an unhealthy focus on others to the detriment of one's own needs—may have a very early start, and can be seen in developmental personality processes. This can be seen in data from toddler-age twins. Children were designated as highly *altruistic* if they were in the top 20 percent in measured prosocial behavior. Another category is related to *self-actualizing* behavior, such as 'shows pleasure when s/he succeeds,' 'continues trying, even when something is hard,' or 'wants to do things by him/herself.' Children were rated as *low* in self-actualizing behaviors if they ranked in the bottom 20 percent of

that category. Twins were thought to potentially show the beginning of a form of pathological altruism if they simultaneously ranked in the top 20 percent of altruistic behaviors and the bottom 20 percent of self-actualizing behaviors. Of 2,496 children, 73 (3 percent) met both criteria. That is, these children were very likely to share, care for other children, and help around, but were not at all likely to be characterized by 'shows pleasure when s/he succeeds,' 'continues trying, even when something is hard,' or 'wants to do things by him/herself.'" This passage references A. Knafo, "The Longitudinal Israeli Study of Twins (List): Children's Social Development as Influenced by Genetics, Abilities, and Socialization," *Twin Research and Human Genetics* 9, no. 6 (2006): 791–98, and R. Goodman, "The Strengths and Difficulties Questionnaire: A Research Note," *Journal of Child Psychology and Psychiatry* 38 (1997): 581–86.

31. M. Reuter et al., "Investigating the Genetic Basis of Altruism: The Role of the COMT Val158Met Polymorphism," *Social Cognitive and Affective Neuroscience* (2010) (E-pub ahead of print). But also see the wonderful article by I. Dar-Nimrod and S. J. Heine, "Genetic Essentialism: On the Deceptive Determinism of DNA," *Psychological Bulletin*, December 13 (2010) (Epub ahead of print), which cautions against determinism in thinking about issues related to genetics.

32. Zahn-Waxler, "The Legacy of Loss: Depression as a Family Affair."

CHAPTER 8: CARING STARTS EARLY

1. Linda Lawrence Hunt, *Bold Spirit: Helga Estby's Forgotten Walk across Victorian America* (New York: Random House, 2003), p. 251.

2. B. S. McEwen, "Steroid Hormones and Brain Development: Some Guidelines for Understanding Actions of Pseudohormones and Other Toxic Agents," *Environmental Health Perspectives* 74 (1987): 177; C. Viglietti-Panzica et al., "Organizational Effects of Diethylstilbestrol on Brain Vasotocin and Sexual Behavior in Male Quail," *Brain Research Bulletin* 65, no. 3 (2005): 225–33.

3. E. J. O'Reilly et al., "Diethylstilbestrol Exposure in Utero and Depression in Women," *American Journal of Epidemiology* 171, no. 8 (2010): 876–82.

4. Carole's mother was eight months pregnant—past the usual stage

when chicken pox is generally found to affect the fetus. But as it turns out, chicken pox can cause severe damage even in late pregnancy. Centers for Disease Control and Prevention, "Varicella Vaccine—Q & A's about Pregnancy," http://www.cdc.gov/vaccines/vpd-vac/varicella/vac-faqs-clinic-preg .htm (accessed June 30, 2009); Gideon Koren, "Congenital Varicella Syndrome in the Third Trimester," *Lancet* 366, no. 9497 (2005). J. W. Gnann Jr., "Varicella-Zoster Virus: Atypical Presentations and Unusual Complications," *Journal of Infectious Diseases* 186, no. S1 (2002); A Yaramis et al., "Cerebral Vasculitis and Obsessive-Compulsive Disorder Following Varicella Infection in Childhood," *Turkish Journal of Pediatrics* 51, no. 1 (2009): 72–75. Smith et al. note: "If VZV transmission occurs as a consequence of maternal infection during the perinatal period, from approximately two days before delivery to five days after, the infant is at risk of severe life-threatening varicella disease." C. K. Smith and A. M. Arvin, "Varicella in the Fetus and Newborn," *Seminars in Fetal and Neonatal Medicine* 14, no. 4 (2009): 209–17. Narkeviciute notes: "Although the risk of foetal abnormalities, herpes zoster in early childhood or neonatal varicella following maternal varicella is small, the outcome for the affected infant may be very serious." Irena Narkeviciute, "Consequences of Varicella in Pregnancy: A Report of Four Cases," *Acta Paediatrica* 96, no. 7 (2007): 1099–1100.

    5. S. B. Barnett and H. D. Rott, "The Sensitivity of Biological Tissue to Ultrasound," *Ultrasound in Medicine & Biology* 23, no. 6 (1997): 805–12; G. Haar, "Ultrasound Bioeffects and Safely," *Proceedings of the Institution of Mechanical Engineers, Part H: Journal of Engineering in Medicine* 224, no. 2 (2010): 363–73; J. S. Abramowicz, "Ultrasound Imaging of the Early Fetus: Is It Safe?" *Imaging* 1, no. 1 (2009): 85–95; J. P. Spencer and M. S. Blumberg, "Short Arm and Talking Eggs: Why We Should No Longer Abide the Nativist-Empiricist Debate," *Child Development Perspectives* 3, no. 2 (2009): 79–87; M. S. Blumberg, *Freaks of Nature: What Anomalies Tell Us about Development and Evolution* (New York: Oxford University Press, 2008); Mark S. Blumberg, *Basic Instinct: The Genesis of Behavior* (New York: Basic Books, 2006); Mark S. Blumberg, *Body Heat: Temperature and Life on Earth* (Cambridge, MA: Harvard University Press, 2004). Mark Blumberg's works in particularly masterful in their depiction of the complex interactions of the environment and the developing body.

    6. P. V. Gejman, A. R. Sanders, and J. Duan, "The Role of Genetics in the Etiology of Schizophrenia," *Psychiatric Clinics of North America* 33, no. 1

(2010): 35–66. See also M. F. Fraga et al., "Epigenetic Differences Arise during the Lifetime of Monozygotic Twins," *Proceedings of the National Academy of Sciences of the United States of America* 102, no. 30 (2005): 10604.

7. Sharon Begley, "DNA as Crystal Ball: Buyer Beware," *Newsweek*, May 18, 2010, http://www.newsweek.com/2010/05/18/dna-as-crystal-ball -buyer-beware.html (accessed December 19, 2010). Iain McGilchrist, *The Master and His Emissary: The Divided Brain and the Making of the Modern World* (New Haven, CT: Yale University Press, 2010), p. 53.

It's wise to be careful when interpreting data related to genes. We just don't know enough yet. For example, just knowing whether someone has genes that have been associated with a disease can't help predict whether a person will actually get the disease. In discussing this counterintuitive finding, *Newsweek*'s Sharon Begley observes this "must reflect the fact that the effect of a gene depends on a person's 'genetic background'—all the other genes he or she has. And it also reflects a person's environment. In some environments a gene does lead to disease; in others, it doesn't."

This desire to categorize—that is, to think in a categorical, deterministic fashion about genes and their effects—also reflects neatly on the differing strengths of the left and right brain. As psychiatrist Iain McGilchrist observes in *The Master and His Emissary*, the left brain has a categorizing drive that is at work all the time in all of us—this is particularly apparent in patients with conditions such as stroke that tend to favor the left hemisphere over the right.

8. T. F. D. Farrow and P. W. R. Woodruff, *Empathy in Mental Illness* (New York: Cambridge University Press, 2007).

CHAPTER 9: THE PRELIMINARY HEARING BEGINS

1. W. H. Auden, "The Guilty Vicarage," in *Harper's*, May 1948, pp. 406–12.

2. What follows is an abbreviated version of the court records in the Fourth Judicial District Court, in and for Millard County, State of Utah, *State of Utah, Plaintiff, v. Carole Alden Sessions, Defendant*, Case No. 061700168, before the Honorable Donald J. Eyre, Fourth District Court, 765 South Highway 99, Fillmore, Utah 84631, Reporter's Transcript of Proceedings, Preliminary Hearing, January 8, 2007. Misspoken words have been largely

eliminated, and the text has been tightened, but care has been taken to preserve context. The order in which witnesses and issues were presented has in some instances been changed.

3. *Voir dire* is a phrase most often used to refer to the preliminary questions put to potential jurors before they are selected to sit on the jury. However, *voir dire* can also be used to refer to the preliminary questions of a witness—most often an expert witness—concerning the expert's qualifications.

As Mike Wims would later point out: "For those of us familiar with the French language who attended the University of Texas School of Law, it was sometimes difficult not to shudder when a law professor with a strong Texan accent pronounced the term '*voir dire*' so that the 'voir' rhymed with the first syllable of voracious and 'dire' rhymed with the first syllable of the musical group 'Dire Straits.'"

Though the term *voir dire* is properly pronounced like the modern French verbs *voir* ("to see") and *dire* ("to say"), the term precedes even Norman French. The word *voir* in this usage actually derives from the Latin *verum*, "that which is true," and is not really related to the modern French word *voir*.

CHAPTER 10: MARTY SESSIONS

1. Ewan McGregor played Renton in Danny Boyle's 1996 drama, *Trainspotting*, which follows the adventures of a group of friends immersed in Edinburgh's drug scene, based on the novel by Irvine Welsh.

2. These reminiscences are based on interviews with Denny Sessions in August 2010. As Denny notes, the events described here have been passed down into family lore, and so may diverge to some extent from actual facts.

3. Guestbook of Thomas LeRoy Sessions, http://www.legacy.com/guestbook/deseretnews/guestbook.aspx?n=martin-sessions&pid=18714546 (accessed August 24, 2010).

4. Steven Okazaki, *Black Tar Heroin, the Dark End of the Street*, 1999, http://www.youtube.com/watch?v=9Yt4Mmn7ofI (accessed August 24, 2010).

5. Anna Ruttenbur's recollections here are based on telephone conversations between Anna Ruttenbur and the author, August 2010.

6. Comments throughout the chapter from Anna Ruttenbur and Edee Sessions-Wagers are from telephone conversations between them and the author during August–September 2010.

7. Edee Sessions's recollections here are based on telephone conversations between Edee Sessions and the author, August 2010.

8. This statement is according to Edee and Denny Sessions and Anna Ruttenbur, speaking from their knowledge of the family as a whole.

9. Patty Henetz, "Spurned Advances Led to Killings, Records Say," *Deseret News*, November 6, 1991.

10. "Judge Declares W. V. Man Incompetent," *Deseret News*, June 3, 1992, http://www.deseretnews.com/article/230163/JUDGE-DECLARES-WV-MAN-INCOMPETENT.html (accessed August 15, 2010).

11. Stephen Hunt, "1991 Shootings: Woman Who Survived Testifies about Murderous Rampage," *Salt Lake Tribune*, February 27, 2008.

12. Linda Thomson, "Details of Killings Emerge: After Years at Utah State Hospital, Tiedemann on Trial for 1991 Slayings," *Deseret News*, February 27, 2008, http://www.deseretnews.com/article/695256762/Details-of-killings-emerge.html (accessed August 15, 2010).

13. "Attorney Says W.V. Man Who Is Charged in 2 Murders, Rape May Not Be Competent," *Deseret News*, November 27, 1991, http://www.deseretnews.com/article/196074/ATTORNEY-SAYS-WV-MAN-WHO-IS-CHARGED-IN-2-MURDERS-RAPE-MAY-NOT-BE—COMPETENT.html (accessed August 15, 2010).

14. Geoffrey Fattah, "High Court to Hear '91 Homicide Case," *Deseret News*, August 28, 2006, http://www.deseretnews.com/article/645196757/High-court-to-hear-91-homicide-case.html (accessed August 15, 2010).

15. Stephen Hunt, "Lone Survivor Testifies in 1991 Slayings," *Salt Lake Tribune*, June 11, 2003.

16. Linda Thomson, "Tiedemann Gets Prison for Slayings," *Deseret News*, May 3, 2008, http://www.deseretnews.com/article/695276101/Tiedemann-gets-prison-for-slayings.html (accessed August 15, 2010).

17. Linda Thomson, "Details of Killings Emerge: After Years at Utah State Hospital, Tiedemann on Trial for 1991 Slayings." See also Geoffrey Fattah, "Jury Delivers Guilty Verdicts on All Counts in Tiedemann Trial," *Deseret News*, February 28, 2008, http://www.deseretnews.com/article/695257234/Jury-delivers-guilty-verdicts-on-all-counts-in-Tiedemann-trial.html (accessed August 15, 2010); Laura Hancock, "Man Charged in '91 Slayings of 3," *Deseret News*, November 14, 2002, http://www.deseretnews.com/article/948553/Man-charged-in-91-slayings-of-3.html (accessed January 13, 2011).

18. Ben Winslow, "Convicted Double Murderer Asks for Release," *Deseret News*, October 3, 2008, http://www.deseretnews.com/article/7002635 84/Convicted-double-murderer-asks-for-release.html (accessed August 16, 2010). See also *State v. Tiedemann*, no. 20050676, Supreme Court of Utah, 2007.

During his first hearing for a release in front of the Board of Pardons and Parole in 2008, Tiedemann refused to take an oath, said he was of no risk to anyone, and asked to be released to go to Norway. Parole board member Chuck Harms told Tiedemann: "I don't think the citizens of this state ought to bear the risk of you being free for a single moment between now and the time you pass away." As Ben Winslow of the *Deseret News* then reported: "The announcement appeared to stun Tiedemann, who sat silently, blinking his eyes rapidly from behind thick glasses. 'Uh, OK,' he replied. 'You'll be sorry.'"

CHAPTER 11: A DETECTIVE AT WORK

1. Michael D. Wims, Charles Ambrose, and Jack B. Rubin, *How to Prepare and Try a Murder Case: Prosecution and Defense Perspectives* (American Bar Association, in press).

2. Quotations and events described here are based on the recollections of Richard Jacobson during interviews with the author in 2009 and 2010.

3. Personal interview between Relda Jacobson and the author, June 5, 2010.

4. Brent E. Turvey and Wayne Petherick, *Forensic Victimology: Examining Violent Crime Victims in Investigative and Legal Contexts* (New York: Elsevier, 2009), p. xvii. The substance of the paragraph is as laid out in the original—only the tense has been changed.

CHAPTER 12: CROSS-EXAMINATION BY MR. SLAVENS— WHY THE HOUSE WAS A WRECK

1. P. J. Buchanan, *Where the Right Went Wrong: How Neoconservatives Subverted the Reagan Revolution and Hijacked the Bush Presidency* (St. Martin's Griffin, 2005), p. 125.

2. Biographical information in this brief section follows from a telephone interview with James Slavens, October 8, 2010.

3. What follows is an abbreviated version of the court records in the Fourth Judicial District Court, in and for Millard County, State of Utah, *State of Utah, Plaintiff, v. Carole Alden Sessions, Defendant*, Case No. 061700168, before the Honorable Donald J. Eyre, Fourth District Court, 765 South Highway 99, Fillmore, Utah 84631, Reporter's Transcript of Proceedings, Preliminary Hearing, January 8, 2007. Misspoken words have been largely eliminated, and the text has been tightened, but care has been taken to preserve context.

CHAPTER 13: FLASHBACK

1. Stella H. Day and Sebrina C. Ekins, *Milestones of Millard: A Century of History of Millard County, 1851–1951* (Art City Publishing Company, 1951), p. 47.

2. State's Memorandum in Opposition to Defendant's 402 Motion to Reduce Conviction, Case No. 061700168 in the Fourth Judicial District Court of Millard County, State of Utah, *State of Utah, Plaintiff, v. Carole Elizabeth Alden, Defendant*, August 20, 2007, pp. 3–5, Judge Donald J. Eyre Jr.

3. Ibid. (The text is taken virtually verbatim from an e-mail Carole wrote to a friend.)

4. Ibid.

5. Ibid.

6. Police inventory, items from inside home, item 20-B.

7. Dialogue reconstructed from the recollections of officials affiliated with the investigation of the gun purchase.

CHAPTER 14: THE SANCTITY OF THE VICTIM

1. Edward Mendelson, "'We Are All Here on Earth to Help Others . . . ,'" *The W. H. Auden Society*, http://audensociety.org/vivianfoster .html (accessed October 19, 2010). Auden, it seems, never claimed credit for the quote, though it was often attributed to him. As noted in Mendelson's article, the source was finally tracked to an audio recording of English music-hall and radio comedian John Foster Hall (1867–1945), who called himself the Reverend Vivian Foster, the Vicar of Mirth.

2. Malcolm Gladwell, "Dangerous Minds," *New Yorker*, November 12,

2007, http://www.newyorker.com/reporting/2007/11/12/071112fa_fact _gladwell?currentPage=all (accessed September 17, 2010).

3. Brent E. Turvey and Wayne Petherick, *Forensic Victimology: Examining Violent Crime Victims in Investigative and Legal Contexts* (New York: Elsevier, 2009).

4. B. E. Turvey, *Criminal Profiling: An Introduction to Behavioral Evidence Analysis* (New York: Academic Press, 2008).

5. Turvey and Petherick, *Forensic Victimology*, pp. xxv–xxvi.

6. Ibid., p. xxxii.

7. David R. Koon, "Politics and Legislation," in *Career Development in Bioengineering and Biotechnology*, edited by G. Madhavan, B. Oakley, and L. Kun (New York: Springer, 2008).

This happened to eighteen-year-old Jennifer Koon, the daughter of David Koon, an industrial engineer at Bausch and Lomb, in New York State. In November 1993, "Jennifer, who was a college sophomore, decided to stop for bagels at a nearby shopping plaza after finishing her shift at the psychology clinic where she worked. As she was leaving the shop at about 11:30 a.m., she was abducted. After being held captive for a time, Jennifer managed to dial 911 on her car phone, but her urgent call for help was for naught—she was raped and shot to death in bright daylight. In this moment of life and death urgency, the 911 dispatcher and her supervisor could not even determine which cell tower was transmitting Jennifer's signal; they had no idea where she was." All they could do was helplessly listen to the last twenty minutes of Jennifer's life.

Jennifer's phone, as it turned out, did not contain location-enabled GPS technology. After Jennifer's death, Koon carried a tape of his daughter's last helpless struggle in his briefcase to inspire him as he waged an engineer's battle to prevent others from being victimized as had his Jennifer. He ran for the New York State Assembly and, after he won, waged a decade-long battle to implement an enhanced 911 system that included GPS technology. This system has since spread to save lives nationwide.

8. Turvey and Petherick, *Forensic Victimology*, p. 20.

9. Ibid., p. xxi, citing J. A. Holstein and G. Miller, "Rethinking Victimization: An Interactional Approach to Victimology," *Symbolic Interaction* 13, no. 1 (1990): 103–22.

10. Brent E. Turvey, "Pathological Altruism: Victims and Motivational Types," in *Pathological Altruism*, edited by B. Oakley et al. (New York: Oxford University Press, in press), p. xxii.

11. "Illegal Alien Makes 'Living' Filing Hundreds of Frivolous (ADA) Lawsuits," *LiveLeak*, 2010, http://www.liveleak.com/view?i=cb6_128439 8099 (accessed September 14, 2010).

12. Charlie Deitch, "Cashing In . . . Or Catching Up: Do Some ADA Lawsuits Potentially Pit Disability Activists against Businesses?" *Pittsburgh City Paper*, May 22, 2008, http://www.pittsburghcitypaper.ws/gyrobase/ Content?oid=oid%3A46860 (accessed September 14, 2010).

13. Ibid.

14. Ibid.

15. Joe Johnson, "Fake Crime Reports Becoming Real Pain: Police, Fed up with Wasting Time, Money, Vow to Charge Pretenders," *Athens Banner-Herald*, February 28, 2010, http://www.onlineathens.com/stories/022810/ new_568808185.shtml (accessed September 11, 2010); Nancy Martinez, "DPS Hopes to Crack Down on False Crime Reports," *University of Southern California Daily Trojan*, March 23, 2010, http://dailytrojan.com/2010/03/23/ dps-hopes-to-crack-down-on-false-crime-reports/ (accessed September 16, 2010).

16. Carey Roberts, "Domestic Violence Fairytales Threaten Constitutional Protections: The Violence against Women Act Includes a Definition of Domestic Violence That Is So Wide You Could Drive a Mack Truck through It," *Pajamas Media*, September 2, 2010, http://pajamasmedia.com/blog/ domestic-violence-fairytales-threaten-constitutional-protections/ (accessed September 16, 2010).

17. Ibid.

18. Skip Downing, "On Course," http://www.oncourseworkshop.com/ (accessed June 13, 2010); S. Downing, *On Course: Strategies for Creating Success in College and in Life*, 6th ed. (Boston: Wadsworth Publishing, 2010).

CHAPTER 15: HELL ON WHEELS

1. Letter from Carole Alden to author.

2. Personal interview with "Penny Packer," July 2009.

3. E-mail from Richard Senft to author, July 8, 2010.

CHAPTER 16: MIKE MCGRATH
APPLIES CRITICAL THINKING

1. Seymour Barofsky, ed., *The Wisdom of Mark Twain* (New York: Citadel Press, 2003), p. 72.

2. These quotes and reminiscences, unless otherwise noted, are from e-mail correspondence between Michael McGrath and the author during 2010.

3. Later researchers agreed there was a problem. See D. V. Canter et al., "The Organized/Disorganized Typology of Serial Murder: Myth or Model?" *Psychology Public Policy and Law* 10, no. 3 (2004): 293–320, which notes that "Despite weaknesses in the *organized/disorganized* classification of serial killers, it is drawn on for 'offender profiles,' of offending, and in murder trials. This dichotomy was therefore tested by the multidimensional scaling of the co-occurrence of 39 aspects of serial killings derived from 100 murders committed by 100 US serial killers. Results revealed no distinct subsets of offense characteristics reflecting the dichotomy." L. B. Schlesinger et al., "Ritual and Signature in Serial Sexual Homicide," *Journal of the American Academy of Psychiatry and the Law Online* 38, no. 2 (2010), noted that

> [r]itual and signature are fantasy-driven, repetitive crime scene behaviors that have been found to occur in serial sexual homicide. Notwithstanding numerous anecdotal case reports, ritual and signature have rarely been studied empirically. In a national sample of 38 offenders and their 162 victims, we examined behavioral and thematic consistency, as well as the evolution and uniqueness of these crime scene actions. The notion that serial sexual murderers engage in the same rituals and leave unique signatures at every scene was not supported by our data. In fact, the results suggest that the crime scene conduct of this group of offenders is fairly complex and varied.

Malcolm Gladwell, "Dangerous Minds," *New Yorker*, November 12, 2007, http://www.newyorker.com/reporting/2007/11/12/071112fa_fact_gladwell?currentPage=all (accessed September 17, 2010).

4. As noted in Brent E. Turvey, "Criminal Profiling in Court," 2007,

Forensic Solutions LLC, http://www.corpus-delicti.com/prof_archives
_court.html#pd (accessed July 26, 2010), citing Gregg McCrary's January
24, 2000, deposition related to *Alan Davis et al. v. State of Ohio*, no. 312322,
p. 121.

5. *Investigation of Allegations of Cheating on the FBI's Domestic
Investigations and Operations Guide (DIOG) Exam* (US Department of Justice, Office of the Inspector General, Oversight and Review Division, 2010).

6. See also Gladwell, "Dangerous Minds"; B. Snook et al., "The Criminal Profiling Illusion: What's Behind the Smoke and Mirrors?" *Criminal
Justice and Behavior* 35, no. 10 (2008): 1257; Craig Jackson et al., "Against
the Medical-Psychological Tradition of Understanding Serial Killing by
Studying the Killers," *Amicus Curiae* (2010), article in press; Ian Sample,
"Psychological Profiling 'Worse Than Useless,'" *Guardian*, September 14,
2010, http://www.guardian.co.uk/science/2010/sep/14/psychological-profile
-behavioural-psychology (accessed January 11, 2011).

7. Turvey, "Criminal Profiling in Court."

8. In reality, there is no hard number. Estimates of false allegations of
sexual assault vary from "never" to 90 percent. McGrath has always found
problems with the lowball estimates and has equal difficulty believing estimates that exceed 40 to 50 percent. He feels a reasonable estimate, based on
careful analysis of the studies cited in this endnote, as well as many other
studies, is 25 percent. As noted by Brent E. Turvey and M. McGrath, "False
Reports," in *Criminal Profiling: An Introduction to Behavioral Evidence
Analysis*, 4th ed., edited by Brent E. Turvey (London: Academic Press, in
press):

> [F]alse reports of crime occur in many contexts and for many rea-
> sons. This is far from a small problem of isolated reports. The Uni-
> versity of Southern California Department of Public Safety (campus
> police) has recently warned students that it will no longer tolerate
> false crime reports and will bring in the LAPD to prosecute such
> claims. [Martinez.] A campus police spokesman stated that one pat-
> tern that has emerged is students falsely reporting a crime, such as a
> robbery, to elicit sympathy from parents when grades are poor. Police
> in Clarke County, Georgia, are fed up with the phenomenon: "This is
> becoming an epidemic and we're taking a stance" [Johnson.]
>
> Examples of false reports from Clarke County include: a UGA

female law student reported a robbery and beating to garner sympathy during a divorce; a male UGA student reporting a beating and robbery to obtain free medical care after injuring himself while intoxicated; a soldier on leave who reported a robbery at knifepoint because he had spent too much money and did not want his wife to know. An Athens-Clarke police spokesman noted accurately that false reports of crime not only waste taxpayer money and police time, they also harm the community by inflating crime rates and perceptions of safety.

Every so often, a notable false report will be mentioned in the press, and unofficial false report rates will be disclosed to the public. . . . Those studying rape and sexual assault do not typically examine false reports, let alone talk about them. This is due in no small part to the fact that many researchers fear being maligned, blacklisted, or professionally sanctioned should their results not agree with the prevailing sexual-political climate. [Footnote within the original text states: "This opinion is based on discussions with fellow investigators and forensic examiners. It is also based on the fact that a number of the articles reviewed for this paper received scathing commentary from the professional community unrelated to reliability and validity. A common complaint was that the identification and prosecution of false reporters causes legitimate victims to fear reporting their crime to law enforcement. As such, it has been argued that presenting the false report numbers, any numbers, harms victims and casework by preventing legitimate victims from coming forward for fear of not being believed, or even being prosecuted for a crime."] For the reader who till now has assumed that false reports of crime in general, and sexual assault specifically, are nonexistent or extremely rare, nothing could be further from the truth.

Turvey and McGrath, "False Reports," also reviews the provenance of many of the different statistics generally given for false rape reporting. See within that review the following and other studies: J. Baeza and Brent E. Turvey, "False Reports," in *Criminal Profiling: An Introduction to Behavioral Evidence Analysis*, 2nd ed., edited by Brent E. Turvey (London: Academic Press, 2002); Brent E. Turvey, "False Reports," in *Criminal Profiling: An Introduction to Behavioral Evidence Analysis*, 3rd ed., edited by Brent E.

Turvey (London: Academic Press, 2008); M. McGrath, "False Allegations of Rape and the Criminal Profiler," *Journal of Behavioral Profiling* 1, no. 3 (2000); Brent E. Turvey and M. McGrath, "False Allegations of Crime," in *Forensic Victimology: Examining Violent Crime Victims in Investigative and Legal Contexts*, edited by B. E. Turvey and W. Petherick (London: Academic Press, 2009); E. Greer, "The Truth behind Legal Dominance Feminism's Two Percent False Rape Claim Figure," *Loyola of Los Angeles Law Review* 33 (1999): 947; D. P. Bryden and S. Lengnick, "Rape in the Criminal Justice System," *Journal of Criminal Law and Criminology* 87, no. 4 (1997); M. D. Feldman, C. V. Ford, and T. Stone, "Deceiving Others/Deceiving Oneself: Four Cases of Factitious Rape," *Southern Medical Journal* 87, no. 7 (1994): 736; K. L. Gibbon, "False Allegations of Rape in Adults," *Journal of Clinical Forensic Medicine* 5, no. 4 (1998): 195–98; D. Haws, "The Elusive Numbers on False Rape," *Columbia Journalism Review* 36, no. 4 (1997): 16–18; Joe Johnson, "Fake Crime Reports Becoming Real Pain: Police, Fed Up with Wasting Time, Money, Vow to Charge Pretenders," *Athens Banner-Herald*, February 28, 2010; J. Jordan, "Beyond Belief? Police, Rape and Women's Credibility," *Criminology and Criminal Justice* 4, no. 1 (2004): 29; E. J. Kanin, "False Rape Allegations," *Archives of Sexual Behavior* 23, no. 1 (1994): 81–92; D. B. Kennedy and M. Witkowski, "False Allegations of Rape Revisited: A Replication of the Kanin Study," *Journal of Security Administration* 23 (2000): 41–46; K. A. Lonsway, J. Archambault, and A. Berkowitz, "False Reports: Moving Beyond the Issue to Successfully Investigate and Prosecute Non-Stranger Sexual Assault," National Center for the Prosecution of Violence Against Women (circa 2007), http://www.ndaa.org/publications/ newsletters/the_voice_vol_3_no_1_2009.pdf (accessed September 11, 2010); K. A. Lonsway, "Unfounded Cases and False Allegations, Chapter in the National Center for Women and Policing: Successfully Investigating Acquaintance Sexual Assault: A National Training Manual for Law Enforcement," National Center for the Prosecution of Violence against Women, 2001, http://www.womenandpolicing.org/publications.asp (accessed September 11, 2010). P. N. S. Rumney, "False Allegations of Rape," *Cambridge Law Journal* 65, no. 1 (2006): 128–58.

9. Interestingly, some feminists who have read this manuscript have objected to the citation of the "one in four college students is raped" statistic, saying it presents a straw man argument that no one believes. As Christina Hoff Sommers notes, based on the 1988 Koss study,

"One in four" has since become the official figure on women's rape victimization cited in women's studies departments, rape crisis centers, women's magazines, and on protest buttons and posters. Susan Faludi defended it in a *Newsweek* story on sexual correctness. Naomi Wolf refers to it in *The Beauty Myth*, calculating that acquaintance rape is "more common than lefthandedness, alcoholism, and heart attacks." "One in four" is chanted in "Take Back the Night" processions, and it is the number given in the date rape brochures handed out at freshman orientation at colleges and universities around the country. Politicians, from Senator Joseph Biden of Delaware, a Democrat, to Republican Congressman Jim Ramstad of Minnesota, cite it regularly, and it is the primary reason for the Title IV, "Safe Campuses for Women" provision of the Violence against Women Act of 1993, which provides twenty million dollars to combat rape on college campuses. [References omitted.]

C. H. Sommers, *Who Stole Feminism? How Women Have Betrayed Women* (Touchstone Books, 1995), p. 212, see in general chap. 10, pp. 209–26. The recent (2010) *ABC News/Nightline* article cited in the text, purportedly based on Department of Justice statistics, shows that the one in four rape statistic has real staying power. The crux of the problem revolves around a definition of rape that is worded so loosely and ambiguously that it encompasses events that few would consider to be rape—see Sommers's book for a detailed analysis. For a sense of current widespread use of the "one in four" statistic, see: One in Four Inc., 2008, national organization headquarters: New London, Connecticut, http://www.oneinfourusa.org/index.php (accessed September 12, 2010); UCSC Rape Prevention Education Rape Statistics, http://www2.ucsc .edu/rape-prevention/statistics.html (accessed September 12, 2010); Crisis Connection: College Campuses and Rape, http://www.crisisconnectioninc .org/sexualassault/college_campuses_and_rape.htm (accessed September 12, 2010); feminist.com, 2008, http://www.feminist.com/antiviolence/facts.html (accessed September 12, 2010). But also see: Michael P. Wright, "Deflating the Date Rape Scare: A Look at Campus Police Records," 1998, Responsible Opposing.com, http://www.responsibleopposing.com/comment/1in4.html (accessed September 12, 2010); Chris (last name not given), "Rape Statistics: 1 in 4?" September 11, 2009, http://aspiring economist.com/index.php/2009/ 09/11/rape-statistics-1-in-4/ (accessed September 12, 2010).

10. McGrath refers readers to Sommers, *Who Stole Feminism?* chap. 10, pp. 209–26; J. W. Dixon and K. E. Dixon, "Gender-Specific Clinical Syndromes and Their Admissibility under the Federal Rules of Evidence," *American Journal of Trial Advocacy* 27 (2003): 25–54; M. McMahon, "Battered Women and Bad Science: The Limited Validity and Utility of Battered Woman Syndrome," *Psychiatry, Psychology and Law* 6, no. 1 (1999): 23–49; Mary Ann Dutton, "What Is Battered Woman Syndrome?" 2009, Wings of a Dove Domestic Violence Shelter, http://www.facebook.com/topic.php?uid =150816125945&topic=11377 (accessed May 8, 2010). See also Wendy McElroy, "Rape Scandal Turns Sympathy into Skepticism," April 21, 2004, Fox News, http://www.foxnews.com/story/0,2933,117690,00.html (accessed May 13, 2010); S. Taylor and K. C. Johnson, *Until Proven Innocent: Political Correctness and the Shameful Injustices of the Duke Lacrosse Rape Case* (St. Martin's Griffin, 2008); Ampersand (pseudonym), "No, Ms Magazine Never 'Hired' Mary Koss," *Alas! A Blog*, July 31, 2010, http://www .amptoons.com/blog/archives/2010/07/31/no-ms-magazine-never-hired -mary-koss/ (accessed August 11, 2010).

11. Even though the "free pass" idea may push emotional hot buttons for feminists, it is a proposition for which abundant evidence exists. (See the following section "Suppressing the Evidence.") There are inadvertent negative consequences to well-meaning but overwrought efforts to draw attention to rape as a major societal problem. As McGrath points out with his typically nononsense demeanor, "If I were a woman I would be so annoyed with this crap, for three reasons: 1) it is BS 2) it belittles the real women who have suffered an actual sexual assault and 3) it infantilizes women when someone else decides they were raped and they were apparently too stupid to realize it."

12. Cynthia McFadden, "Many Campus Assault Victims Stay Quiet, or Fail to Get Help: One in Four College Women Will Be Raped before They Graduate, According to Justice Department Study," *ABC News/Nightline*, 2010, http://abcnews.go.com/Nightline/college-campus-assaults-constant-threat/story?id=11410988 (accessed September 11, 2010). Citing Rana Sampson, "Acquaintance Rape of College Students: Problem-Oriented Guides for Police Series No. 17," *US Department of Justice*, http://www.cops .usdoj.gov/pdf/e03021472.pdf (accessed September 15, 2010).

13. Anny Jacoby, "College Campus ape Rate 10 Times Higher Than Detroit's? Don't Believe Everything the Justice Department Tells You . . . ," September 19, 2010, http://annyjacoby.wordpress.com/2010/09/19/college

-campus-rape-rate-10-times-higher-that-detroit%E2%80%99s-don%E2%80 %99t-believe-everything-the-justice-department-tells-you (accessed February 4, 2011).

14. Brent E. Turvey and Wayne Petherick, *Forensic Victimology: Examining Violent Crime Victims in Investigative and Legal Contexts* (New York: Elsevier, 2009), pp. 239–40. Specifically, Walker states that battered woman syndrome was listed in the *DSM-III-TR* (1987) under section 309.81, but there *is* no section 309.81. The *Forensic Victimology* discussion from pages 237–48 describes many other problems with Walker's work from a scientific perspective.

15. Sporadic criticism of Walker's work has been published, but her standard response is a deflection: an accusation that critics are against battered women. See, for example, Michael McGrath, Lenore Walker, and Arnold Robbins, "More on Battered Women Syndrome: The Debate Continues . . ." *Psychiatric Times*, October 26, 2009, http://www.psychiatrictimes .com/display/article/10168/1481281 (accessed May 1, 2010).

In related work, Diana Russell put her research assistants through sixty hours of "consciousness-raising" as part of their training for the data collection underpinning her book *Rape in Marriage*. There was enormous variability in the resulting data—one assistant, for example, discovered rape history in 90 percent of her respondents. In this regard, sociologist Augustine Brannigan observes, "In other words, she [Russell] didn't take 'no' for an answer. The problem is that it doesn't seem to be sufficient to conclude there is a grave problem, but it has to be framed as an epidemic in order for it to be taken seriously. Such a strategy can lead to the trivialization of the academic reports." Personal communication between Augustine Brannigan and the author, May 5, 2010. See also Murray A. Straus, Richard J. Gelles, and Suzanne K. Steinmetz, *Behind Closed Doors: Violence in the American Family*, Transaction revised from original 1980 edition (New Brunswick, NJ: Transaction Publishers, 2006). Straus has felt the brunt of career blackballing for publication of his findings.

16. E-mail communication, Mike McGrath to the author.

17. For far more detail, see the following: Straus, "Bucking the Tide in Family Violence Research"; M. A. Straus, "Women's Violence toward Men Is a Serious Social Problem," *Current Controversies on Family Violence* 2 (2005): 55–77; Murray A. Straus, "Current Controversies and Prevalence Concerning Female Offenders of Intimate Partner Violence: Why the Overwhelming Evi-

dence on Partner Physical Violence by Women Has Not Been Perceived and Is Often Denied," *Journal of Aggression, Maltreatment & Trauma* 18 (2009): 552–71; Murray A. Straus, "Processes Explaining the Concealment and Distortion of Evidence on Gender Symmetry in Partner Violence," *European Journal on Criminal Policy and Research* 13 (2007): 227–32.

18. M. A. Straus, *Beating the Devil Out of Them: Corporal Punishment by Parents and Its Effects on Children* (Boston: Macmillan, 1994).

19. Straus, "Bucking the Tide in Family Violence Research."

20. Ibid.

21. Straus, "Partner Physical Violence."

22. Examples of studies and results include the following (data from ibid.):

Study	Severity of Assault	Perpetrator Male	Female
National Co-Morbidity Study	Minor	17.4%	17.7%
(Kessler, 2001)	Severe	6.5%	6.2%
National Alcohol and Family	Overall rate	9.1%	9.5%
Violence Survey (Straus, 1995)	Severe	1.9%	4.5%
Dunedin Health and Development Study (Moffitt & Caspi, 1999)	Overall rate	27.0%	34.0%
National Violence against Women Survey (Tjaden & Thoennes, 2000)	Overall rate	1.3%	0.9%
Youth Risk Behavior Survey (Eaton et al., 2006)	Overall rate	8.8%	8.9%
National Youth Survey (Wofford-Mihalic,	Overall rate	20.2%	34.1%
Elliott, & Menard, 1994)	Severe	5.7%	3.8%
National Longitudinal Study of Adolescent Health (Whitaker et al., 2007)	Overall rate	19.3%	28.4%

Social workers involved with battered women feel certain that it could not be true that women initiate partner violence at the same rates as men—after all, their experience and all their training leads them to feel that women *for sure* are the main recipients of domestic violence. Others are simply left bewildered—how can it be true that "the percentage of women who physically assaulted a male partner is as high or higher than the percentage of men who physically assaulted a female partner, and that this applies to severe violence such as kicking, choking, and attacks with objects and weapons, as well as to minor violence . . . women initiate [partner violence] at the same or higher rates as men, and they are the sole perpetrator at the same or higher rates." (Murray A. Straus, "Current Controversies and Prevalence Concerning Female Offenders of Intimate Partner Violence: Why the Overwhelming Evidence on Partner Physical Violence by Women Has Not Been Perceived and Is Often Denied," *Journal of Aggression, Maltreatment & Trauma* 18 [2009]: 552–71.) If that really were true, wouldn't everybody know it?

In two incisive journal articles, "Why the Overwhelming Evidence on Partner Physical Violence by Women Has Not Been Perceived and Is Often Denied" and "Processes Explaining the Concealment and Distortion of Evidence on Gender-Symmetry in Partner Violence," Straus tackled precisely that question. (Ibid.; Straus, "Processes Explaining the Concealment and Distortion of Evidence on Gender Symmetry in Partner Violence," pp. 227–32.) Straus found that researchers are unwilling to accept that partner violence is equally perpetrated by both men and women because men predominate in almost all other crimes—especially violent crimes. Women are also more likely to be hurt in any violent encounter, which brings them more into the public eye. But the most serious reason that many remain unaware of the true statistics involved in male and female partner violence is due to "the efforts of feminists to conceal, deny, and distort the evidence . . . these efforts include intimidation and threats, and have been carried out not only by feminist advocates and service providers, but also by feminist researchers who have let their ideological commitments overrule their scientific commitments" (ibid.).

In methodical fashion, Straus laid out seven methods used by feminists to conceal, deny, and distort evidence—providing copious documentation for each charge (ibid.). These methods included:

- Suppressing evidence
- Avoiding the gathering of data inconsistent with the belief that partner violence is caused by a patriarchal social and family system. (In reality, there are many causes of partner violence and types of violent relationships.)
- Citing only studies that show male perpetration of violence
- Concluding that results support feminist beliefs when they do not

- Creating "evidence" through citations that don't actually support the assertion (See also endnote 3, chap. 7 for an example.)
- Obstructing the publication of articles and funding of research that might contradict the idea that male dominance is the cause of partner violence
- Harassing, threatening, and penalizing researchers who produce evidence that contradicts feminist beliefs

Straus is not alone in his charges. Feminist Erin Pizzey, who founded the UK domestic violence charity Refuge, has received death threats and boycotts as a consequence of her statements that domestic violence is reciprocal between the sexes, with women just as capable of violence as men (Erin Pizzey, "How Feminists Tried to Destroy the Family," *Mail Online* January 22, 2007, http://www.dailymail.co.uk/news/article-430702/How-feminists-tried-destroy-family.html (accessed October 29, 2010). Sociology professor Suzanne Steinmetz, author of the book *The Battered Husband* and coauthor of the "First National Family Violence Survey," has also received death threats, and an ACLU meeting she spoke at received a bomb threat (Wendy McElroy, "Feminists Deny Truth on Domestic Violence," *FoxNews .com*, May 30, 2006, http://www.foxnews.com/story/0,2933,197550,00 .html [accessed October 30, 2010].) Lenore Walker's work, in other words, may well be the tip of the iceberg in lack of solid scientific research regarding battered women.

23. Shannan Catalano, *Intimate Partner Violence in the United States* (Bureau of Justice Statistics, 2006); C. M. Rennison and S. Welchans, "Intimate Partner Violence (No. NCJ-178247)" (Washington, DC: Department of Justice, 2000); Straus, "Women's Violence toward Men Is a Serious Social Problem."

24. As Straus notes:

In the 1970's, cases of child abuse had increased by about 10% per year and hundreds of shelters for battered women were opened. There was virtually complete consensus that the United States was experiencing an epidemic of child abuse and wife-beating. This did not seem right to me because of the tremendous growth of "protective factors" such as the increasing educational level of the population, increasing age at marriage and age at birth of the first child, fewer children per couple, growing availability and use of family therapy, decreasing use of [corporal punishment], national programs to increase awareness of child abuse, and the nation-wide establishment of child protective services which presumably provide assistance that will lower the probability of subsequent abuse. These same changes are also protective factors for wife-beating, to which must be added increased gender equality and the efforts to end domestic violence by the women's movement. . . .

In 1985, the second National Family Violence Survey allowed Richard Gelles and me to test that theory. We found that child physical abuse had decreased by 47%, and wife-beating had decreased by 27% (Straus & Gelles, 1986). These results were greeted with doubt by child protective workers and hostility by feminists. The doubt was because it contradicted their daily experience of more and more cases. The hostility occurred because we found a large decrease in male violence toward female partners, but no decrease for [partner violence] by women, and because we suggested this might be the result of the domestic violence campaign ignoring female perpetration. The *Christian Science Monitor* interviewed Richard Berk, a leading feminist criminologist, wherein (18 November 1985, pp. 3–4) he said, "Given all we know about the pattern of crime statistics, a 47% drop is so unprecedented as to be unbelievable. Never before has there been a drop of that magnitude, that rapidly." On the contrary, other crime rates did change that much and that fast. The homicide rate increased by more than 100% between 1963 and 1973. Then, between 1980 and 1984, homicide dropped at a faster annual rate than our studies found for male [partner violence]. I believe this is another example of an ideological or theoretical commitment blinding social scientists to the evidence. Since then, a national survey by Kaufman Kantor using the same questions in 1992 found a continuation of the decrease in assaults by men, and again no decrease for women (Straus, 1995; Straus, Kaufman Kantor, & Moore, 1997). Most recently, the research of Finkelhor and Jones has found sustained decreases in rates of child physical abuse (Finkelhor, 2008; Jones & Finkelhor, 2003).

Straus, "Bucking the Tide in Family Violence Research."

CHAPTER 17: A LOVE AFFAIR WITH ART, WOOING THE PRESS, AND A CONVENIENT DEATH

1. Jeremy McCarter, "Drama Queen: Sarah Bernhardt Was Part Gaga, Part Streep," *Newsweek*, September 27, 2010, p. 59, http://www.newsweek .com/2010/09/16/palin_is_a_pale_imitation_of_this_sarah.html (accessed February 2, 2011).

2. Vince Horiuchi, "Artist's Works Are Her Therapy," *Salt Lake Tribune*, June 26, 2005.

3. Ibid.

4. Letter from Carole Alden to the author.

5. "Beware of Lizard," *Deseret News*, 1993, http://www.deseretnews .com/article/267732/CAPTION-ONLY—BEWARE-OF-LIZARD.html (accessed June 2, 2010).

6. Richard P. Christenson, "Artists Define, Break Down Boundaries," *Deseret News*, March 7, 1993, http://www.deseretnews.com/article/279329/ ARTISTS-DEFINE-BREAK-DOWN-BOUNDARIES.html?pg=2 (accessed June 2, 2010).

7. Brandon Griggs, "Arts Festival Comes Alive," *Salt Lake Tribune*, June 23, 2006.

8. "Doll Museum Featuring Dinosaur, Dragon Exhibit," *Deseret News*, October 11, 1994, http://www.deseretnews.com/article/380691/DOLL -MUSEUM-FEATURING-DINOSAUR-DRAGON-EXHIBIT.html (accessed June 2, 2010).

9. "Bike Was Boy's Only Possession," *Deseret News*, September 8, 1991, http://www.deseretnews.com/article/181980/BIKE-WAS-BOYS-ONLY -POSSESSION.html (accessed June 2, 2010).

10. Dennis Lythgoe, "Replacement of Boy's Bike Proves Bad News Can Have a Happy Ending," *Deseret News*, September 26, 1991, http://www .deseretnews.com/article/print/185059/REPLACEMENT-OF-BOYS-BIKE -PROVES-BAD-NEWS-CAN-HAVE-A-HAPPY-ENDING.html (accessed June 2, 2010).

11. Ibid.

12. Francisco Kjolseth, "Hatching a Surprise—Holiday Spirit Brings Exotic Emus to Young Bird Lover Battling Cancer; Holden Girl Is Given a

Surprising Present: Exotic Emu Chicks," *Salt Lake City Tribune*, January 2, 2002.

13. Ibid.

14. Lynn Arave, "New Pets, Good News Cause for Celebration," *Deseret News*, January 2, 2002, http://www.deseretnews.com/article/887315/New-pets-good-news-cause-for-celebration.html (accessed June 2, 2010).

15. E-mail from Krystal Rusek to author, September 28, 2010.

16. W. R. Anderson et al., "The Urologist's Guide to Genital Piercing," *BJU International* 91, no. 3 (2003): 245–51.

17. Ibid.

18. C. Young and M. L. Armstrong, "What Nurses Need to Know When Caring for Women with Genital Piercings," *Nursing for Women's Health* 12, no. 2 (2008): 128–38.

19. Ibid.

20. Letter from Carole Alden to the author.

21. Ibid.

22. Ibid.

23. Sheila Isenberg, *Women Who Love Men Who Kill* (New York: Simon & Schuster, 1992), p. 138.

24. Ibid., pp. 199–200.

25. Personal interview with "Penny Packer," July 2009.

26. "Forced to Wear a Chastity Belt!" *Pick Me Up*, February 7, 2008, http://www.pickmeupmagazine.co.uk/real_lives/Forced_to_wear_a_chastity_belt_article_177843.html (accessed June 10, 2010).

27. Letter from Carole Alden to the author.

28. Personal interview between Rosemary Salyer and the author, June 6, 2010.

29. Letter from Carole Alden to the author.

30. Telephone interview, LaRee Bristow and the author, July 2, 2010.

CHAPTER 18: WHY SO DIFFERENT?

1. G. Apollinaire and P. F. Read, *The Cubist Painters* (University of California Press, 2004), p. 9.

2. Personal interview between Irene Scott and the author, April 30, 2009.

3. Although no one saw Ed Gein kill his brother, there were a number of oddities at the scene. For example, Henry was supposedly asphyxiated during a brushfire on the property, bruising his head on a rock as he fell. But although the body was lying on scorched earth, there were no burns. At the time, no one had reason to suspect the soft-spoken, mild-mannered, ever-helpful Ed. Harold Schechter, *Deviant: The Shocking True Story of the Original "Psycho"* (Pocket, 1998), pp. 31–32.

4. Robert D. McFadden, "Prisoner of Rage—A Special Report: From a Child of Promise to the Unabom Suspect," *New York Times*, May 26, 1996, http://query.nytimes.com/gst/fullpage.html?res=9B05E7D91139F935A1575 6C0A960958260&pagewanted=all (accessed September 4, 2010).

5. J. Hinckley and J. A. Hinckley, *Breaking Points* (Chosen Books, 1985).

6. N. C. Sharp, "The Human Genome and Sport, Including Epigenetics, Gene Doping, and Athleticogenomics," *Endocrinology & Metabolism Clinics of North America* 39, no. 1 (2010): 20–15.

7. A. Knafo and S. Israel, "Genetic and Environmental Influences on Prosocial Behavior," in *Prosocial Motives, Emotions, and Behavior: The Better Angels of Our Nature*, edited by M. Mikulincer and P. R. Shaver (Washington, DC: American Psychological Association Publications, 2009).

8. Personal interview with Irene Scott.

CHAPTER 19: CAROLE AT WORK

1. Stella H. Day and Sebrina C. Ekins, *Milestones of Millard: A Century of History of Millard County, 1851–1951* (Art City Publishing Company, 1951), p. 601.

2. Randy Morris's recollections ensue from a telephone interview between Randy Morris and the author, July 9, 2010, and e-mail communication from Randy Morris to the author, August 11, 2010.

3. Scott Ross's recollections are from a telephone interview between Scott Ross and the author, July 9, 2010.

4. Leonard Hardy's recollections are from a telephone interview between Leonard Hardy and the author, July 10, 2010.

5. All quotes from Richard Senft are from e-mails and a telephone interview with the author during July–September 2010.

6. Jane Nathanson and Gary Patronek, "Animal Hoarding—How the Semblance of a Benevolent Mission Becomes Actualized as Egoism and Cruelty," in *Pathological Altruism*, edited by Barbara Oakley et al. (New York: Oxford University Press, in press).

7. Allan N. Schore, *Affect Regulation and the Origin of the Self: The Neurobiology of Emotional Development* (Hillsdale, NJ: Lawrence Erlbaum Associates, 1994), p. 104.

8. A. N. Schore, *Affect Dysregulation and Disorders of the Self*, edited by Daniel J. Siegel, Norton Series on Interpersonal Neurobiology (New York: W. W. Norton, 2003), p. 37.

9. Nathanson and Patronek, "Animal Hoarding," citing S. Bonas, J. McNicholas, and G. M. Collis, "Pets in the Network of Family Relationships: An Empirical Study," *Companion Animals and Us: Exploring the Relationships between People and Pets* (2000): 209–36.

10. A nice overview that gives insight into the many factors involved is M. Radke-Yarrow and E. Brown, "Resilience and Vulnerability in Children of Multiple-Risk Families," *Development and Psychopathology* 5, no. 4 (2009): 581–92. See also E. E. Werner, "Risk, Resilience, and Recovery: Perspectives from the Kauai Longitudinal Study," *Development and Psychopathology* 5, no. 4 (2009): 503–15.

11. Nathanson and Patronek, "Animal Hoarding."

12. Ibid.

13. Sue-Ellen Brown, "Self Psychological Theoretical Constructs of Animal Hoarding," *Society & Animal, Journal of Human-Animal Studies* (2009), as cited in Nathanson and Patronek, "Animal Hoarding."

CHAPTER 20: ALLEN LAKE

1. L. Chang, *Wisdom for the Soul: Five Millennia of Prescriptions for Spiritual Healing* (Washington, DC: Gnosophia Publishers, 2006), p. 284.

2. A pseudonym.

3. This chapter is based on a personal interview by the author in Delta, Utah, with Allen Lake, June 19, 2009; and also a telephone conversation, September 2010.

Chapter 21: I'm Right and You're Wrong

1. K. J. Connolly and M. Martlew, *Psychologically Speaking: A Book of Quotations* (Leicester, UK: British Psychological Society, 1999), p. 5.

2. Robert Burton, *On Being Certain: Believing You Are Right Even When You're Not* (St. Martin's Griffin, 2008).

3. Robert Burton, "Pathological Certitude," in *Pathological Altruism*, edited by B. Oakley et al. (New York: Oxford University Press, in press).

4. Ibid.

5. Ibid.

6. Ibid.

7. Ibid.

8. David Brin, "Self-Addiction and Self-Righteousness," in *Pathological Altruism*, edited by B. Oakley et al.

9. Burton, "Pathological Certitude."

10. Madeline Li and Gary Rodin, "Altruism and Suffering in the Context of Cancer Caregiving: Implications of a Relational Paradigm," in *Pathological Altruism*, edited by Barbara Oakley et al.

11. Karen G. Jackovich, "Sex, Visitors from the Grave, Psychic Healing: Kubler-Ross Is a Public Storm Center Again," *People* 12, October 29, 1979, http://www.people.com/people/archive/article/0,,20074920,00.html (accessed July 29, 2010).

12. Ibid.

13. "Behavior: The Conversion of K," *Time*, November 12, 1979, http://www.time.com/time/magazine/article/0,9171,946362-2,00.html (accessed July 29, 2010).

14. Ibid.

15. Li and Rodin, "Altruism and Suffering in the Context of Cancer Caregiving."

16. Robert Burton, "Pathological Certitude."

17. D. L. Smith, *The Most Dangerous Animal: Human Nature and the Origins of War* (New York: St. Martin's Griffin, 2009), p. 114.

18. Iain McGilchrist, *The Master and His Emissary: The Divided Brain and the Making of the Modern World* (New Haven, CT: Yale University Press, 2010), pp. 25–28.

19. Ibid., pp. 27–28.

20. Ibid., pp. 72, 77–79.

21. Ibid., p. 84.

22. Ibid., p. 234. citing V. S. Ramachandran and S. Blakeslee, *Phantoms in the Brain: Probing the Mysteries of the Human Mind* (Quill, 1999), pp. 131–32.

23. McGilchrist, *The Master and His Emissary*, p. 235.

24. Ibid., pp. 192–93.

CHAPTER 22: A VICTIM'S SUPPORTERS

1. J. Winokur, *The Big Curmudgeon: 2,500 Irreverently Outrageous Quotations from World-Class Grumps and Cantankerous Commentators* (New York: Black Dog & Leventhal, 2007), p. 36.

2. Ben Winslow, "Woman to Take Plea Deal in Murder Case," *Deseret Morning News*, June 22, 2007.

3. Ibid.

4. Quotes in this section are based on a telephone interview between Sylvia Huntsman and the author, May 5, 2009.

CHAPTER 23: THE WAR ROOM

1. Johann Wolfgang Goethe, *Maxims and Reflections of Goethe* (A translation of *Sprüche in Prosa: zum ersten Mai erläutert und auf ihre Quellen zurückgeführt von G. v. Loeper*, Berlin, 1870), New Edition, translated by Bailey Saunders (New York: Macmillan, 1906), p. 90.

2. All "War Room" conversations are based on composite recollections of those involved and portray a general sense of attitudes and opinions.

3. Letter from Stephen L. Golding, PhD, to James Slavens RE: *State v. Sessions*, January 8, 2007.

CHAPTER 24: MARTY'S SECRETS

1. Leo F. Buscaglia, *Born for Love: Reflections on Loving* (New York: Ballantine, 1994), p. 232.

2. The stories of Marty's grandmother, and related stories of Marty's younger years, are based on the recollections of Marty's younger brother Dennis Sessions, from interviews conducted in August–September 2010.

3. Denny attributes his own redemption to the kindness of strangers. Out of prison in a halfway house, he went to buy a snack from the catering truck. Unbeknownst to Denny, two $20 bills he had crumpled in his pocket slipped out as he was stuffing in change. The caterer saw the bills fall and called out, but Denny didn't hear and disappeared around the corner.

That $40 was all Denny had for lunch for two weeks, so he simply had to do without. Two weeks later, money once again in hand, Denny went back out to the truck—he was bowled over when the caterer handed him the two twenties from two weeks before.

"If it had been me," Denny says ruefully, "I would have kept that money. It made me stop right there and rethink my life. I realized I wanted to be as honest as that guy was. It didn't happen overnight. But I changed my path. Now, seventeen years later, I have a good life—I like to think I'm almost the way that caterer was."

Just as deception ruined Marty's life, honesty helped heal Denny.

Denny offers up the psychological outlook he's found that helps steer him away from addiction—even as he realizes it's not the full answer: "If you can let go of your anger," he says, "you can move on. A lot of it is basically that simple. The way we feel is a direct result of the way we think, and the only way we can change how we feel is to change the way we think."

4. Based on extensive correspondence with Carole Alden.

CHAPTER 25: MEDIA MAESTRO

1. Michael D. Wims, Charles Ambrose, and Jack B. Rubin, *How to Prepare and Try a Murder Case: Prosecution and Defense Perspectives* (American Bar Association, in press).

2. "Wife Kills 'Depraved' Hubby Who Made Her Wear Chastity Belt," *National Enquirer*, UK ed., March 26, 2007, pp. 36–37.

3. Ibid.

4. Letter from Carole Alden to the author.

5. "Forced to Wear a Chastity Belt!" *Pick Me Up*, February 7, 2008, http://www.pickmeupmagazine.co.uk/real_lives/Forced_to_wear_a _chastity_belt_article_177843.html (accessed June 10, 2010).

6. John Cooke, "Woman Marries for Love—Then Kills for Survival," *National Enquirer*, April 7, 2008, p. 48.

7. "Forced to Wear a Chastity Belt!"

8. Ibid.

9. Bruce E. Wexler, *Brain and Culture: Neurobiology, Ideology, and Social Change* (Cambridge, MA: MIT Press, 2006), p. 96.

10. Ibid., p. 109.

11. Ibid., p. 104.

12. Ibid. See also E. Nagy et al., "The Neural Mechanisms of Reciprocal Communication," *Brain Research* 1353 (2010): 59–67.

13. Carolyn Zahn-Waxler and Carole Van Hulle, "Empathy, Guilt, and Depression: When Caring for Others Becomes Costly to Children," in *Pathological Altruism*, edited by Barbara Oakley et al. (New York: Oxford University Press, in press).

14. Ibid.

15. Letter from Carole Alden to the author.

CHAPTER 26: PRELIMINARY HEARING— THE GRAND FINALE

1. Umberto Eco, *Foucault's Pendulum*, trans. William Weaver (New York: Harcourt, 2007), p. 49.

2. The information regarding Michael Wims is based on a personal interview, telephone interviews, and e-mails between Michael Wims and the author, 2010.

3. Personal interview with Pamela Wims, May 10, 2010.

4. Michael D. Wims, Charles Ambrose, and Jack B. Rubin, *How to Prepare and Try a Murder Case: Prosecution and Defense Perspectives* (American Bar Association, in press).

5. The following information is based on testimony recorded in the Fourth Judicial District Court, in and for Millard County, State of Utah, *State of Utah,*

Plaintiff, v. Carole Alden Sessions, Defendant, Case No. 061700168, before the Honorable Donald J. Eyre, Fourth District Court, 765 South Highway 99, Fillmore, Utah 84631, transcript, preliminary hearing, January 8, 2007.

6. Letter from Carole Alden to the author.

7. Ruling on State's Motion to Disqualify Defense Counsel, Case No. 061700168, Judge Donald J. Eyre, August 28, 2006.

8. Letters from Carole Alden to the author; police sources.

9. Letters from Carole Alden to the author.

10. Motion to Stay the Proceedings and Supporting Memorandum, Case No. 061700168 in the Fourth Judicial District Court of Millard County, State of Utah, *State of Utah, Plaintiff, v. Carole Elizabeth Alden, Defendant*, September 21, 2006, p. 3, Judge Donald J. Eyre Jr. citing the August 14 hearing, 2006.

11. Interview, Mike Wims and the author, July 20, 2010.

CHAPTER 27: MARTY'S GOOD SIDE

1. Iain McGilchrist, *The Master and His Emissary: The Divided Brain and the Making of the Modern World* (New Haven, CT: Yale University Press, 2010), p. 133.

2. Comments throughout the chapter from Anna Ruttenbur and Edee Sessions-Wagers are from telephone conversations between them and the author during August–September, 2010.

3. Lisa Rosetta, "Killer Paints Picture of Marriage Gone Bad," *Salt Lake Tribune*, September 3, 2006.

4. Ibid.

5. Interview between Russ Crook and the author, June 16, 2009.

6. All quotations from Joe Trujillo are from a telephone interview between Joe Trujillo and the author, July 8, 2010.

7. State's Memorandum in Opposition to Defendant's 402 Motion to Reduce Conviction, Case No. 061700168 in the Fourth Judicial District Court of Millard County, State of Utah, *State of Utah, Plaintiff, v. Carole Elizabeth Alden, Defendant*, August 20, 2007, pp. 3–5, Judge Donald J. Eyre Jr., p. 7.

8. This beautiful campground features sweeping views of the Pahvant range and backs onto pasture land with idyllic grazing herds of cattle and horses. When friendly hosts Ann and Dick Flones happily chat with visitors during the evening ice cream socials, it looks like a Norman Rockwell

painting. The campground also offers (if you know where to look) a view of the back of the Millard County Jail, where Carole was housed in the year following the homicide.

9. Nate Carlisle, "Wife Sentenced in Manslaughter," *Salt Lake Tribune*, September 7, 2007.

10. Nate Carlisle, "Accused Slayer of Husband Calls Him Abusive, Depraved," *Salt Lake Tribune*, January 9, 2007.

11. All quotes and reminiscences from Edee Sessions are from telephone interviews between Edee Sessions and the author, August–September 2010.

12. These reminiscences are based on interviews with Denny Sessions in August 2010.

13. Ibid.

14. Rosetta, "Killer Paints Picture of Marriage Gone Bad."

CHAPTER 28: HOW LITTLE WE KNOW ABOUT PSYCHIATRIC DISORDERS

1. *Daily Reflections: A Book of Reflections by A. A. Members for A. A. Members* (Alcoholics Anonymous World Services, 1990), p. 336.

2. Daniel Carlat, *Unhinged: The Trouble with Psychiatry—A Doctor's Revelations about a Profession in Crisis* (New York: Free Press, 2010), p. 80.

3. Ibid.

4. Yu Gao and Adrian Raine, "Successful and Unsuccessful Psychopaths: A Neurobiological Model," *Behavioral Sciences & the Law* 28, no. 2 (2010): 194–210.

5. Iain McGilchrist, *The Master and His Emissary: The Divided Brain and the Making of the Modern World* (New Haven, CT: Yale University Press, 2010), p. 85.

6. S. Akhtar and H. Parens, *Lying, Cheating, and Carrying On: Developmental, Clinical, and Sociocultural Aspects of Dishonesty and Deceit* (Jason Aronson, 2009).

7. H. R. Agrawal et al., "Attachment Studies with Borderline Patients: A Review," *Harvard Review of Psychiatry* 12, no. 2 (2004): 94–104.

8. W. M. Dinn et al., "Neurocognitive Function in Borderline Personality Disorder," *Progress in Neuro-Psychopharmacology and Biological Psychiatry* 28, no. 2 (2004): 329–41.

9. E-mail communication from Joseph Carroll to the author, August 29, 2010. See "What Is Literary Darwinism," interview with David DiSalvo, *Neuronarrative*, http://neuronarrative.wordpress.com/2009/02/27/what-is-literary-darwinism-an-interview-with-joseph-carroll/, posted February 27, 2009 (accessed January 13, 2011).

10. Ibid.

11. Paul T. Mason and Randi Kreger, *Stop Walking on Eggshells: Taking Your Life Back When Someone You Care About Has Borderline Personality Disorder* (Oakland, CA: New Harbinger Publications, 1998), p. 19.

12. "Wife Kills 'Depraved' Hubby Who Made Her Wear Chastity Belt," *National Enquirer,* UK ed., March 26, 2007.

13. Nate Carlisle, "Accused Slayer of Husband Calls Him Abusive, Depraved," *Salt Lake Tribune*, January 9, 2007.

14. Letter from Carole Alden to the author.

15. Akhtar and Parens, *Lying, Cheating, and Carrying On.*

16. R. B. Krueger, "The *DSM* Diagnostic Criteria for Sexual Sadism," *Archives of Sexual Behavior* 39, no. 2 (2010): 325–45.

17. F. M. Saleh and F. S. Berlin, "Sexual Deviancy: Diagnostic and Neurobiological Considerations," *Journal of Child Sexual Abuse* 12, no. 3 (2004): 53–76.

18. Ibid.

19. F. M. Saleh and F. S. Berlin, "Sex Hormones, Neurotransmitters, and Psychopharmacological Treatments in Men with Paraphilic Disorders," *Journal of Child Sexual Abuse* 12, no. 3 (2004): 233–53.

20. P. A. Cross and K. Matheson, "Understanding Sadomasochism," *Journal of Homosexuality* 50, no. 2 (2006): 133–66.

21. Personal interview with "Penny Packer," July 2009.

22. B. A. Aguirre, *Borderline Personality Disorder in Adolescents: A Complete Guide to Understanding and Coping When Your Adolescent Has BPD* (Beverly, MA: Fair Winds, 2007), p. 119.

23. Richard C. W. Hall and Ryan C. W. Hall, "False Allegations: The Role of the Forensic Psychiatrist," *Journal of Psychiatric Practice* (September 2001): 343–46.

24. E-mail from Randi Kreger to the author, November 2010.

25. Ibid.

26. The musings about how to better understand battered women are based on ideas outlined by Carolyn Zahn-Waxler, August, 2010.

27. Linda G. Mills, *Violent Partners: A Breakthrough Plan for Ending the Cycle of Abuse* (New York: Basic Books, 2008), p. xii.

28. E-mail correspondence between Mike Wims and the author, September 2010.

One might think that preexisting personality traits could make a person less culpable for murder in legal terms, but that's generally not the case. That makes sense—after all, wouldn't any personality traits figure in any crime?

In fact, in most jurisdictions only a *severe* mental disease or defect that renders a person *unable to appreciate the nature and quality or the wrongfulness of his acts* can serve as a defense. Just having a personality disorder doesn't automatically mean someone has a severe mental disease. A person who has been diagnosed with antisocial personality disorder, for example, is not automatically considered to have a severe mental disease or defect. For instance, central features of "antisocial personality disorder," as defined by the psychiatrist's bible, the *DSM*, include deceit, manipulation, and a persistent pattern of violating the basic rights of others by destroying property, stealing, or pursuing illegal occupations. But viewed from a legal perspective, "antisocial personality disorder" is simply a description of a personality—not necessarily a disease. Whether it qualifies as a mental disease, and further, a *severe* mental disease, can be an issue argued in court. So a forensic mental health expert would give an opinion, perhaps supported or contradicted by other experts, and the judge or jury would determine whether the criminal defendant has a personality disorder and if so, whether it is a "severe mental disease" *and* the defendant is *as a result of the severe mental disease* unable to appreciate the nature and quality or the wrongfulness of his acts. Few personality disorders ultimately qualify for this defense. As a consequence, prisons are full of people who show the traits of antisocial personality disorder. As Wims points out: "Some mental health experts have called 'anti-social personality disorder' the same as a diagnosis of 'classic son-of-a-bitch.' So if the bad apple won't turn itself back into a good apple, perhaps we need to pull that apple out of our apple barrel and stick the apple in prison where it belongs."

29. Lenore Walker, *The Battered Woman* (New York: Harper and Row, 1979).

30. Lenore Walker, *Battered Woman Syndrome* (New York: Springer-Verlag, 1984).

31. David L. Faigman, *Legal Alchemy: The Use and Misuse of Science in the Law* (New York: W. H. Freeman, 1999), pp. 72–75.

32. Mills, *Violent Partners*, p. xi.

33. Richard A. Friedman, "Accepting That Good Parents May Plant Bad Seeds," *New York Times*, July 12, 2010, http://www.nytimes.com/2010/07/13/health/13mind.html?_r=1&scp=1&sq=bad%20seed&st=cse (accessed July 16, 2010).

Chapter 29: The Deal

1. Lionel Trilling, *The Liberal Imagination: Essays on Literature and Society* (New York: New York Review of Books, 2008; original ed., 1950), p. 220.

2. R. M. Bilder, "Phenomics: Building Scaffolds for Biological Hypotheses in the Post-Genomic Era," *Biological Psychiatry* 63, no. 5 (2008): 439; R. M. Bilder et al., "Phenomics: The Systematic Study of Phenotypes on a Genome-Wide Scale," *Neuroscience* 164, no. 1 (2009): 30–42.

3. B. Levin, *Women and Medicine*, 3rd ed. (Scarecrow Press, 2002).

4. E-mail communication from Michael Wims, July 19, 2010.

5. Personal interview with Pat Finlinson and Richard Jacobson, June 17, 2009, at the Millard County Sheriff's Office.

6. Brent E. Turvey and Wayne Petherick, *Forensic Victimology: Examining Violent Crime Victims in Investigative and Legal Contexts* (New York: Elsevier, 2009), pp. xxxii–iii.

7. Carole Alden, letter to author.

Chapter 30: Closure

1. Lionel Trilling, *The Liberal Imagination: Essays on Literature and Society* (New York: New York Review of Books, 2008; original ed., 1950), p. 220.

2. John Cooke, "Woman Marries for Love—Then Kills for Survival," *National Enquirer*, April 7, 2008, p. 48.

3. Although I've made a note to myself to never again commit to having two books with the same deadline.

4. Marc D. Hauser, *Moral Minds: How Nature Designed Our Universal Sense of Right and Wrong* (New York: Ecco, 2006).

5. Nicholas Wade, "Harvard Finds Scientist Guilty of Misconduct," *New York Times*, August 20, 2010, http://www.nytimes.com/2010/08/21/

education/21harvard.html?_r=1&ref=nicholas_wade (accessed September 3, 2010). Nicholas Wade, "Harvard Researcher May Have Fabricated Data," *New York Times*, August 27, 2010, http://www.nytimes.com/2010/08/28/science/28harvard.html# (accessed September 3, 2010). Nicholas Wade, "Difficulties in Defining Errors in Case against Harvard Researcher," *New York Times*, October 25, 2010, http://www.nytimes.com/2010/10/26/science/26hauser.html (accessed October 29, 2010).

6. E-mail communications with Marc Hauser, December 22–23, 2010.

7. Ibid.

8. E-mail communication from Joseph Carroll to the author, September 4, 2010.

9. Jonah Lehrer, "The Truth Wears Off: Is There Something Wrong with the Scientific Method?" *New Yorker*, 2010, http://www.newyorker.com/reporting/2010/12/13/101213fa_fact_lehrer?currentPage=all (accessed January 4, 2011).

10. Ibid.

11. Ibid.

12. A prescient study in this regard is Augustine Brannigan, *The Rise and Fall of Social Psychology: The Use and Misuse of the Experimental Method* (New York: Aldine de Gruyter, 2004). See also Stephen Cole, ed. *What's Wrong with Sociology?* (Transaction Publishers, 2001); Rogers Wright and Nicholas Cummings, eds., *Destructive Trends in Mental Health: The Well-Intentioned Path to Harm* (Brunner-Routledge, 2005); D. Carlat, *Unhinged: The Trouble with Psychiatry—A Doctor's Revelations about a Profession in Crisis* (Free Press, 2010).

13. Some text in footnote taken directly from my original article: B. Oakley, "Kiss My APA!" *Psychology Today*, August 10, 2009, http://www.psychologytoday.com/blog/scalliwag/200908/kiss-my-apa (accessed January 3, 2011).

My theory—call it the "Oakley effect"—is that highly intelligent people are often less experienced in accepting and reacting constructively to criticism. (A neuroscientist might say they "have underdeveloped neurocircuitry for integrating negatively valenced stimuli.") If you are often or nearly always right in your interactions with others as you mature, your increased confidence in your own abilities would be accompanied by an inadvertent decrease in your capacity to deal effectively with criticism. After all, your experience would have shown that your critics were usually wrong.

As brilliant people mature and move naturally into positions of authority, they begin to encounter richly complex problems—so complex that no single person can faultlessly teach himself or herself all the key concepts involved, which are often both contradictory and important. Yes, the gifted have an advantage in dealing with such problems, because they've got natural brain-power that allows them to hold many factors in mind at once, bringing for-midable problem-solving skills to bear. But smart people have a natural dis-advantage, too: they're not used to changing their thinking in response to crit-icism when they get things wrong.

In fact, natural smarties—the intellectual elite—often don't seem to learn the art of soliciting the criticism necessary to grasp the core issues of a com-plex problem and then making vital adaptations as a result. Instead, they fall in naturally with people who admire, rather than are critical of, their thinking. This further strengthens their conviction they are right, even as it distances them from people of very different backgrounds who grasp very different, but no less crucial, aspects of complex problems.

14. Ed Douglas, "Darwin's Natural Heir," *Guardian.co.uk*, February 17, 2001, http://www.guardian.co.uk/science/2001/feb/17/books.guardianreview 57 (accessed December 30, 2010).

15. Gillilan, "There's Always a Way."

16. John Cooke, "Woman Marries for Love—Then Kills for Survival," *National Enquirer*, April 7, 2008.

17. Sheryl Gillilan, "There's Always a Way: Carole Alden Continues the Artistic Life Behind Bars," *15 Bytes: Utah's Art Magazine*, 2010, http://www.artistsofutah.org/15bytes/10july/page1.html.

18. Jennifer W. Sanchez, "Utah Inmates Escape through Art," *Salt Lake Tribune*, September 13, 2010, http://www.sltrib.com/sltrib/news/50179924-78/art-prison-says-inmates.html.csp (accessed September 19, 2010).

19. Letter from Carole Alden to Prometheus Books, dated August 8, 2010.

20. Ibid.

21. Iain McGilchrist, *The Master and His Emissary: The Divided Brain and the Making of the Modern World* (New Haven, CT: Yale University Press, 2010), pp. 55–56.

22. Ibid., p. 151.

23. E-mail from Krystal Rusek to the author, September 28, 2010.

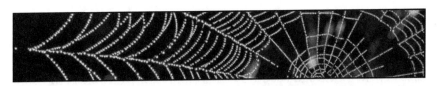

PHOTO AND ILLUSTRATION CREDITS

Page 16. Map based in part on "Landforms of the Conterminous United States—A Digital Shaded-Relief Portrayal," 1991, by Gail P. Thelin and Richard J. Pike, US Geological Survey, Department of the Interior/USGS, http://pubs.usgs.gov/imap/i2206/ (accessed September 19, 2010). Revised final image courtesy Kevin Mendez Aracena.

Page 23. Marty Sessions's side table. Photograph courtesy Alden.

Page 40. Carole and Marty's double-wide trailer, as see main road. Photograph courtesy Stuart Alden.

Page 55. Carole Alden's self-portrait as dragon. Pho' Art Access/VSA Utah.

Page 65. Carolyn Zahn-Waxler. Photograph cour

Page 67. Empathizers-systemizers. Illustration courtesy the author.

Page 72. Two ways empathic people can react when they see someone else in pain. Illustration courtesy Olga Klimecki. With kind permission from O. Klimecki and T. Singer, "Empathic Distress Fatigue Rather Than Compassion Fatigue? Integrated Findings from Empathy Research Is Psychology and Social Neuroscience," in *Pathological Altruism*, edited by B. Oakley, A. Knafo, G. Madhavan, and D. S. Wilson (New York: Oxford University Press, in press).

Page 79. Carole as a baby. Photograph courtesy Stuart Alden.

Page 82. Carole at dog obedience class. Photograph courtesy Stuart Alden.

Page 89. Carole Alden with James Slavens. Photograph courtesy Chris Detrick and the *Salt Lake Tribune*.

Page 92. Marty Sessions's grave. Photograph courtesy the Utah Attorney General's Office.

Page 93. Hallway where Marty Sessions died. Photograph courtesy the Utah Attorney General's Office.

Page 95. The pillow. Photograph courtesy the Utah Attorney General's Office.

Page 102. Marty on his sixth birthday. Photograph courtesy Edee Sessions-Wagers.

Page 105. Marty Sessions. "Anybody who knew my Dad liked him." Photograph courtesy Edee Sessions.

Pages 111–12, 241. "How to Prepare and Try a Murder Case," by Mike Wims, © 2010 by the American Bar Association. Reprinted with permission. All rights reserved. This information or any portion thereof may not be copied or disseminated in any form or by any means or stored in an electronic database or retrieval system without the express written consent of the American Bar Association.

Page 113. The trunk. Photograph courtesy the Utah Attorney General's Office.

Page 115. Back porch cum chicken coop. Photograph courtesy Stuart Alden.

Page 116. Dilapidated Buick. Photograph courtesy Stuart Alden.

Page 118. The hallway where Marty Sessions was killed. Photograph courtesy Stuart Alden.

Page 120. Child's bedroom. Photograph courtesy Stuart Alden.

Page 124. James K. Slavens. Photograph courtesy James K. Slavens.

Page 129. The master bedroom. Photograph courtesy Stuart Alden.

Page 138. Brent Turvey and Mike McGrath on the Great Wall of China. Photograph courtesy Michael McGrath, MD.

Page 149. Carole at age fourteen. There were happy times mixed in with what her parents hoped was simply a typically turbulent teenage phase.

Page 151. Carole, age eighteen, models a dress of her own creation. Photograph courtesy Stuart Alden.

Page 170. "Library Square Sea Dragon" in reflecting pool. Photograph courtesy Steve Wilson Photography.

Page 206. Müller-Lyer optical illusion courtesy Robert Burton, MD.

Page 232. Carole and Marty at the wedding of Carole's daughter Melloney, 2003. Photograph courtesy Stuart Alden.

Page 236. Carole and Marty at Salt Lake Arts Festival, 2006. Photograph courtesy Stuart Alden.

Page 248. Michael Wims. Photograph by David Williams, supplied courtesy Michael Wims.

Page 270. Carole Alden sobs in the courtroom. Photograph courtesy Chris Detrick and the *Salt Lake Tribune*.

Page 304. "Limbo" (Skewered Woman). Photograph courtesy Art Access/VSA Utah.

INDEX

hostility toward research involving family violence, 162–63, 299–300, 351–52n24

influence on battered woman syndrome research, 49, 280

methods used by feminists to conceal, deny, and distort evidence, 350–51n22

sexism in research, 63–64, 285

Fillmore, Utah, 35–36. *See also* KOA Campground in Fillmore, Utah (lovely place)

Fine, Cordelia, a discussion of her *Delusions of Gender*, including an example of creation of evidence through a citation that doesn't actually support the assertion, 323–25n3

Finlinson, Patrick, deputy attorney
appointment as prosecutor for Carole Alden case, 87
background of, 34–36, 125
discussions in the "War Room" about Carole Alden's culpability in the crime, 217–26
as an exemplary prosecutor, 303, 311
reflects on the outcome of the case, 288

flexibility, mental
hypothesized deficit in highly intelligent people—"Oakley effect," 366–67n12
as part of empathy, 57

Forensic Victimology (Turvey and Petherick)
how the book came about, 138–39
Michael McGrath's criticism of battered woman syndrome in, 47, 160

Gein, Ed (model for Norman Bates in *Psycho*), in relation to nature versus nurture, 182–83, 355n3

gender differences. *See* women

genes
the counterintuitive finding that just knowing whether someone has genes that have been associated with a disease can't help predict whether a person will actually get the disease, 335n7

influence on problematic personalities, 280, 327–29n9

interaction with environment, 46, 184, 280

related to altruism, 75, 184

related to empathy, 59

genital piercings. *See* piercings, body

Geschwind-Galaburda theory, 67–68, 326n8

Gilbert, Neil, on inflated numbers in rape statistics, 160

Gilmore, Gary (murderer who was executed by firing squad), in relation to nature versus nurture, 183

Golding, Stephen, forensic psychologist, weighs in on Carole Alden's suitability for bail, 217–19, 224, 285

Greathouse, Josie, Officer
dresses Carole Alden out after arrest, 41–42, 270
untimely death of, 303
was told by Carole that Marty was "too plowed" to get her, 94

Greenland, Sander
control group and its equivalence to comparison group, 318n8
debunks Lenore Walker's methodology for BWS, 319–21n9
quotation about basic misinterpretations of statistics, 43

guilt
and codependency, 60
empathic distress, and depression, 71
and empathy, 69–70
as female-oriented emotion, 70

"Guilty Vicarage, The" (Auden), 85

Hall, John Foster, quote "We are all here on earth to help others; what on earth the others are here for, I don't know," 137

hallway where Marty was killed, picture of, 93, 118

Hardy, Leonard, reminiscences about Carole's work for the City of Delta, 189–91, 197–98

Harman, Francis, B., *Milestones of Mil-*